IMAGES
of America

PUNTA GORDA

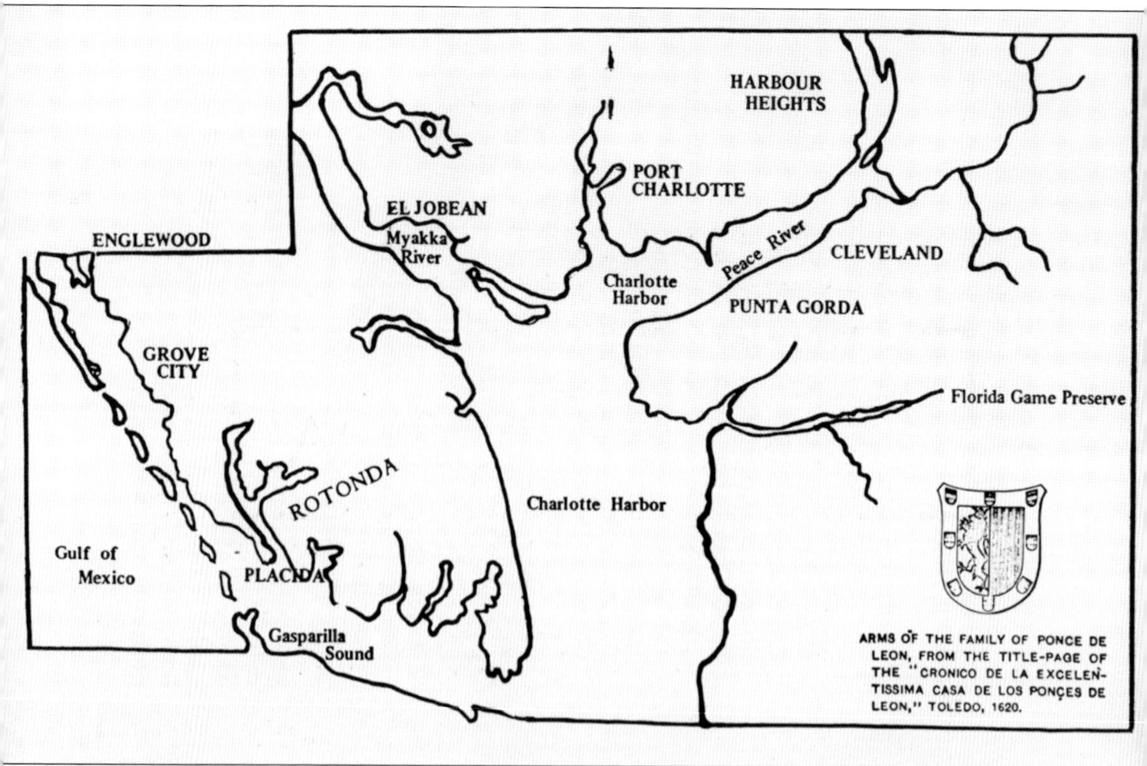

Early Map of Charlotte Harbor. This map depicts the location of Punta Gorda. The town rests at a point where the Peace River meets Charlotte Harbor. The name *Punta Gorda* means "Broad Point" or "Fat Point" in the language of the Spanish conquistadors. Juan Ponce de León was known to have arrived in the Charlotte Harbor area as early as 1521 in his search for the Fountain of Youth. (Punta Gorda Historical Society.)

On the Cover: Punta Gorda Fish Company Workers. Shown are employees of the Punta Gorda Fish Company, one of the largest fishing operations in the area. The company was organized in 1897. Pictured from left to right are Harry R. Dreggors, Andrew "Mullet" Owens, Tom Coleman, Harry R. Goulding, "Bum" Mansel Graham, Sammy Holmes, and William H. Monson. (U. S. Cleveland Collection.)

IMAGES
of America

PUNTA GORDA

Ann M. O'Phelan and Scot Shively
with the Blanchard House
and the Punta Gorda Historical Society

ARCADIA
PUBLISHING

ISBN 978-0-7385-6799-0

Published by Arcadia Publishing
Charleston, South Carolina

Printed in the United States of America

Library of Congress Control Number: 2009923615

For all general information contact Arcadia Publishing at:
Telephone 843-853-2070
Fax 843-853-0044
E-mail sales@arcadiapublishing.com
For customer service and orders:
Toll-Free 1-888-313-2665

Visit us on the Internet at www.arcadiapublishing.com

This book is dedicated to Bernice Andrews Russell, a well-known humanitarian, social activist, and dedicated historian for the Punta Gorda African American community. And to Fran Campbell, Eloise McDougal, Helen Wrobbel, Audrey Muccio, Virginia Vaughn, Donna Sanford, Nancy Lisby, and Linda Wilson—all members of the Punta Gorda Historical Society. Also to Claire Zachritz and Ken Grevlich of the Punta Gorda Historic Railroad Depot and Antique Mall.

It's impossible to tell all of the history of Punta Gorda in one book. There are plenty more stories to be told, images to be seen, and other sources to learn from, including reading books and other materials by U. S. Cleveland, Vernon Peeples, Lindsey Williams, Angie Larkin, Byron Rhode, Barbara Thorp Gunn, and the local newspaper, the Sun-Herald.

A percentage of the authors' proceeds will be donated to the Punta Gorda Historical Society and the Blanchard House Museum.

Contents

ACKNOWLEDGMENTS

This book was created with help from the Punta Gorda Historical Society, an organization dedicated to preserving and maintaining historic structures, landmarks, and streets in the city of Punta Gorda. The society celebrated its 25th year in 2008 and takes pride in having encouraged the City to provide land on which historic buildings in danger of demolition could be placed. The History Park on Shreve Street now houses the 1886 Trabue Land Sales Office, once owned by Punta Gorda founder Col. Isaac Trabue and used as the town's first "post office;" the 1890s "Cigar House," which housed two families who were employed by the El Palmetto Cigar Manufacturing Company; and the Price House, a 1914 house-turned-inn—all thanks to their efforts.

The historical society is housed in the historic Punta Gorda Woman's Club building in downtown Punta Gorda. The building was constructed in 1927 on land donated by Judge William Fenmore Cooper of Cook County, Illinois. It was created to house clubs for women that later consolidated to form one group, the Punta Gorda Woman's Club. The clubs were formerly known as the Women's Civic Association, the Married Ladies Club, and the Fortnightly Club. The building was also designed to provide facilities where various events could take place; hence it features a grand hall with a stage, a kitchen, and meeting rooms.

The building has had other uses as well. The Punta Gorda Public Library was located in a section of the building until 1957, the building served as a USO during World War II, and Charlotte High School used the hall for commencement exercises. The Tourist Club, the Parents-Teachers Association, and other organizations also have used the building, and wedding receptions and other events are still held there.

The Women's Club Building was added to the National Register of Historic Places on April 5, 1991. Nine year later, in 2000, the deed to the building was transferred to the Punta Gorda Historical Society.

Special thanks go to the Blanchard House Museum for a generous amount of input and images; Fran Campbell and Eloise McDougal for their input and images and Linda Wilson for her collection of photographs—they are all members of the Punta Gorda Historical Society; Kathy Burnam, marketing director, Fishermen's Village Waterfront Mall, Resort, and Marina, for her assistance with images; Jill Shively for her input and thorough review and Anne M. Shively for editing; John Allen for his review and assistance identifying the images; and Kim Lovejoy, executive director, Military Heritage and Aviation Museum, for military history assistance and images.

Unless otherwise noted, all images are courtesy of the Punta Gorda Historical Society.

Introduction

This book was also created with the generous help of the Blanchard House Museum of African-American History and Culture of Charlotte County. The Blanchard House Museum, established in 2004, was the vision of Bernice Andrews Russell. Russell was a humanitarian, social activist, and historian for the local African American community. She was a descendant of one of the first African American pioneer families to settle in Punta Gorda. Russell's pride in her roots and the cultural value of "giving back" motivated her to document the history, culture, and contributions of African Americans in Charlotte County.

Bernice Russell began the journey toward establishing an African American museum in the 1980s. She organized a traveling exhibit that was located in the Colored Waiting Room at the Old Punta Gorda Train Depot. In 1997, Russell purchased the 1925 home of Joseph and Minnie Blanchard. He was an African American boat pilot, a fisherman, and a key member of early Punta Gorda's fishing industry.

For More Information:
Blanchard House Museum of African-American History and Culture of Charlotte County
406 Martin Luther King Boulevard
Punta Gorda, FL 33950
941-575-7518
www.blanchardmuseum.org

Punta Gorda Army Airfield
Charlotte County Airport
28000 Airport Road
Punta Gorda, FL 33982
941-639-1101

Punta Gorda Chamber of Commerce
252 West Marion Avenue No. 121
Punta Gorda, FL 33950
941-639-3720
www.puntagorda-chamber.com

Punta Gorda Historical Mural Society
716 Monaco Drive
Punta Gorda, FL 33950
941-575-0785
www.puntagordamurals.com

Punta Gorda Historical Society
118 Sullivan Street
Punta Gorda, FL 33950
941-639-1887

Punta Gorda History Park
501 Shreve Street
Punta Gorda, FL 33950
941-639-1887

Punta Gorda Historic Railroad Depot and Antique Mall
1009 Taylor Road
Punta Gorda, FL 33950
941-639-6774

Military Heritage Museum
At Fisherman's Village
1200 West Retta Esplanade, Unit 48
Punta Gorda, FL 33950
www.mhaam.org/index.html

Fishermen's Village Waterfront Mall, Resort, and Marina
1200 West Retta Esplanade
Punta Gorda, FL 33950
941-575-3007
www.fishville.com

Charlotte Sun and Weekly Herald
23170 Harborview Road
Port Charlotte, FL 33980
941-206-1000
www.sunnewspapers.net

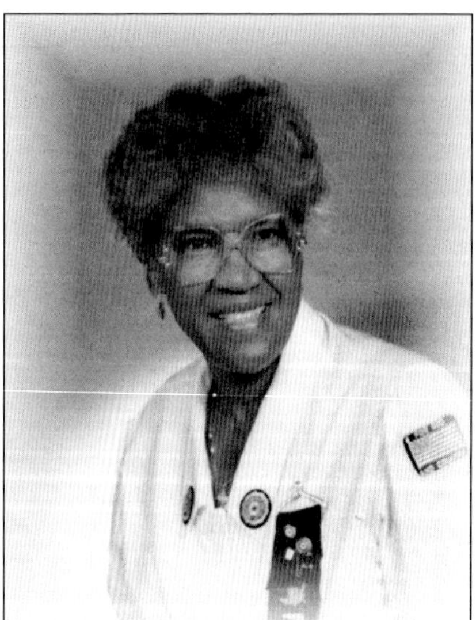

BERNICE A. Russell (1923–1999). Bernice Andrews Russell was a humanitarian, social activist, and historian for the local African American community. (Blanchard House Museum of African-American History and Culture of Charlotte County.)

THE BEGINNING

The Calusa Indians were believed to have inhabited the Charlotte Harbor area about 3,000 years ago. The Calusas were a warrior tribe and were also known as "The Shell People." They used seashells for trade and tools and piled the shells high to create massive shell mounds, many of which are still standing today. Although the city of Punta Gorda traces its roots back to 1539, when Hernando de Soto landed at Live Oak Point on the Peace River, Ponce de León was known to have arrived in the Charlotte Harbor area as early as 1521. Ponce de León came to the area in search of the Fountain of Youth, a spring of water that supposedly had the power to restore youth. When he landed on the shores and tried to colonize the area, his party was attacked so fiercely that they retreated to Cuba, where he later died of his wounds. While the American Indians were successful in getting Ponce de León to leave the area, more Spaniards arrived and eventually conquered the American Indians. The name *Punta Gorda* means "Broad Point" or "Fat Point" in the language of the Spanish conquistadors, who in fact also were the area's early commercial fishermen. A key figure in the Charlotte Harbor area's commercial fishing industry was Pedro Menendez D'Aviles. He brought commercial fishing to the area in 1566. In the late 19th century, cattle ranchers and homesteaders moved into the area and began to make their mark. Along with settlers came the railroad, and Punta Gorda was the end of the line. Once the railroad came, settlers, tourists, and industry arrived. The railroads were key to the area's growth. Punta Gorda rests on the waters of Charlotte Harbor near the base of the Peace River. On the opposite side of the harbor lies Port Charlotte. The harbor was named after the British queen Charlotte, wife of King George III of England, in the late 1700s after the Spanish lost control of the area to the British colonists. The Peace River was named by the Spanish, who called it Rio de la Paz, meaning "river of peace." Punta Gorda was incorporated on December 7, 1887.

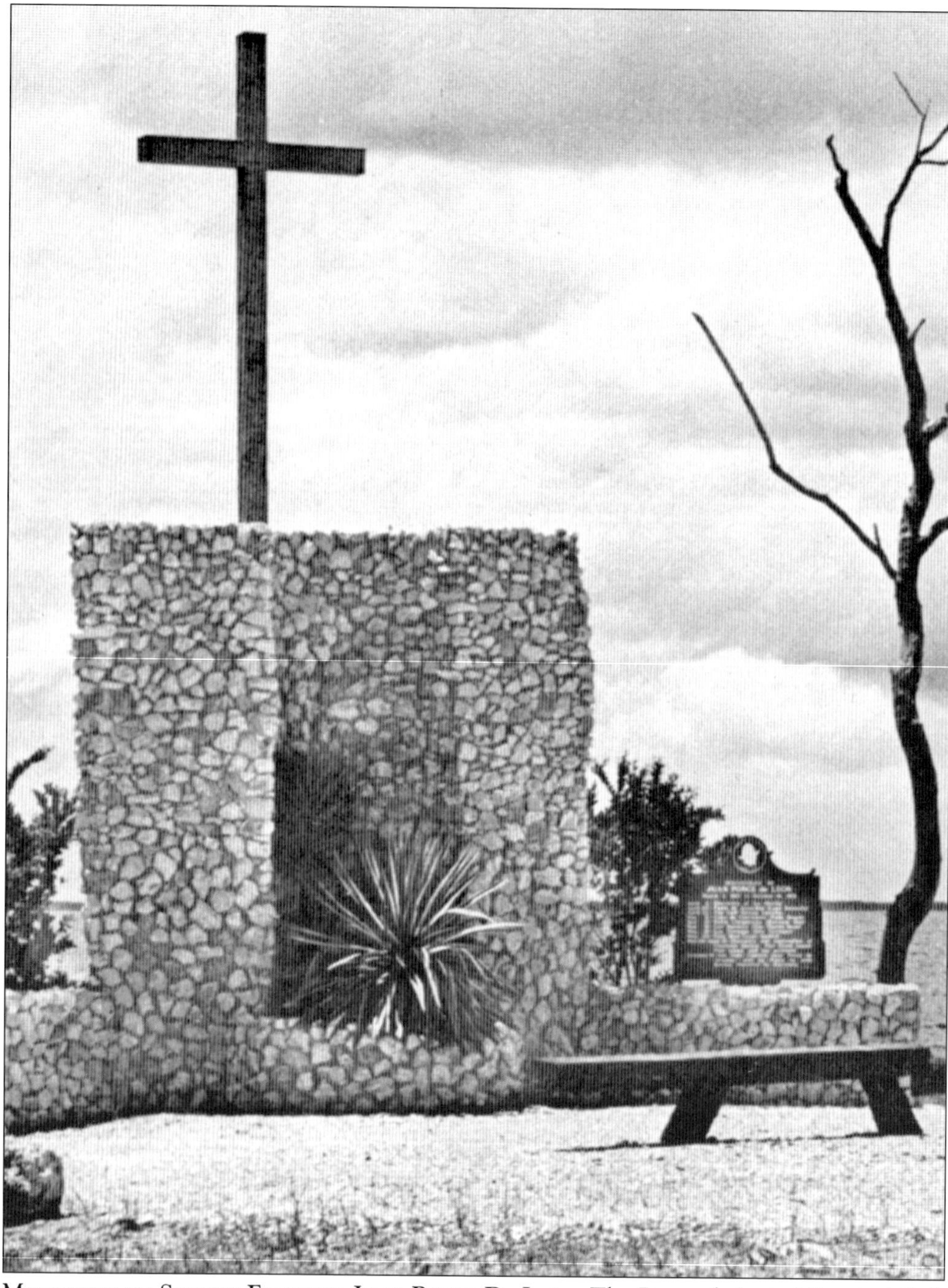

MONUMENT TO SPANISH EXPLORER JUAN PONCE DE LEÓN. The Ponce de León Historical Park Shrine is located at Ponce de León Park on Marion Avenue in Punta Gorda. He is believed to have set foot in the area in the early 16th century, as he was searching for the Fountain of Youth. He fought with the Native Americans and suffered an arrow wound in 1521. Afterward, he fled to Cuba, where he died of his injury. The 10-acre park is located at 3400 West Marion Avenue. There is also a Ponce de León monument in Gilchrist Park at 400 West Retta Esplanade in Punta Gorda.

One

RAILROADS

The history of railroading in Florida dates back to the early 1800s, although it wasn't until the late 1800s that the railroads began connecting the state of Florida. The first railroad that traveled into Punta Gorda was the Florida Southern Railroad, with a line that extended from Arcadia to Punta Gorda in 1886. Col. Isaac Trabue, one of Punta Gorda's early settlers, approached the Plant System of railway and steamship lines and requested that the track be laid. Henry Bradley Plant was the founder of the Plant System. He reportedly did not get along well with Trabue. Trabue actually gave the railroad a large tract of land to ensure they would lay the tracks down the south side of the Peace River to his new town, Trabue. In February 1904, an extension running from Punta Gorda to Fort Myers was built by the Atlantic Coast Line (ACL) Railroad. That was after Florida Southern Railroad declared bankruptcy and was taken over by the Atlantic Coast Line in 1902.

The railroads made it easier to transport bulk goods, such as sugar, and agricultural goods from Florida to the Northern states and brought building materials, settlers, and tourists back to Florida. One of the key goods shipped north was the fresh fish caught in the local waters, first packed with ice.

Punta Gorda's third railroad depot was built in 1928 by the Atlantic Coast Line. This depot replaced the 1897 one located by the Railroad Wharf. The depot was also the southernmost train station in the United States at the time it was built. The Punta Gorda Railroad Depot served the ACL, hauling mostly freight until 1971, when the railroad ceased operations. The building remained closed for a few years but was then acquired by the late Fred Babcock, industrialist and rancher. He in turn gave the Punta Gorda Historical Society money to purchase the depot from him in 1996. Since then, the building has been restored, and the freight room now serves as the Punta Gorda Historic Railroad Depot and Antique Mall. The building was listed on the National Register of Historic Places in 1990, and in 2008, a historical marker was placed on the grounds.

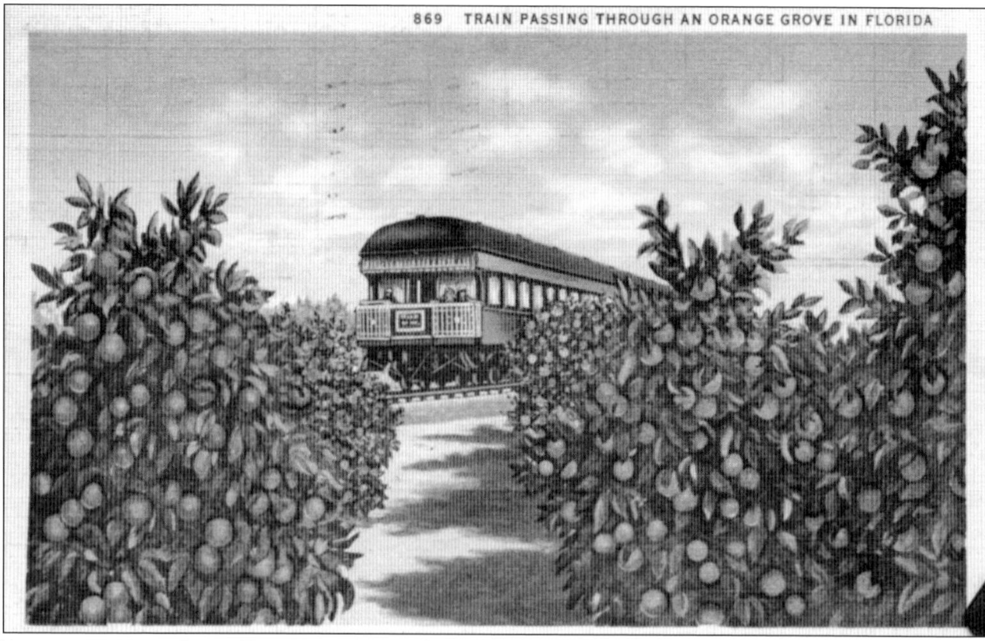

POSTCARD OF AN EARLY FLORIDA TRAIN. This early postcard depicts the significance and popularity of railroads in Florida. Although railroads were used for shipping, tourists loved riding them, too. By 1890, the railroads were nearly completed, and travel to the state was relatively easy. By the early 1900s, thousands of tourists came to Florida to enjoy the new hotels, warm weather, and natural beauty. (Punta Gorda Historic Railroad Depot and Antique Mall.)

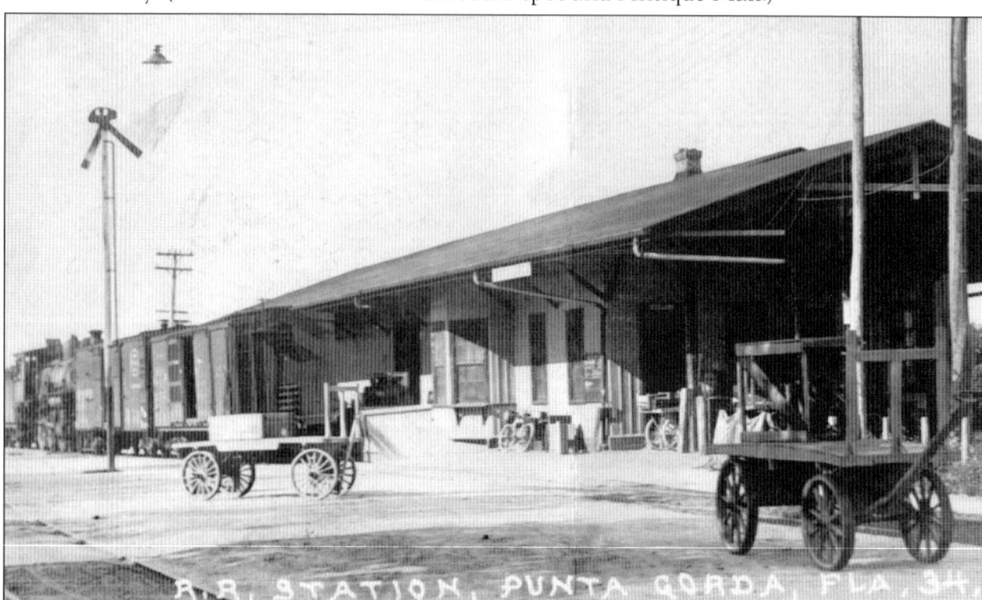

THE 1897 PUNTA GORDA RAILROAD DEPOT. Punta Gorda's second railroad station was erected in 1897 near the Railroad Wharf. The first trains that came to Punta Gorda came along the Florida Southern Railway. The railway line ran out to the 4,000-foot Long Dock. The dock had to extend far enough into the Peace River to reach sufficiently deep water in order for boats to load goods. (Punta Gorda Historic Railroad Depot and Antique Mall.)

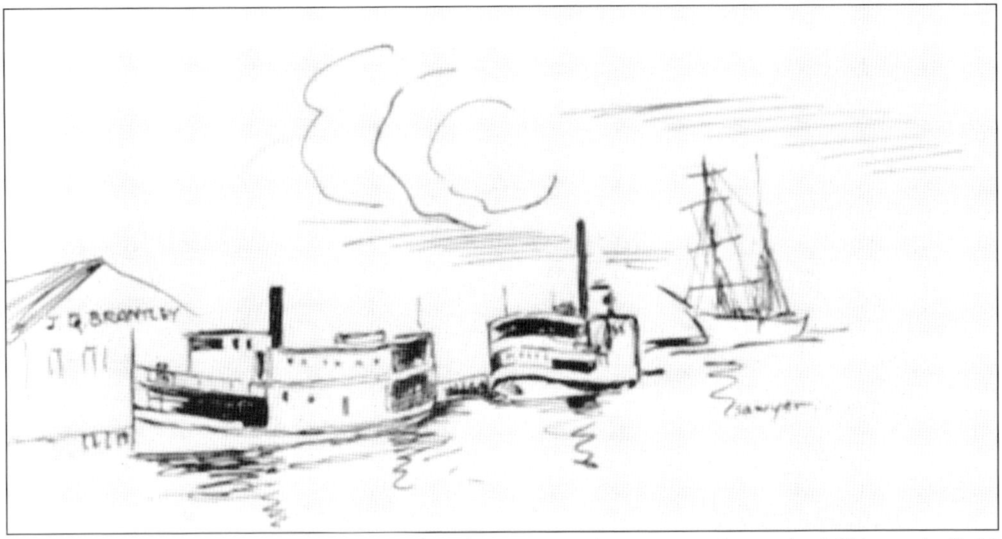

DRAWING BY PHILIP AYERS SAWYER. This drawing is of two steamships, the *Hildergarde* (left) and the *H. B. Plant* (center), that were built at Jacksonville in 1899. The *H. B. Plant* traveled the Tampa–to–Manatee River or the Punta Gorda runs. Punta Gorda was a major stop for steamships that went between New Orleans and Havana, Cuba, and other ports in the Caribbean. Unfortunately the *H. B. Plant* burned at a Tampa pier in 1913. The Charlotte Harbor Lighthouse was completed in September 1890 and no doubt helped guide some of these ships in and out of the Punta Gorda docks. The steamships docked at Punta Gorda and other ports to unload goods that were then loaded onto railcars. (Florida Photographic Collection, the Florida Memory Project.)

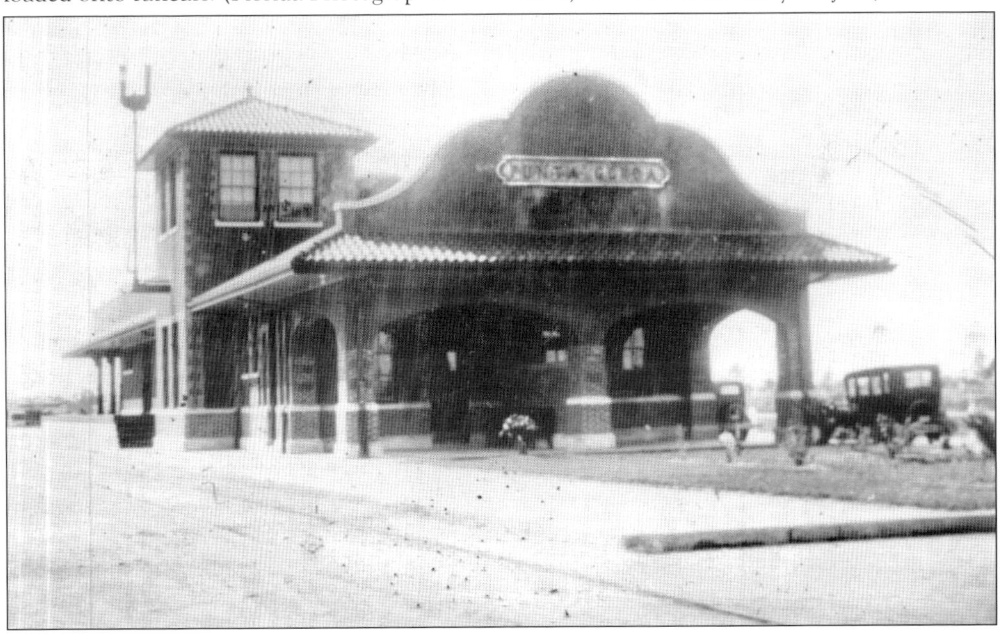

THE PUNTA GORDA RAILROAD DEPOT. The Punta Gorda Railroad Depot was built in 1928, before the stock market crashed. It was the country's southernmost depot at the time. Although the depot serviced mostly freight trains, passengers were also carried. The Mediterranean Revival style of the building was popular in the United States in the 1920s and 1930s. It is a style similar to a Mediterranean resort.

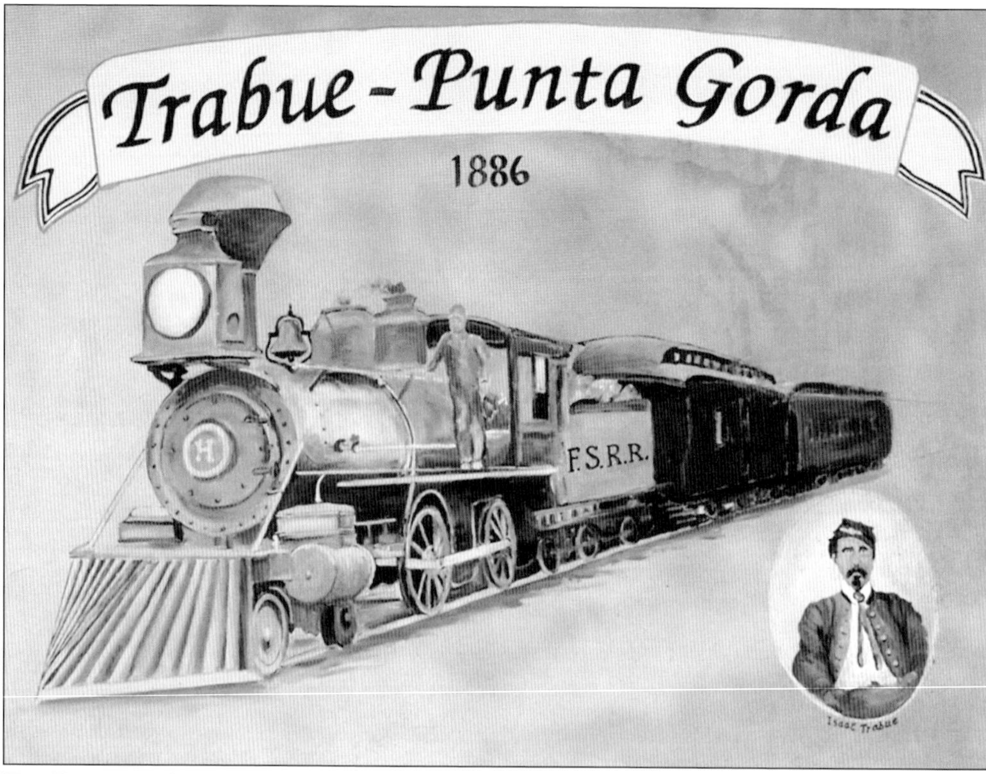

The Railroad Arrives, by Betty Reese. This oil painting celebrates the arrival of the railroad to the town of Trabue in 1886. Col. Isaac Trabue persuaded Florida Southern Railway to extend its line from Bartow to his town. On July 24, 1886, the first train of the Florida Southern Railroad arrived in Trabue and began its regular passenger service. Reese's depiction of Colonel Trabue is based on a Civil War photograph. This image was photographed by Dr. and Mrs. David Phelen and later donated to the Punta Gorda Historical Society. (Punta Gorda Historic Railroad Depot and Antique Mall.)

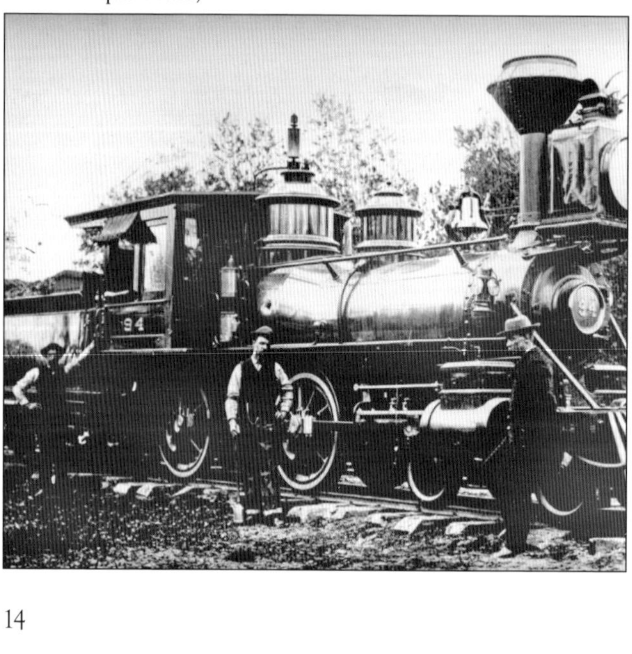

Steam Locomotive. In 1886, the first steam locomotive arrived in Trabue with workmen who came down to help build the regal Hotel Punta Gorda, later known as Hotel Charlotte Harbor after it was sold in 1924. During the late 1800s and early 1900s, early steam locomotives hauled heavy loads filled with freight and passengers to the Punta Gorda Railroad Depot. The first train to arrive in Trabue was a wood-burning Baldwin locomotive that operated on narrow 3-foot-gauge iron rails. (Punta Gorda Historic Railroad Depot and Antique Mall.)

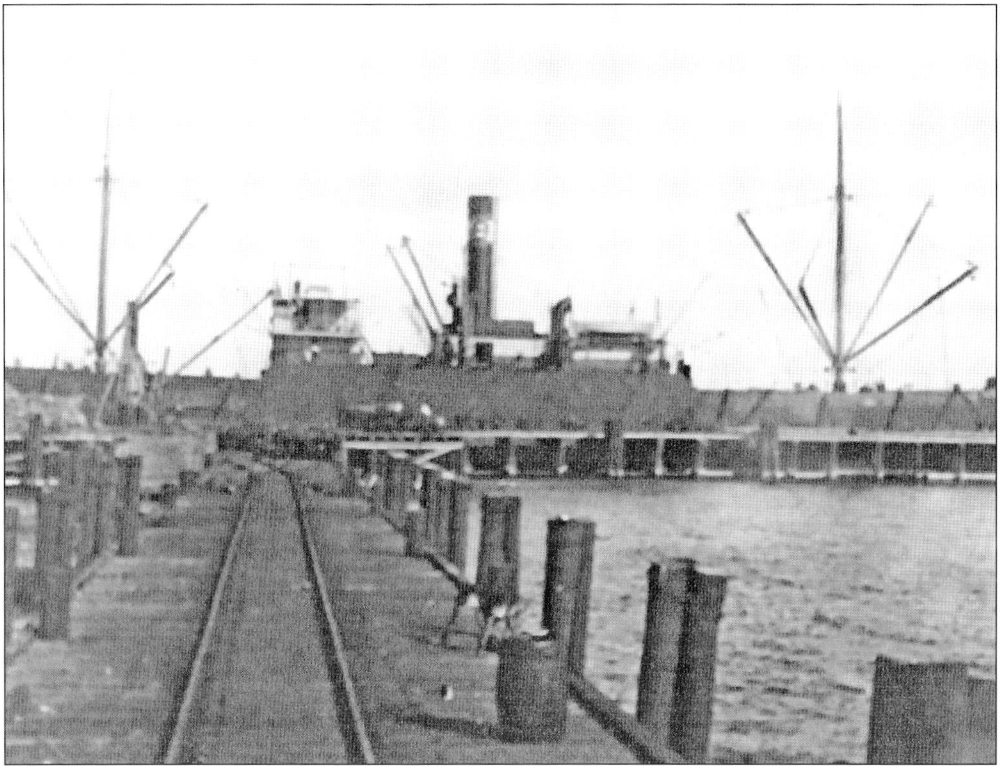

The 4,400-ton Ship *Jean* in Charlotte Harbor. Steamboats, such as the ship *Jean*, used steam power to drive propellers or paddle wheels. Steamers, as they were also known, carried both goods and passengers who were coming to and from Florida. Capt. Peter Nelson's note with this photograph states, "This is the ship Jean, 4400 tons, last one I brought into Charlotte Harbor." This ship is docked at the end of the railroad line on Punta Gorda's Long Dock. (Florida Photographic Collection, the Florida Memory Project.)

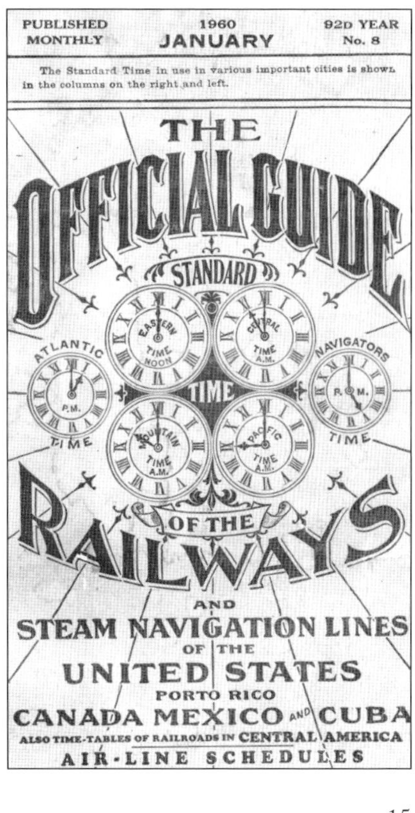

The Official Guide to Railways and Steam Navigation Lines of the United States. This is the front cover of *The Official Guide to Railways and Steam Navigation Lines of the United States, Porto Rico, Canada, Mexico, and Cuba.* The book dates to January 1960, but the history of the guide goes back much earlier. The guides were originally produced by National Railway Publication Company of New York City in 1868 after the National Association of General Passenger and Ticket Agents called for a "railway guide" to be published. The guides were designed to provide routing and shipping information and were found at every train station from coast to coast. (Punta Gorda Historic Railroad Depot and Antique Mall.)

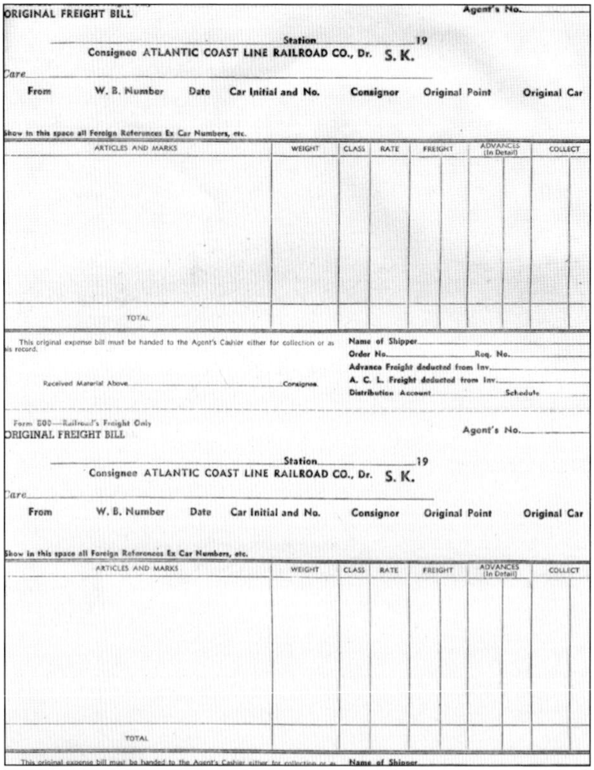

ORIGINAL FREIGHT BILL Agent's No.

Station ____ 19

Consignee ATLANTIC COAST LINE RAILROAD CO., Dr. S. K.

Care

From	W. B. Number	Date	Car Initial and No.	Consignor	Original Point	Original Car

Show in this space all Foreign References Ex Car Numbers, etc.

ARTICLES AND MARKS	WEIGHT	CLASS	RATE	FREIGHT	ADVANCES (In Detail)	COLLECT
TOTAL						

This original expense bill must be handed to the Agent's Cashier either for collection or as his record.

Name of Shipper
Order No. ____ Req. No.
Advance Freight deducted from Inv.
A. C. L. Freight deducted from Inv.
Distribution Account ____ Schedule

Received Material Above ____ Consignee

Form 500—Railroad's Freight Only

ORIGINAL FREIGHT BILL Agent's No.

Station ____ 19

Consignee ATLANTIC COAST LINE RAILROAD CO., Dr. S. K.

Care

From	W. B. Number	Date	Car Initial and No.	Consignor	Original Point	Original Car

Show in this space all Foreign References Ex Car Numbers, etc.

ARTICLES AND MARKS	WEIGHT	CLASS	RATE	FREIGHT	ADVANCES (In Detail)	COLLECT
TOTAL						

This original expense bill must be handed to the Agent's Cashier either for collection or as

Name of Shipper

Atlantic Coast Line Railroad Company's Freight Bill. This is a copy of an Atlantic Coast Line Railroad Company original freight bill. A bill like this is made out in triplicate form. The original and one copy are given to the shipper. The shipper sends the original copy to the person who is receiving the shipment and keeps a copy for himself. The railroad company also keeps a copy. In 1928 and later, when the Punta Gorda Railroad Depot was in operation, freight bills might have been filled in for bulk goods and agricultural goods. Three quarters of the structure's function was dedicated to freight handling. (Punta Gorda Historic Railroad Depot and Antique Mall.)

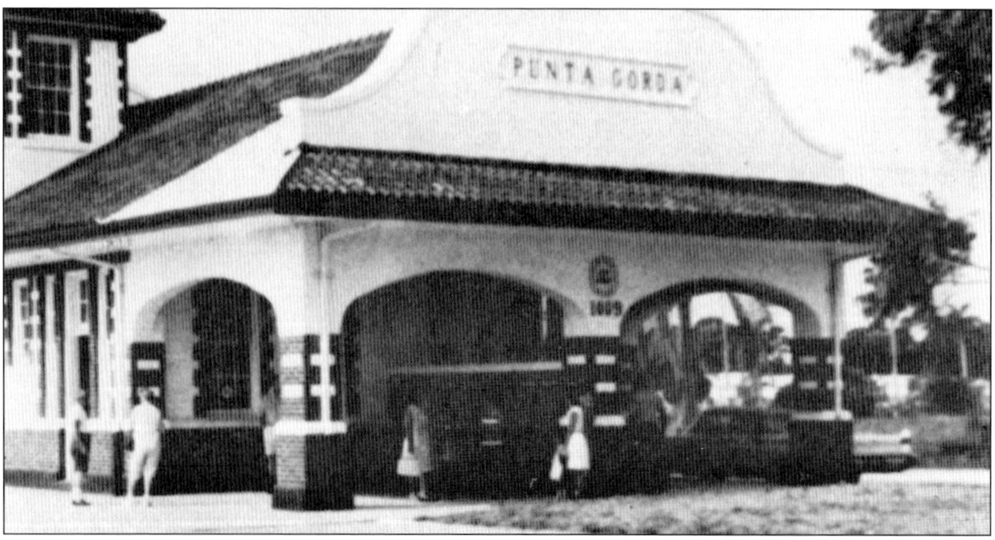

The Punta Gorda Railroad Depot. This early photograph of the Punta Gorda Railroad Depot shows passengers strolling about waiting for a train. They are standing close to the ticketing area located at the front of the depot. The ticketing areas were segregated, as were the bathrooms. Without air-conditioning, the heat in the building would have been sweltering during the summer months. Not to mention that there would be plenty of bugs and mosquitoes to contend with. Charlotte Harbor began its mosquito control program in 1935, according to *Fact and Fable: Charlotte County* (published by First Federal Savings and Loan Association of Charlotte County in 1976).

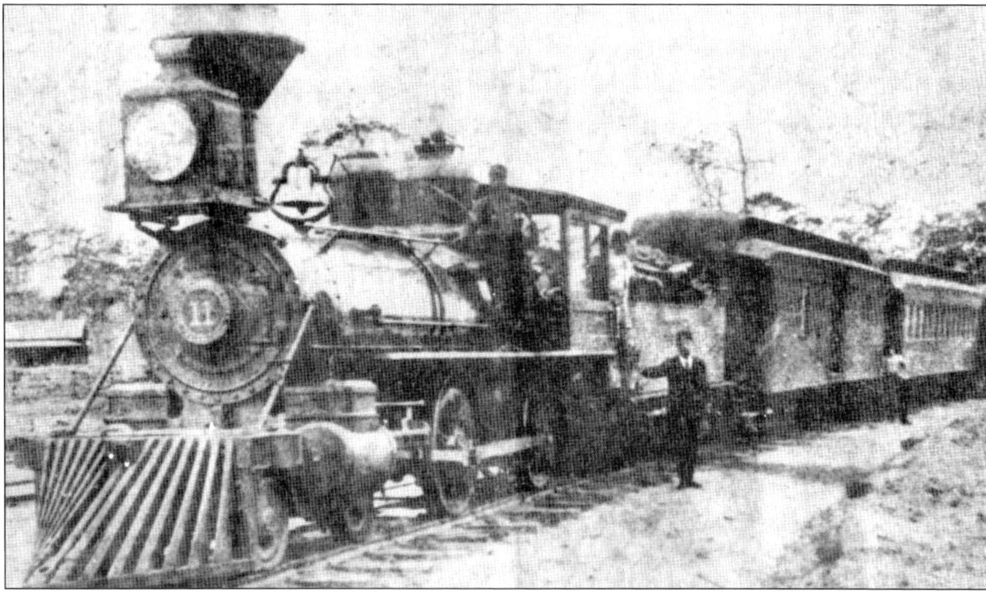

FLORIDA SOUTHERN RAILWAY TRAIN. This 1886 photograph shows the Charlotte Harbor Division of the Florida Southern Railway Company making its way down the Peace River from Bartow. The train is a steam engine with passenger cars. Florida Southern actually became part of the Gulf Line Railway and ceased operations in 1921. The Peace River is a 106-mile-long river that originates south of Bartow in Polk County, Florida, and flows into Charlotte Harbor. (From the *Arcadian*, Thursday, May 6, 1971; Kingston Antiques.)

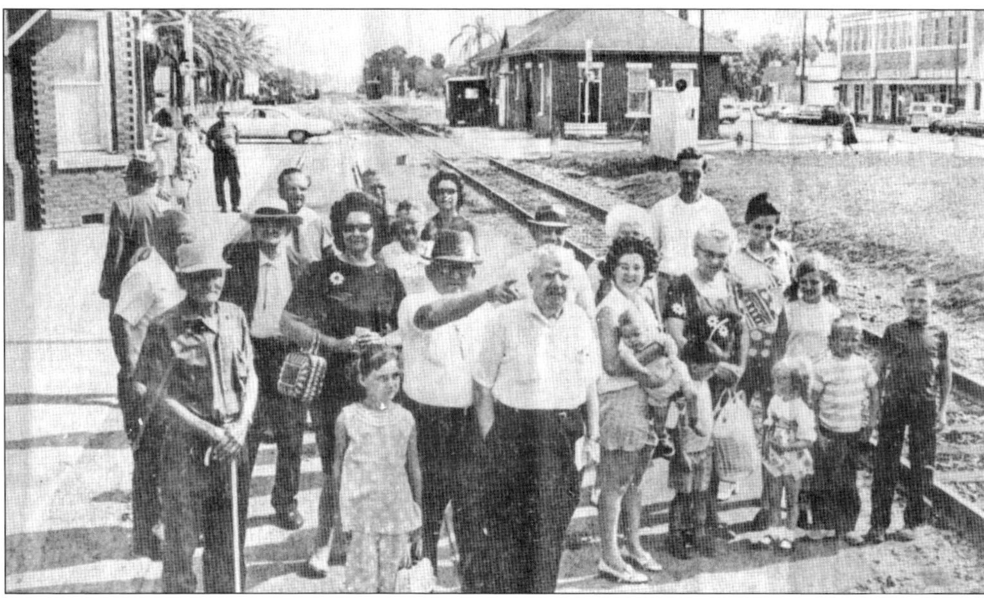

TRAIN LEAVES THE STATION FOR THE FINAL TIME. A crowd gathers to say good-bye to the train leaving Arcadia for the final time. The former Atlantic Coast Line freight and passenger depots still stand in Arcadia and are used for businesses. Punta Gorda's depot was built by the same railroad, the Atlantic Coast Line. Arcadia is in DeSoto County, north of Punta Gorda. Charlotte County, where Punta Gorda lies, was formed in 1921 right after DeSoto County was divided. (Kingston Antiques.)

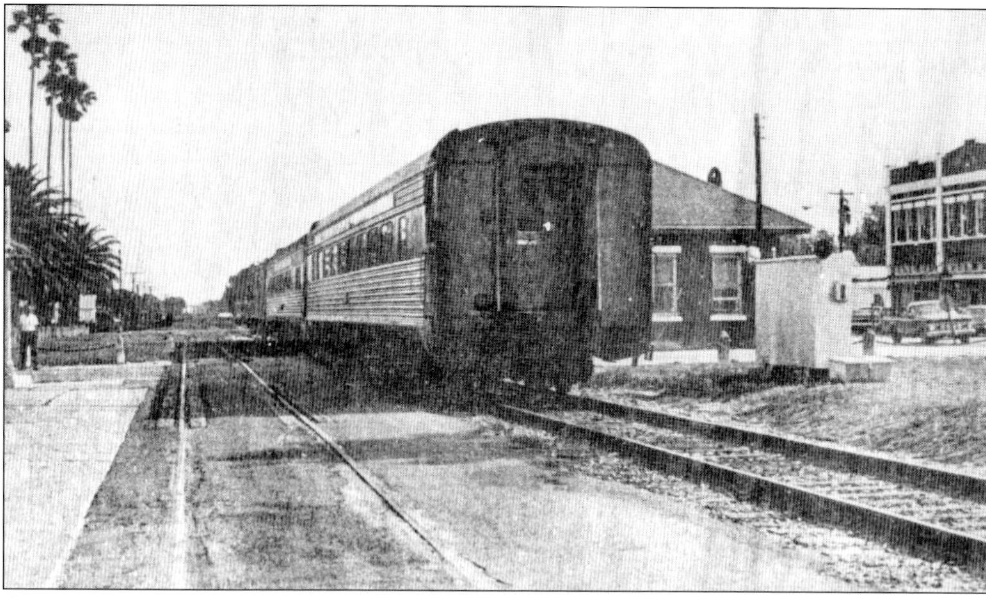

ARCADIA TRAIN STATION. The last passenger train leaves the Arcadia Station in 1971. Trains began losing their advantage as key transportation options when highways improved and automobiles and trucks gained in popularity. During World War II, Congress passed the Federal Aid Highway Act. This act began the creation of a modern, four-lane interstate highway system, which people used instead of the railroad. Also, trucking became a more predominant means of transporting goods as a result of the new interstate highway system. (Kingston Antiques.)

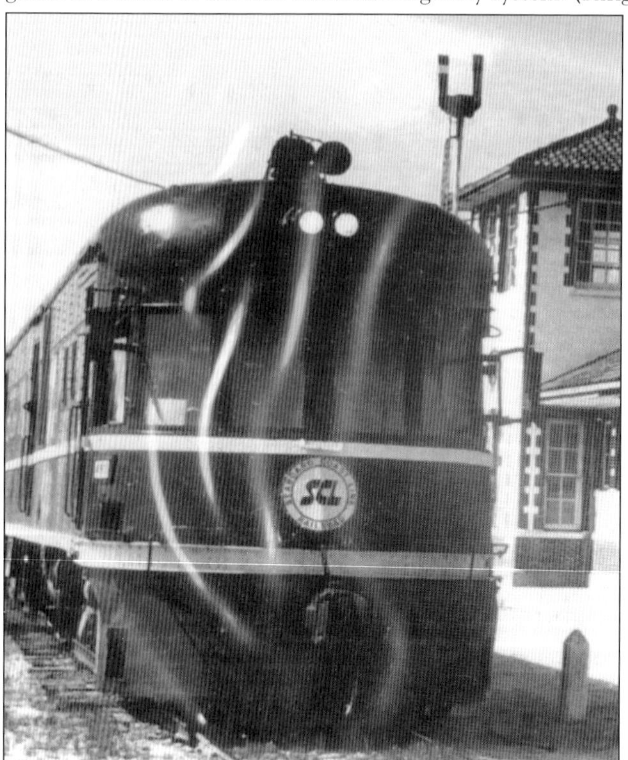

"DOODLE BUG" NO. 4900. The photograph dates to the 1960s when the "Doodle Bug" No. 4900 is stopped at the Punta Gorda Railroad Depot. Seaboard Coast Line Railroad's (SCL) Doodle Bug No. 4900 was built in St. Louis as a gas/ electric motorcar. The car had two stainless steel coaches. Beginning in the 1930s, railroads began modernizing trains by making them lighter and more streamlined using aluminum or stainless steel. The name "doodle bug" describes a self-propelled railroad car that was used for passenger or mail service. Seaboard's *Orange Blossom Special* train rides from New York City became the inspiration for a bluegrass song by Ervin T. Rouse. (Punta Gorda Historic Railroad Depot and Antique Mall, Linda Wilson collection.)

The Punta Gorda Railroad Depot. This 1960s photograph of the Punta Gorda Railroad Depot shows off the Spanish-style design. The building is one of only six that were built in a similar style and fashion by the Atlantic Coast Line and the only one still standing. The depot originally had segregated bathrooms and waiting areas for "Whites" and "Coloreds," as segregation was practiced at the time of its construction. In 1971, the ACL discontinued passenger service. (Punta Gorda Historic Railroad Depot and Antique Mall, Linda Wilson collection.)

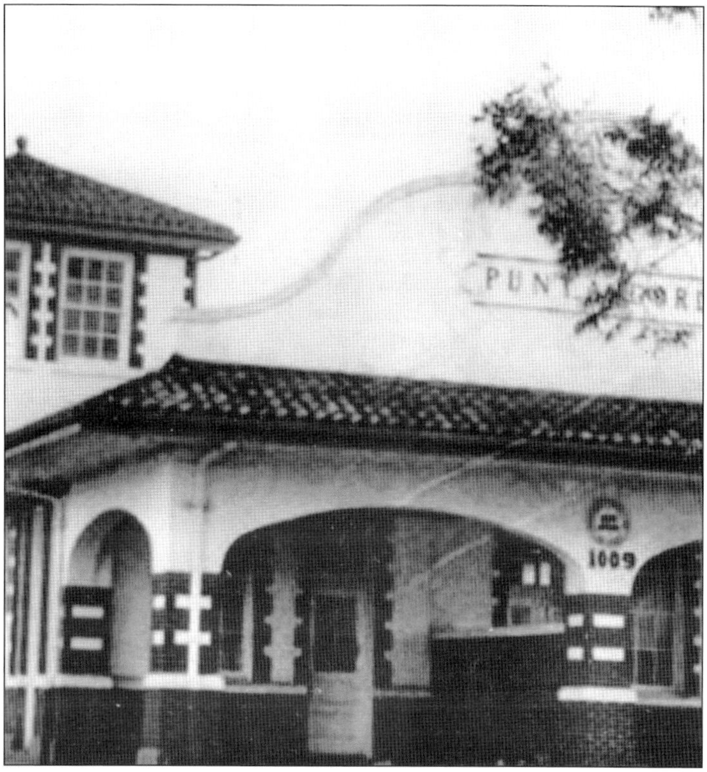

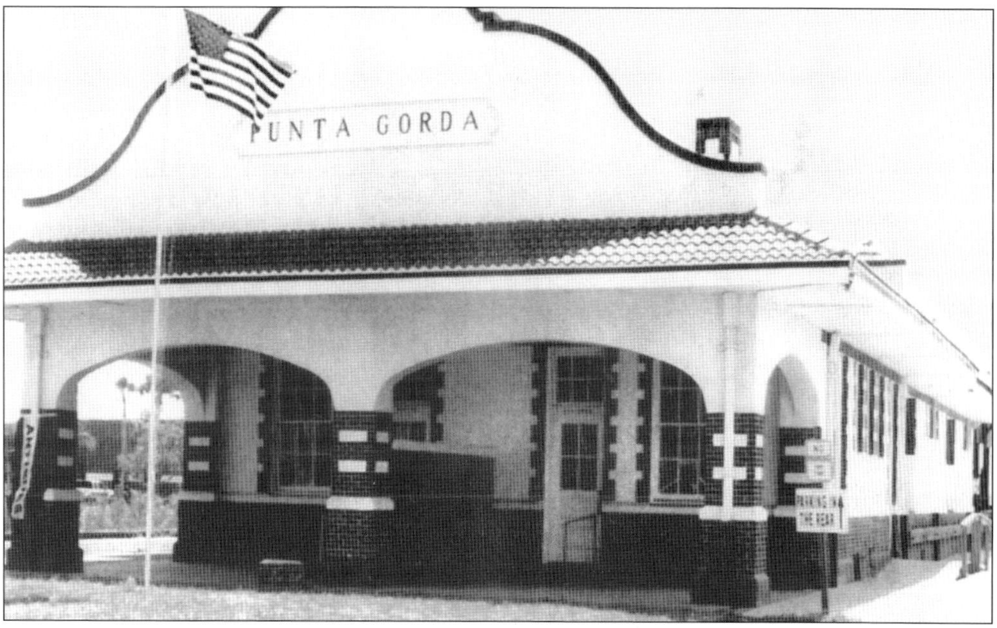

The Depot. The Punta Gorda Railroad Depot is located on Taylor Street and is the last railroad station constructed in Punta Gorda. Punta Gorda remained the country's southernmost railroad terminal until the line was extended to Fort Myers in 1904. The Atlantic Coastline Railroad Depot in Fort Myers now serves as the Southwest Florida Museum of History. The Punta Gorda Railroad Depot now serves as the Punta Gorda Historic Railroad Depot and Antique Mall.

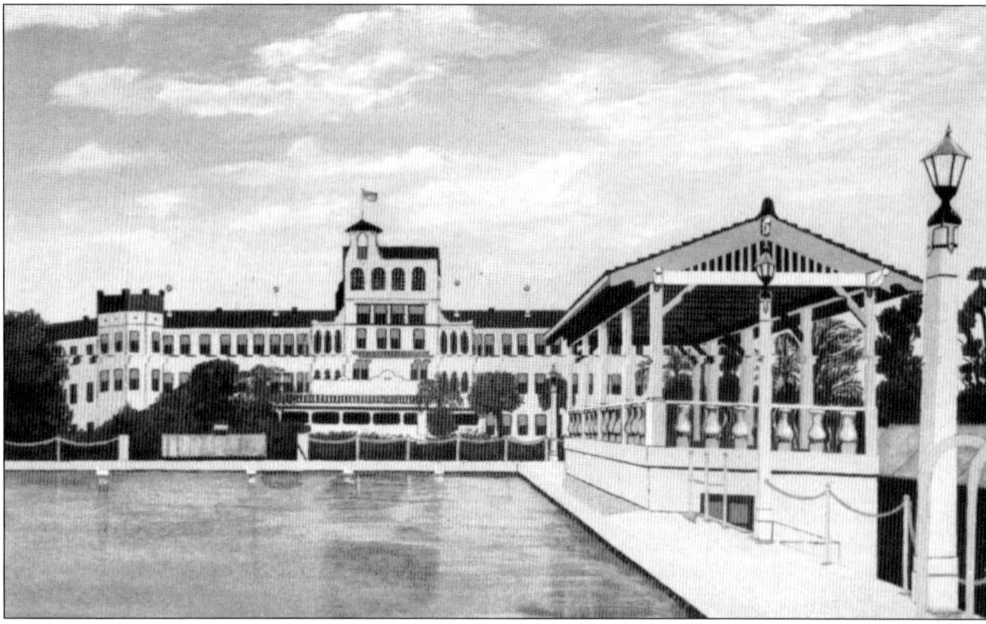

Hotel Charlotte Harbor. The key to the success of the Florida Southern Railway (later known as the Atlantic Coast Line) was the Hotel Punta Gorda. Hordes of visitors from the North came down to vacation via the railway system. All building materials used for the hotel also came down via the railway. The hotel was purchased by Barron Collier in 1925 and was remodeled with a grand reopening in January 1927. The hotel was renamed the Hotel Charlotte Harbor.

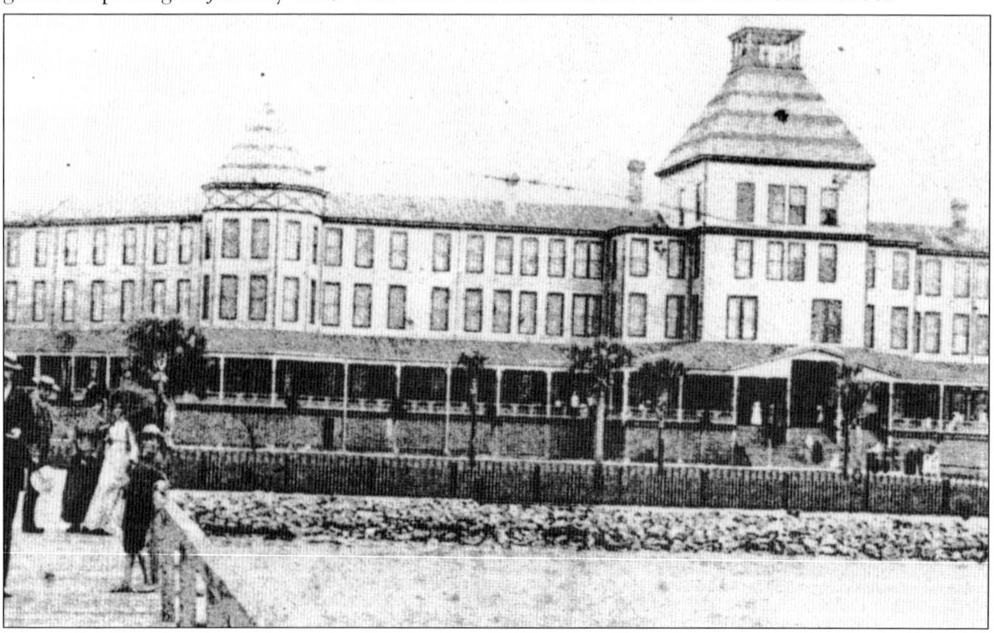

Hotel Punta Gorda, Late 1880s. In this early photograph, guests stroll along the hotel's 1,200-foot-long pier used to dock their yachts and boats. They came from the North by train in order to enjoy the beautiful hotel, the sunny skies, and the Charlotte Harbor waters. The railroad was the key mode of transportation for early southwest Florida before the highway system improved during World War II.

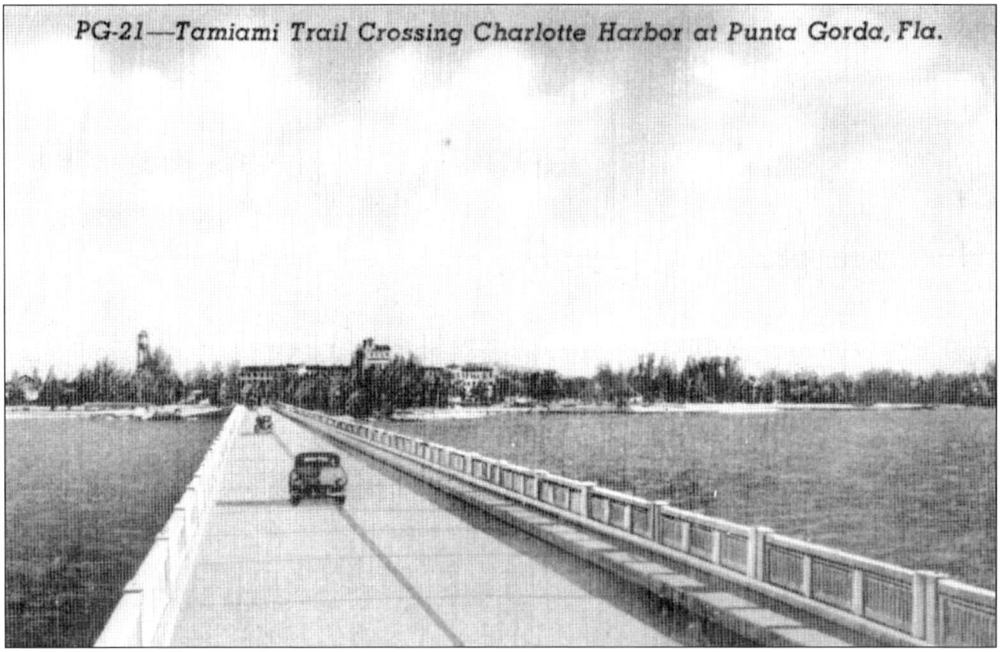

The Bridge across the Peace River. This early postcard shows the bridge across the Peace River headed toward Port Charlotte. Once the highway system was improved during World War II, as a result of the Federal Aid Highway Act, cars became the more dominant means of getting to and from Punta Gorda.

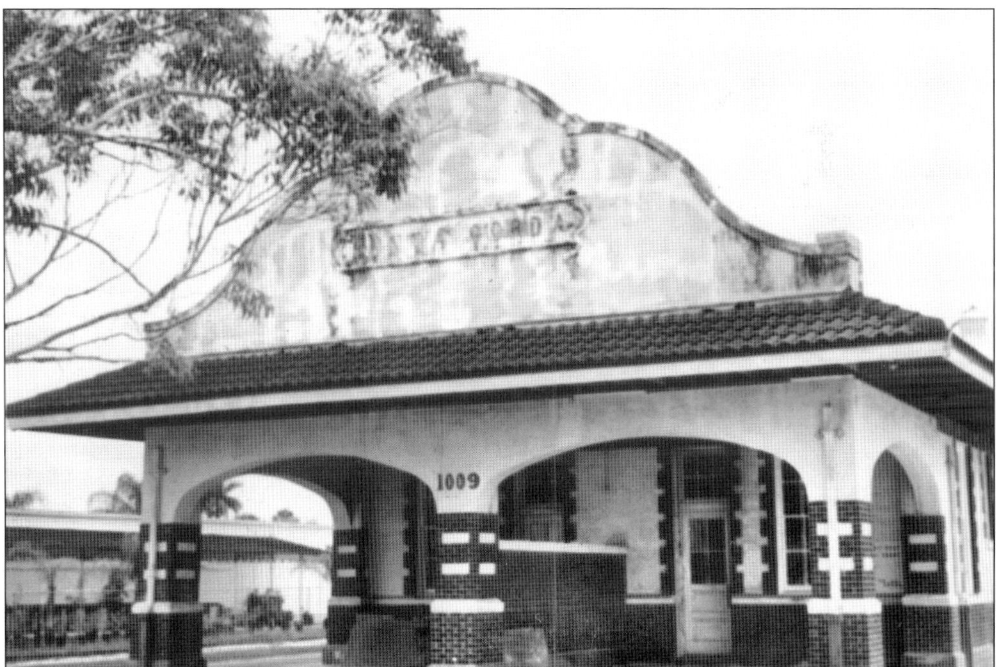

Train Depot in Need of Restoration. After 1971, when the railroad ceased operations, the depot remained closed for a few years. The late Fred Babcock acquired the depot and then gave the Punta Gorda Historical Society money to purchase the depot from him in 1996.

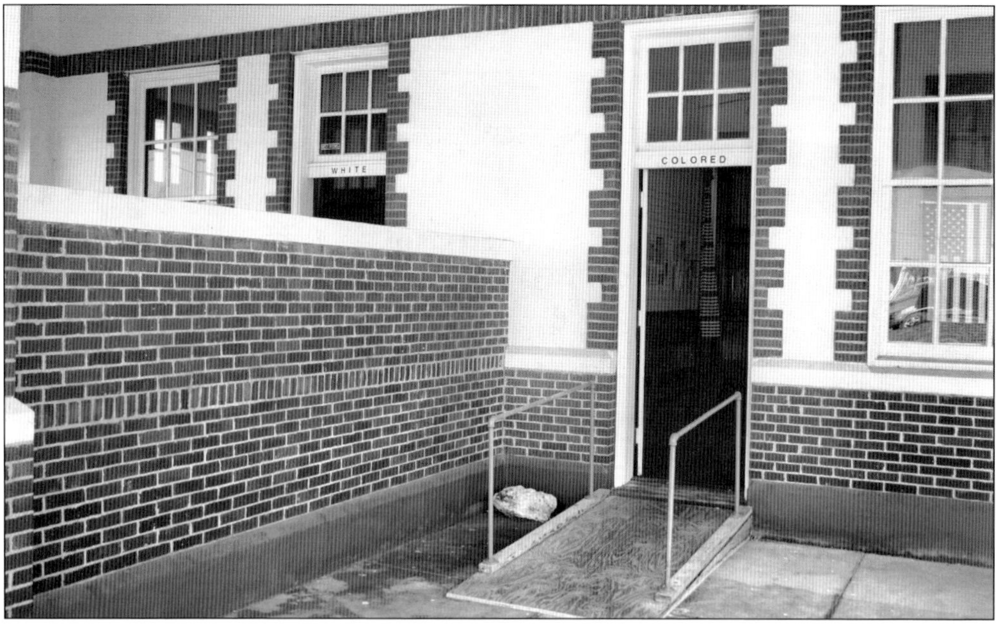

Punta Gorda Railroad Depot's Segregated Waiting Rooms. The ticketing areas were segregated, as were the bathrooms. This ticketing area is for "colored" only. Segregation was the law in the South and in Punta Gorda when the railroad depot was built in 1928. The "colored" waiting room doorway was separated from the "white" doorway by a brick wall. (Photograph by Scot Shively; Blanchard House Museum of African-American History and Culture of Charlotte County.)

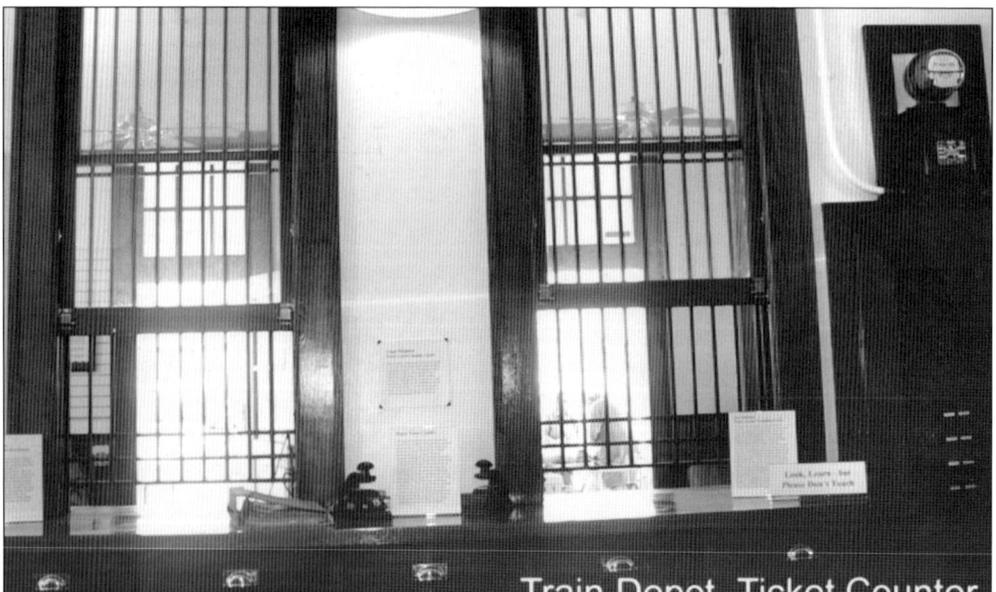

Ticketing Counter. The depot's ticketing counter is seen from the ticket agent's point of view. The two separate windows are reminiscent of the days of segregation and the Jim Crow laws of "separate but equal." The "colored" waiting room is the window on the left, while the "white" waiting room is on the right. (Photograph by Dr. and Mrs. David Phelen; Punta Gorda Historical Society.)

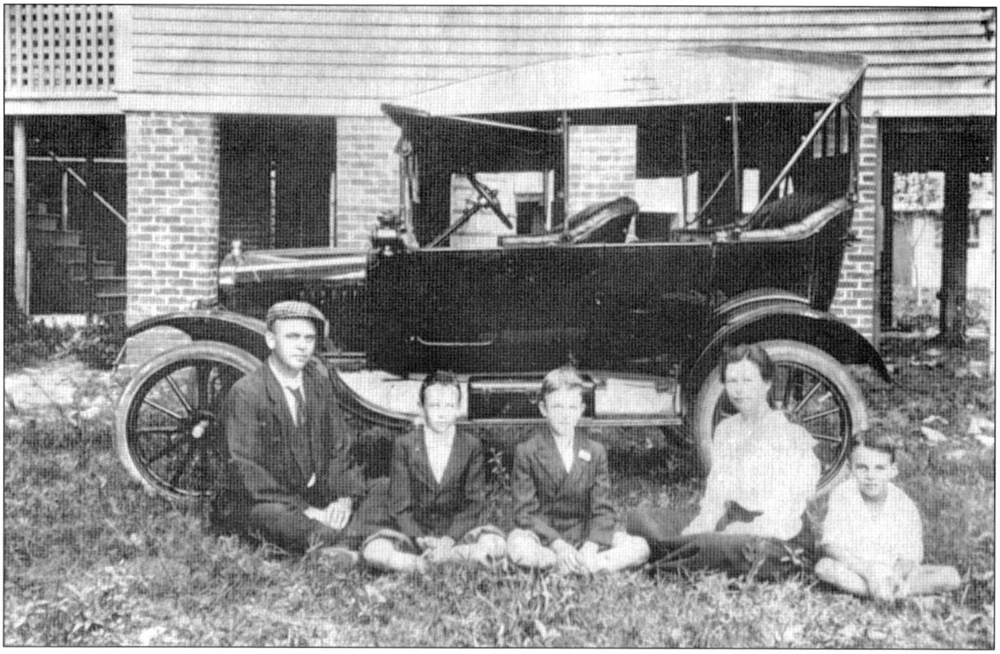

EDGAR ROUNDTREE AND FAMILY. Edgar Roundtree and his family pose for a photograph with their automobile. Edgar was the first station agent to work at the Punta Gorda Historic Railroad Depot. He was in charge of the station and the Punta Gorda railway operations. His job would have included working as a ticket agent and perhaps even as baggage handler and telegraph operator.

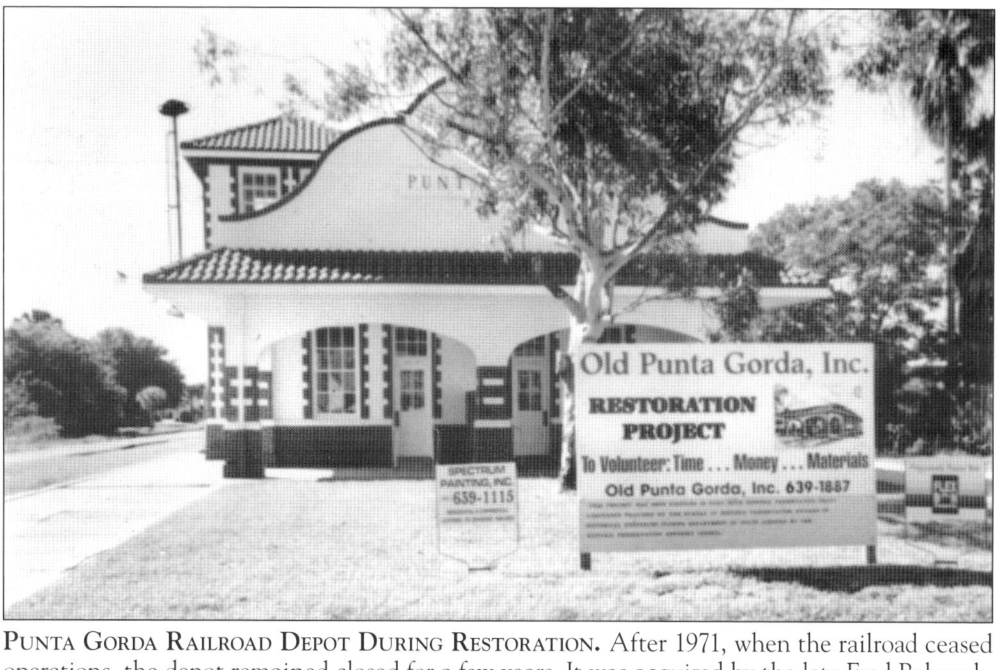

PUNTA GORDA RAILROAD DEPOT DURING RESTORATION. After 1971, when the railroad ceased operations, the depot remained closed for a few years. It was acquired by the late Fred Babcock, who in turn gave the Punta Gorda Historical Society money to purchase the depot from him in 1996. It has since been restored and now houses an antique mall. A railroad museum is planned for the ticketing area.

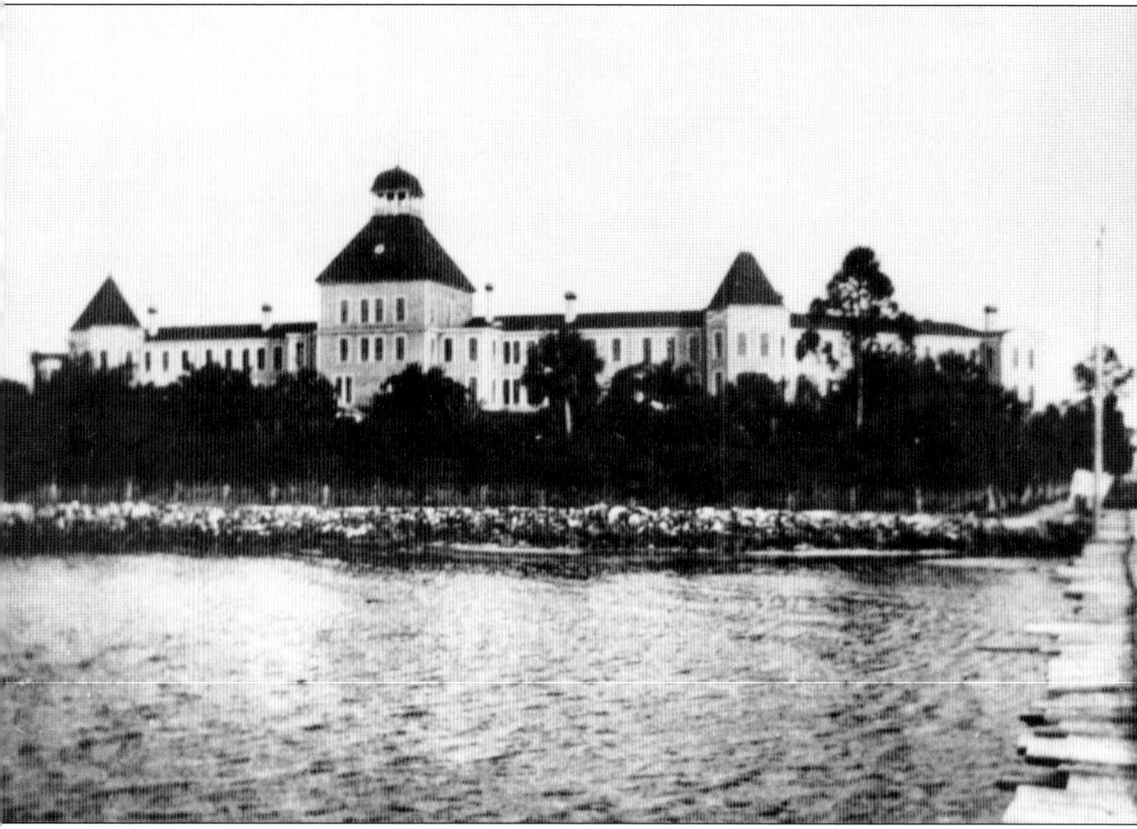

Hotel Punta Gorda. On the Long Dock were several businesses and a rail line that was used to load and unload goods. Long Dock wasn't the only dock in Punta Gorda. Hotel Punta Gorda also had a long dock for the guests to use for their boats and yachts. The dock seen at far right is the City Dock at the foot of Sullivan Street. (*Fact and Fable: Charlotte County.*)

Two

Early Settlers

As the southernmost end of the rail line, Punta Gorda was the last stop. This final length of track brought a mixed bunch of characters off the trains and to the area. There were rich ones and poor ones. There were highly regarded ones and shady ones. There were African Americans and whites. All of them played key roles in the early settlement years. One of Punta Gorda's early pioneers was George Brown. He was an African American shipbuilder who was also known as Florida's first "equal opportunity employer." Brown hired both African American workers and white workers. Another key African American was Robert Meacham. He was the third postmaster and was said to have been appointed in 1890 by Isaac Trabue. Trabue arrived in the area to create his own town, Trabue, on land he purchased from British investors in 1885. However, the area was renamed Punta Gorda when the city was later incorporated. Trabue was out-voted in the decision to incorporation the town, and so he eventually returned to his home state of Kentucky.

Punta Gorda was officially incorporated in 1887 by a group of 34 men, four of whom were African American. The group met at Hector's Billiard Parlor and Drugstore to incorporate the city. Later that year, after it was officially incorporated, a five-member council was formed and official mayoral elections took place. Interesting to note is that out of the five council members, four of them were not American citizens. The only one who was a native Floridian was Albert Gilchrist. Gilchrist was elected governor of Florida in 1909.

Other key people who came to the area were Cornelius Vanderbilt, who was a partial owner of the regal Hotel Punta Gorda, and the Howard brothers, who arrived in the 1870s at Charlotte Harbor and were among the first settlers of the area. The Howard brothers homesteaded their land and grew oranges and vegetables.

Along with notable persons, shadier characters also arrived and brought their share of troubles with them. In fact, 40 murders occurred between 1890 and 1904. City marshal John H. Bowman was shot and killed in front of his family while sitting in his own front parlor on January 29, 1903.

But mostly people came to the area in search of a better life.

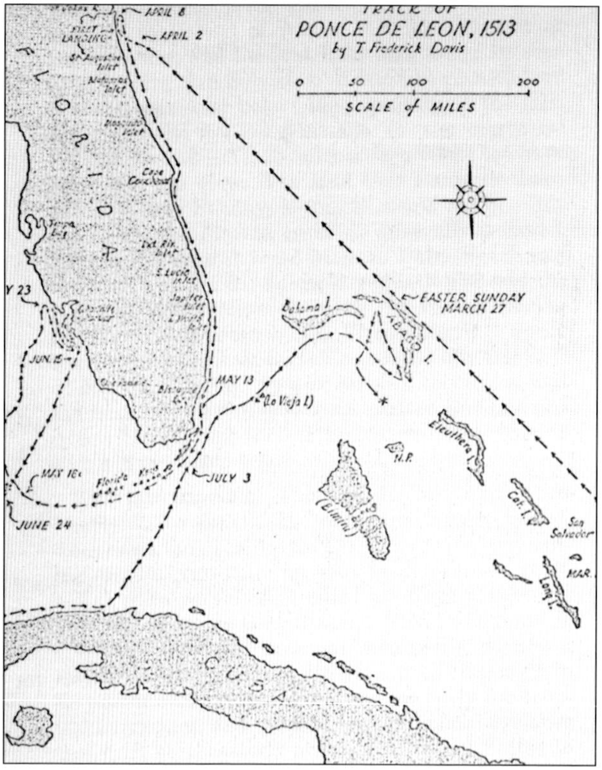

Map Depicting Ponce De León's Travels. This map shows the trek that Ponce de León took to the Charlotte Harbor area in 1521. Juan Ponce de León came back to Florida to build a farming colony in the Charlotte Harbor area. His first trip to the area was in 1513. He arrived with settlers, horses, tools, and other useful items. The Calusa Indians attacked, and Ponce de León was shot by an arrow, causing a serious wound. Ponce de León and his settlers abandoned the settlement and sailed back to Cuba, where he later died of his wounds.

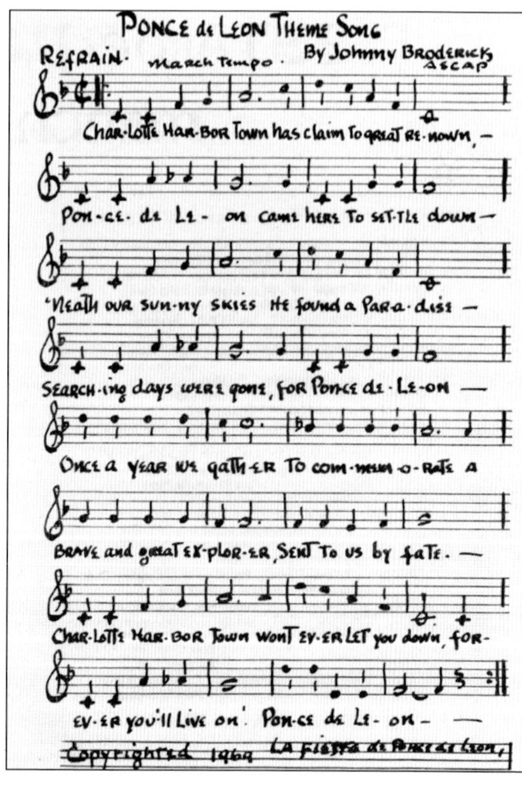

The "Ponce De León Theme Song." The "Ponce de León Theme Song," by Johnny Broderick, was part of Charlotte Harbor's centennial celebration. Punta Gorda was officially incorporated in 1887, and the centennial celebration took place 100 years later in 1987. Ponce de León came to the area first in 1513 and returned in 1521, but other famous explorers came to the area as well. There was de Narvaez in 1527 and de Soto in 1539, but Ponce de León is perhaps the most famous.

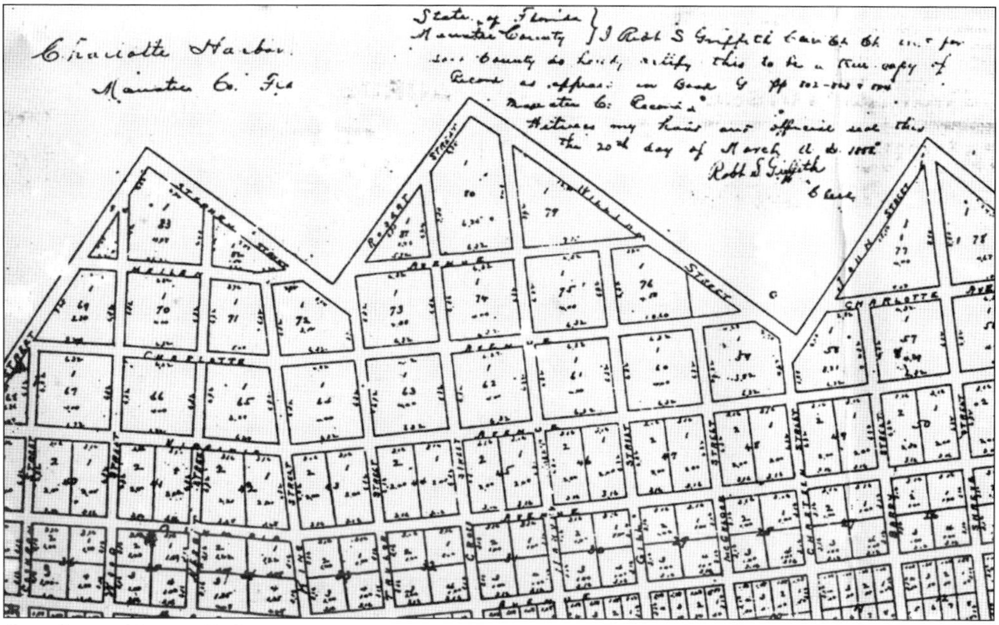

COL. ISAAC TRABUE'S ORIGINAL 1885 PLAT OF THE TOWN. On February 5, 1883, Kentucky native Isaac Trabue purchased 30 acres of land on the south bank of the Peace River, sight unseen, for $300 from John Cross, a land developer. Isaac Trabue and his wife, Virginia, came down to look over the purchased property and were not at all happy with what they found. He had the land platted into lots and named the new town after himself, Trabue.

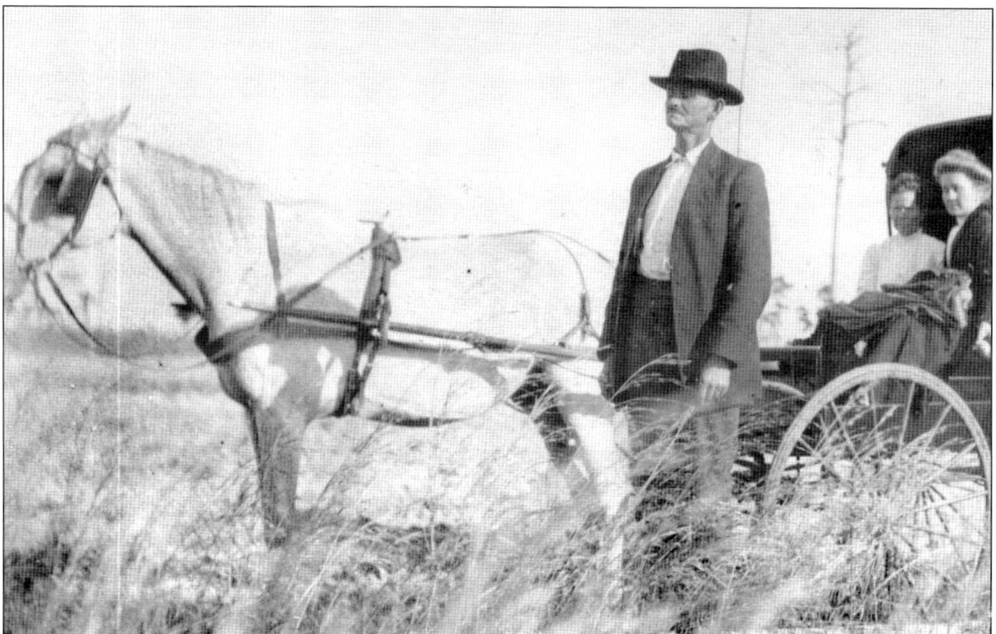

HORSE AND BUGGY. Early settlers used horses and buggies as a means of transportation. Horses arrived in Florida as early as 1521, when Ponce de León brought horses, cattle, and other livestock. Cracker horses, as Florida horses were commonly known as, were used as buggy horses and working horses. They were often the sources of power for many family farms. (Eloise McDougal.)

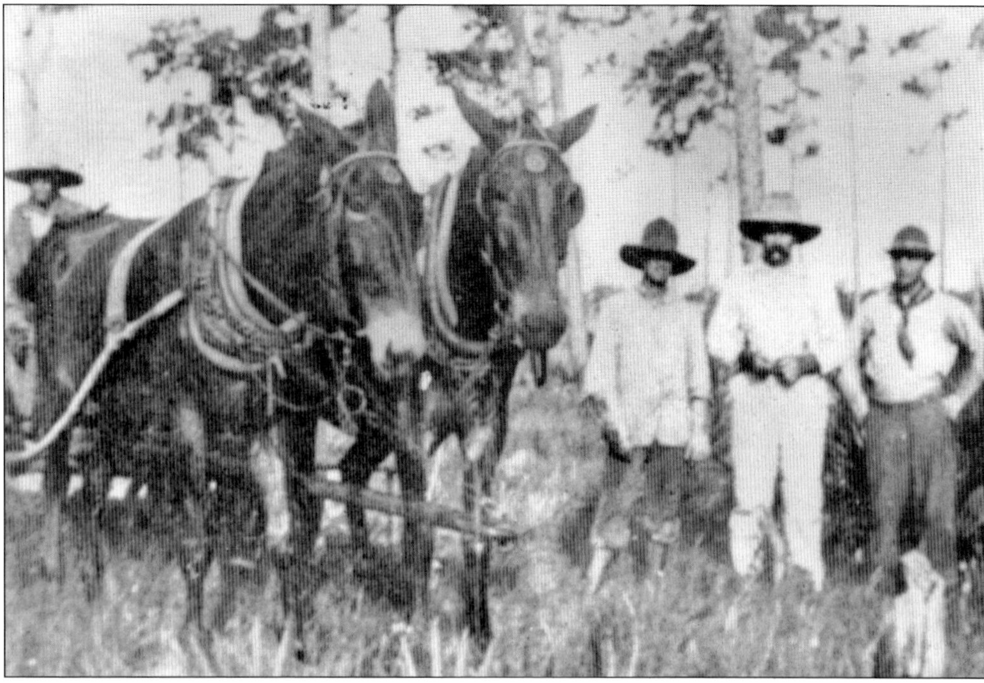

Punta Gorda Street Department Crew. This early photograph shows the Street Department Crew in the 1890s clearing a street right-of-way in Punta Gorda. Back then, the scrub palmettos and roots were scraped off to cut the new street. (U. S. Cleveland Collection.)

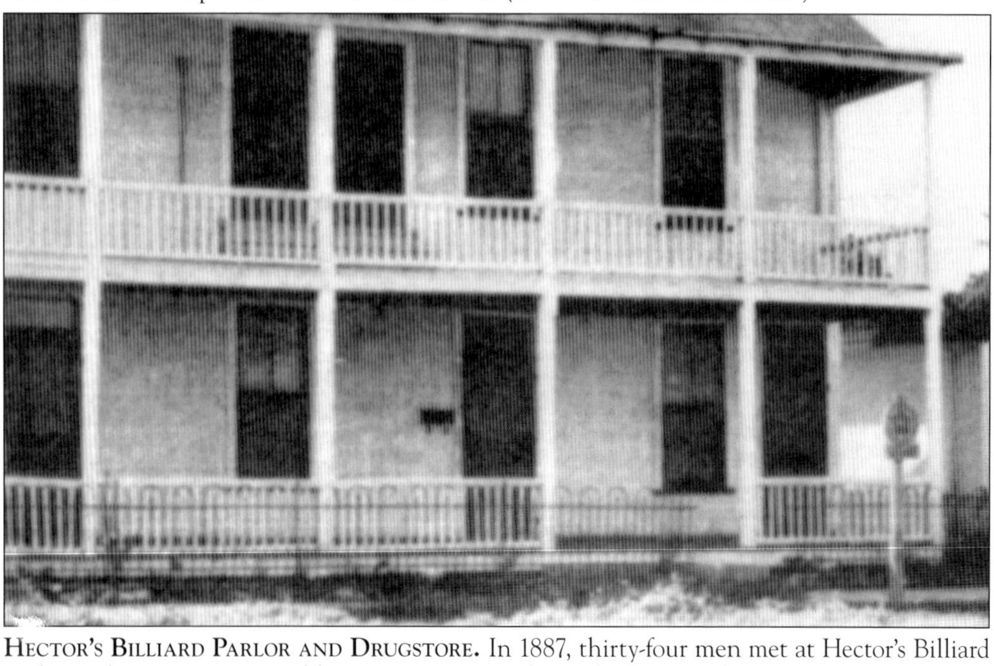

Hector's Billiard Parlor and Drugstore. In 1887, thirty-four men met at Hector's Billiard Parlor and Drugstore, owned by Tom Hector, and voted to create the municipality of Punta Gorda. They met around the pool table located on the second floor. The first floor of the building contained the drugstore. The home was later owned by the Connolly family. (*Ceremonial Journal*; Charlotte Harbor Area Historical Society.)

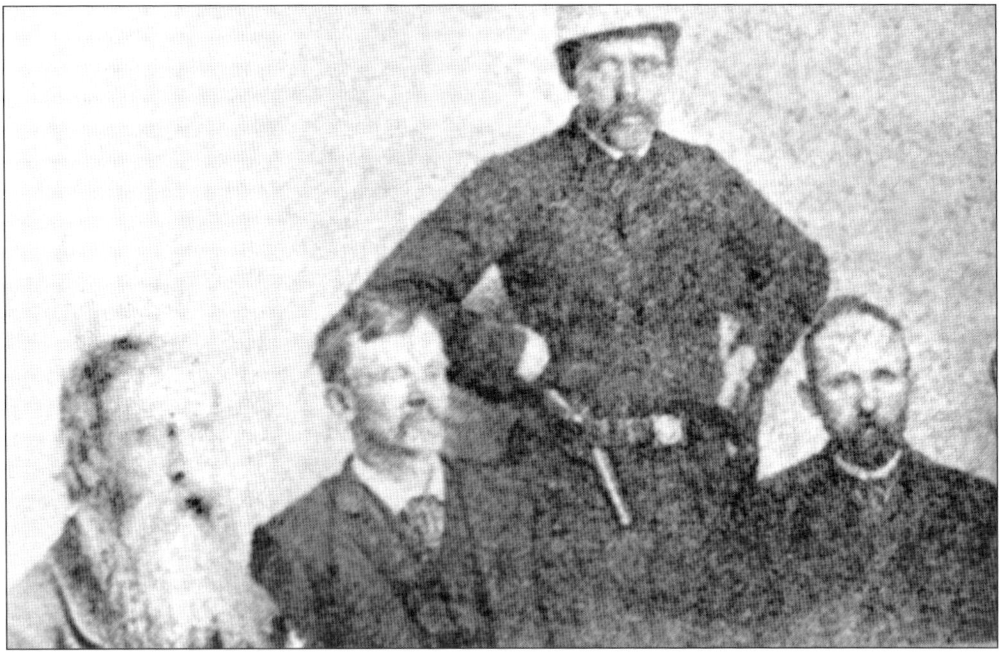

CITY COUNCIL IN 1887. This photograph depicts some of the members of Punta Gorda's first city council in 1887. From left to right are Tom Hector, who was a city clerk; J. O. Swisher; John Fishback; and Dr. W. H. Burland. Perhaps the photograph was taken at Hector's Billiard Parlor and Drugstore, where the meeting to incorporate Punta Gorda took place in 1887.

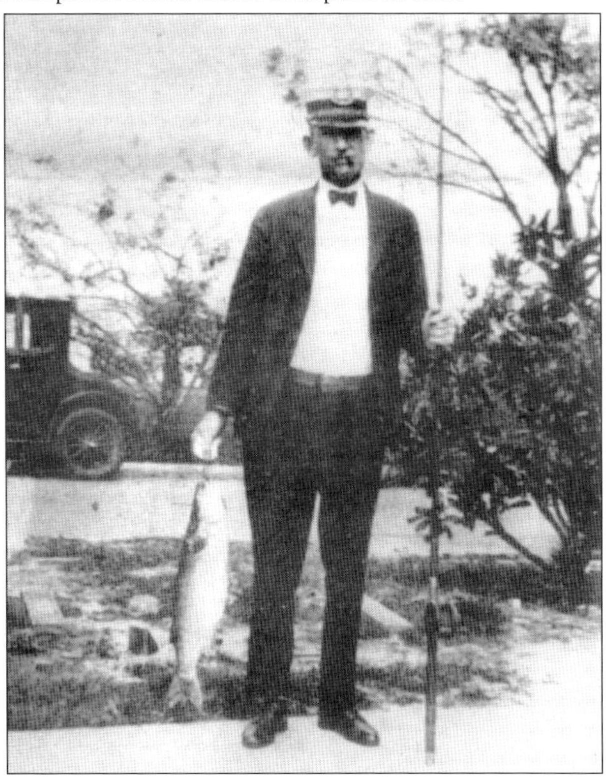

LESLIE LEWIS. Leslie "Lee" Lewis was Punta Gorda's first chief of police. He was also an avid fisherman, like many of the early settlers. In his free time away from enforcing the law, no doubt he fished as often as he could. The city of Punta Gorda is about 18 miles square and is located in Charlotte County. Charlotte County was formed in 1921 after DeSoto County was divided into five counties.

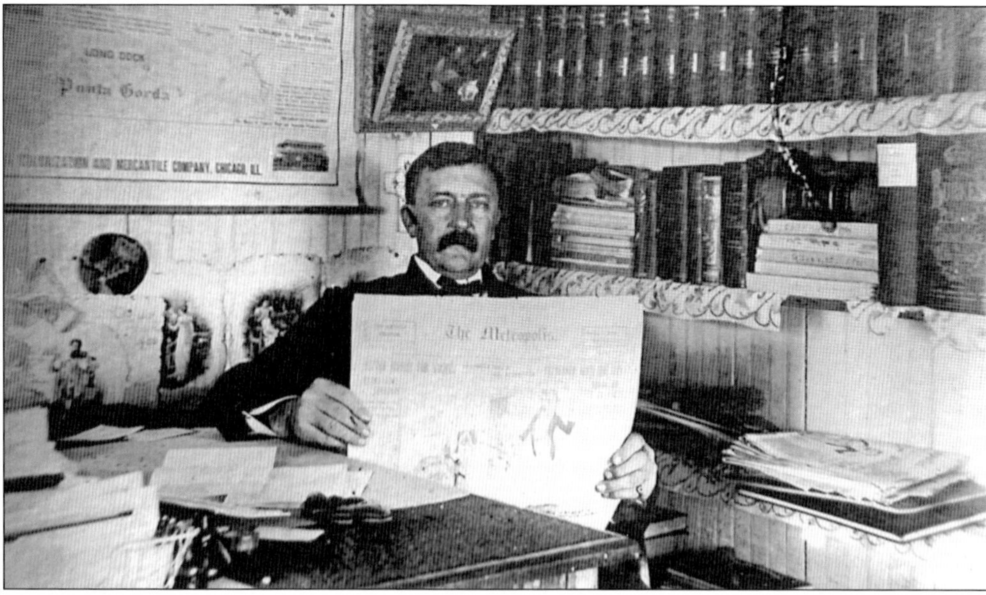

ALBERT GILCHRIST IN HIS OFFICE. Albert Gilchrist, a surveyor and real estate broker, was one of Punta Gorda's five original councilmen. Punta Gorda was officially incorporated in 1887, shortly after mayoral elections took place and the council was formed. Gilchrist initially came to the area to become an orange grower. In 1893, he was elected state representative, and in 1909, he became the 20th governor of Florida. Gilchrist County, Florida, is named after him. Gilchrist also donated the royal palm trees located on Marion Avenue in 1900.

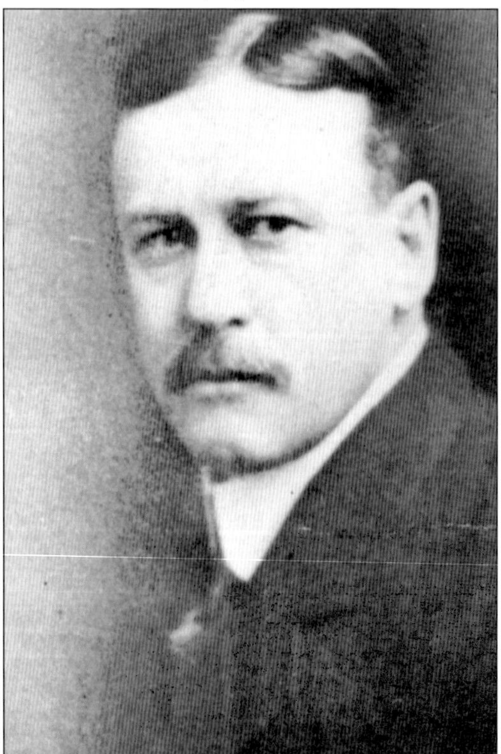

JOHN MILTON MURDOCK. John Milton Murdock was a land speculator from Chicago. He owned the Murdock Land Company and negotiated various purchases of land around the Charlotte Station and Northern Railway Depot in the early 1900s. Many speculators, like Murdock, took advantage of the Great Florida Land Boom in the 1920s, before the Great Depression began in 1929.

Col. Isaac Trabue. Isaac Trabue, a Unionist Kentucky lawyer, purchased 30 acres of land located on the Peace River's south shore in 1884 to found his town of Trabue. The area on the north shore of the Peace River was called Hickory Bluff and is now know as Charlotte Harbor. Trabue purchased waterfront acreage to encourage the Florida Southern Railway to build its track this far south. In 1885, he platted the town of Trabue and set aside a city block for the planting and cultivation of pineapples. In 1887, the city was renamed Punta Gorda by a group of 34 men who met at Hector's Billiard Parlor and Drugstore to incorporate the city. This was much to Trabue's dismay. (U. S. Cleveland Collection.)

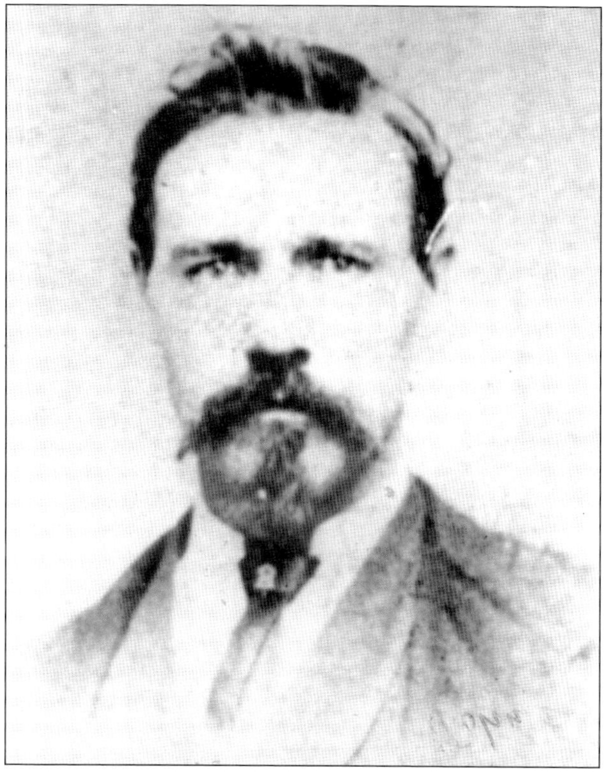

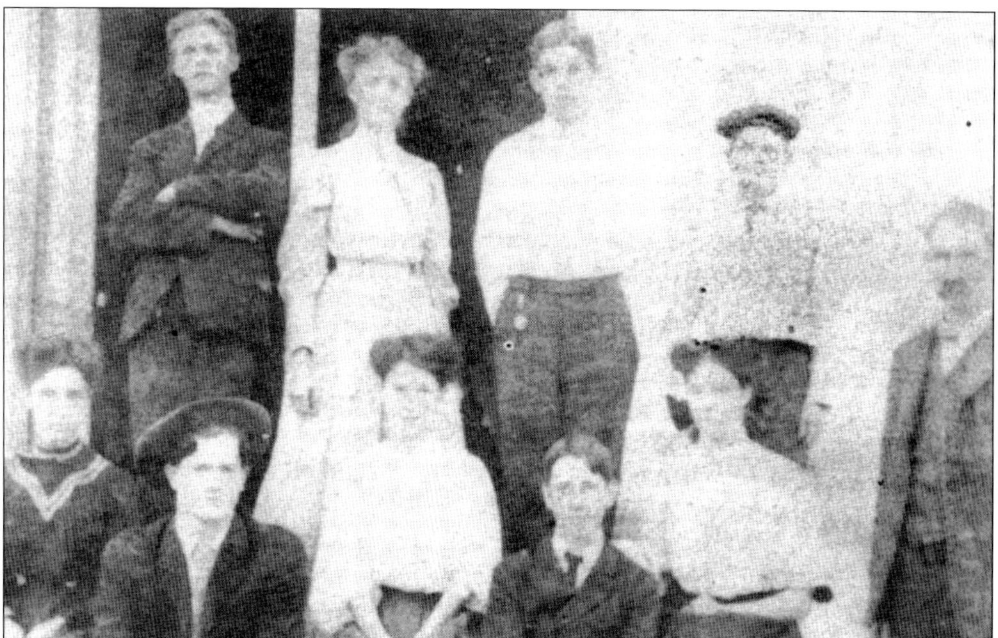

Punta Gorda High School Class of 1906. The Punta Gorda High School class of 1906 was quite small. Professor Foulk was the teacher, and the class had only one senior, Beatrice Meechaw. From left to right are (first row) Undine Jordon, Julian Jordan, Beatrice Meechaw, Gordon Liberty, and Mae Straughn; (second row) Alan Whiteaker, Libby Peka, Karl Fries, and unidentified.

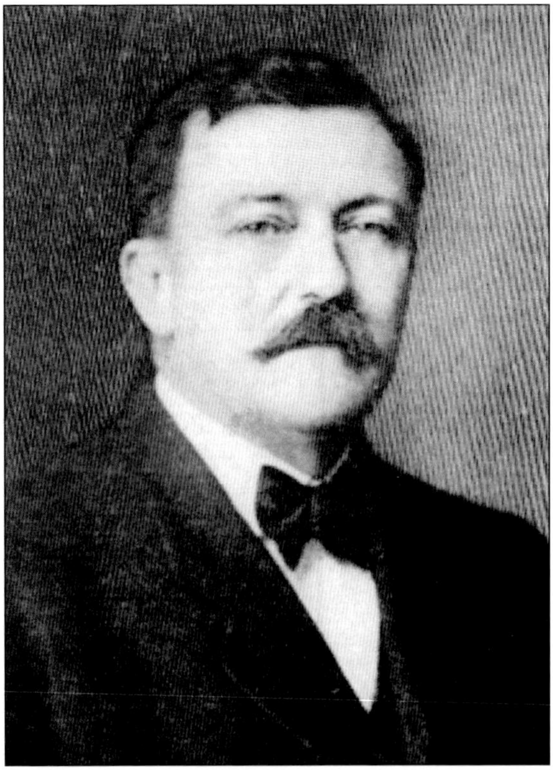

Albert Gilchrist. Gilchrist was Florida's 20th governor from 1909 to 1913. He studied at the Carolina Military Institute and at the U.S. Military Academy at West Point. Gilchrist served his country during the Spanish-American War and worked as a civil engineer, a real estate agent, and a citrus grower in Punta Gorda. As governor, Gilchrist worked toward bettering the state by endorsing legislation that produced a tuberculosis sanitarium, a pure food law, and even a hospital for impoverished crippled children. He ran for the U.S. Senate in 1916 but did not win. (Florida Photographic Collection, the Florida Memory Project.)

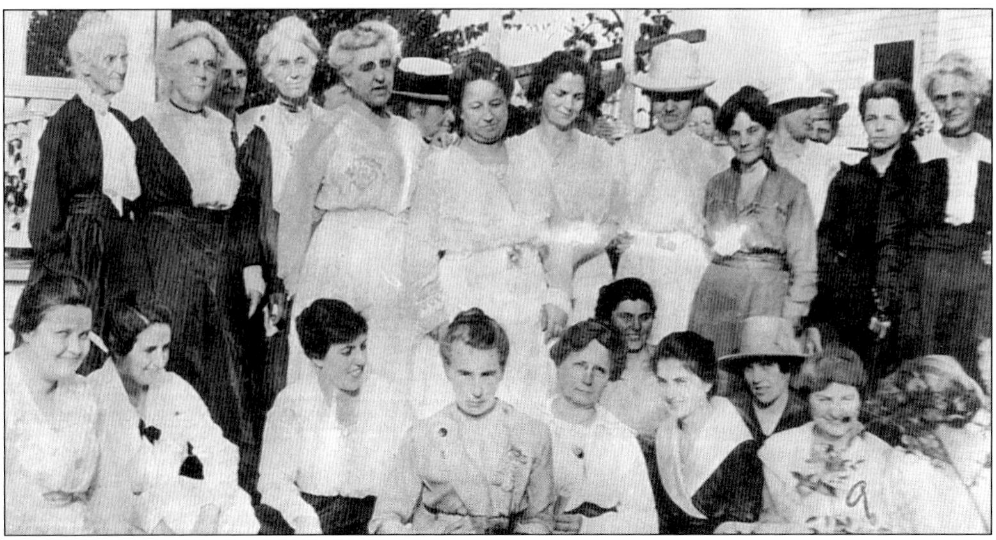

Woman's Club Members in 1927. This 1927 photograph shows the Woman's Club Members. In 1925, three local women's groups—the Woman's Civic Association, the Married Ladies Club, and the Fortnightly Club—consolidated and formed the Punta Gorda Woman's Club. The Woman's Civic Association worked on projects such as building the bathhouse. Members of the Married Ladies Club engaged in polite conversation at meetings and were required to wear hats and gloves. They were called the "tea drinkers." The Fortnightly Club was a literary club. They studied works by Robert Browning and William Shakespeare and read *The Divine Comedy*. (Punta Gorda Historical Society, Linda Wilson collection.)

MIDWIFE CORNELIA PONDER. Cornelia Ponder was born in 1874 in Georgia and came to Punta Gorda around the turn of the 20th century. Cornelia received medical training and was a practical nurse. At one time, Cornelia was Punta Gorda's only midwife tending to expectant mothers, both black and white. Cornelia was very religious and brought hundreds of Punta Gorda's children into the world. (Blanchard House Museum of African-American History and Culture of Charlotte County.)

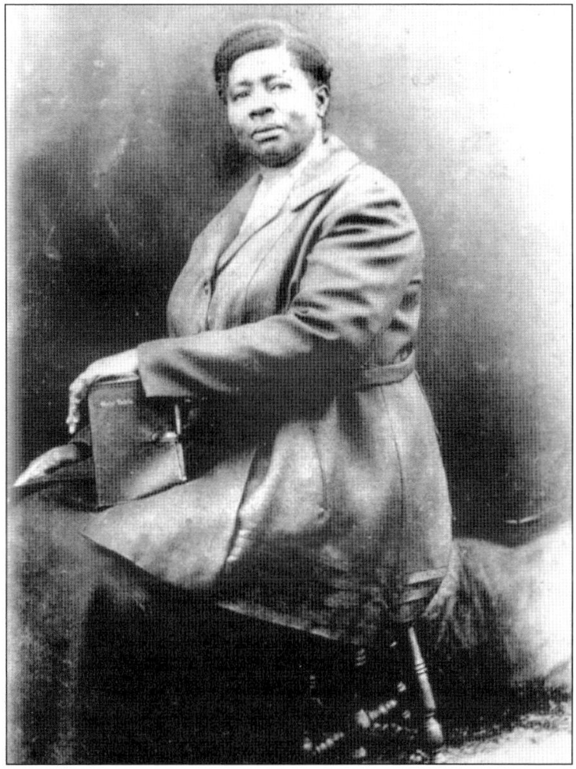

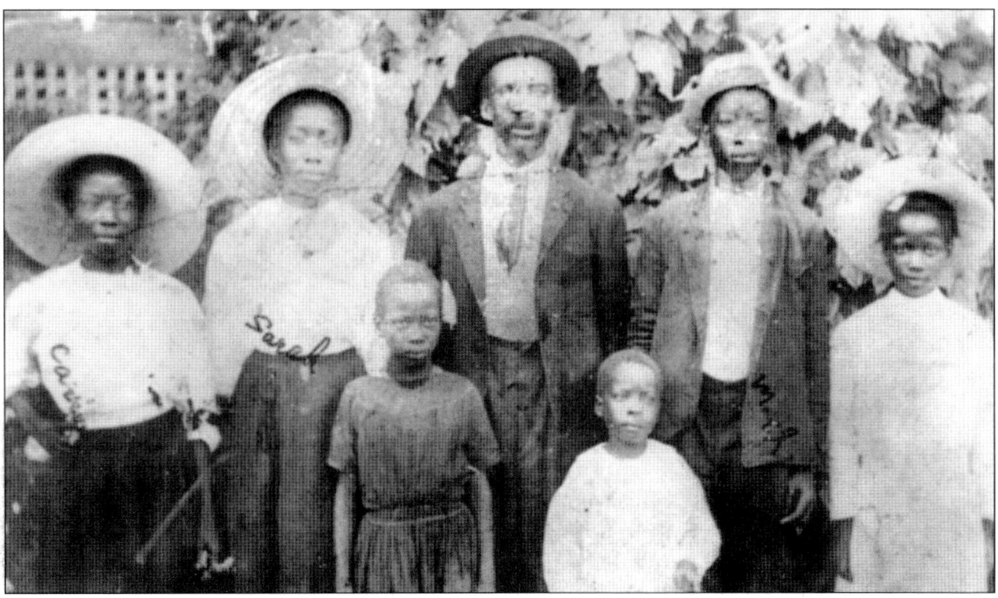

DAN C. SMITH AND FAMILY AROUND 1911. Dan C. Smith came to the area that would become Punta Gorda in 1886 as part of the Florida Southern Railroad survey team led by engineer Albert Gilchrist. Dan and fellow team member Sam Kennedy remained in Punta Gorda, purchased land, and settled down to become the African American community's patriarchs. This Smith family photograph was taken shortly after Dan's wife Louisa's death in 1911. (Blanchard House Museum of African-American History and Culture of Charlotte County.)

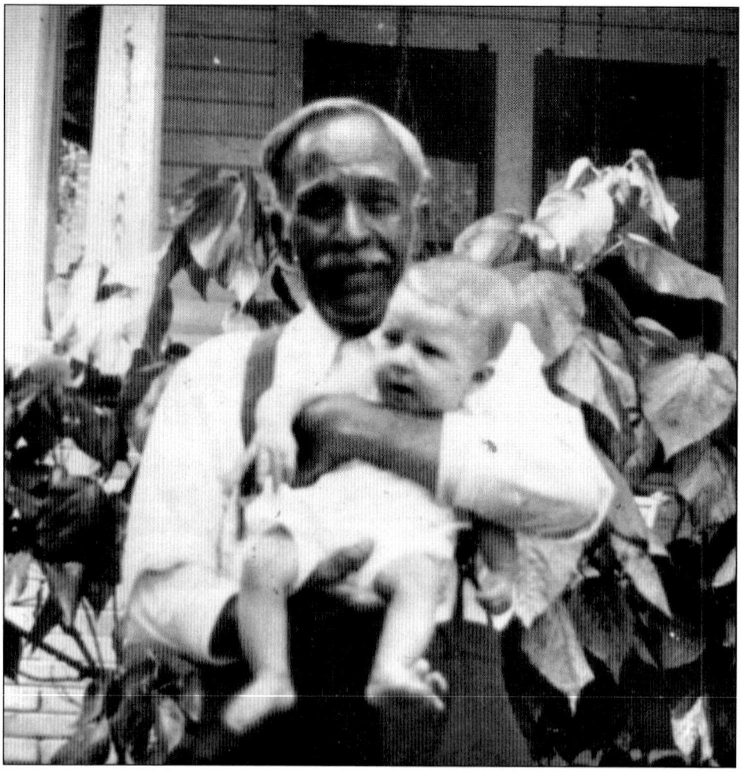

"Mister" George Brown. George Brown, an accomplished carpenter and cabinetmaker, came as part of a crew of black men in 1890 to build barges for the Peace River Phosphate Company. "Mister" Brown was a prominent businessman and landowner, owning at one time about half the land that is now the city of Punta Gorda. (Blanchard House Museum of African-American History and Culture of Charlotte County.)

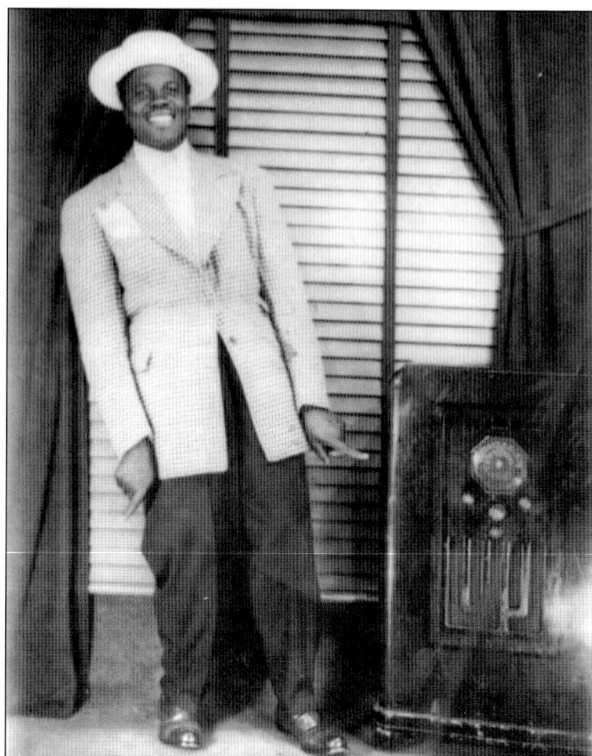

James Prince Ready for a Night on the Town. James Prince is dressed and ready to spend the evening "Down the street" in Punta Gorda. Cochran Street was the main street of the African American community in Punta Gorda during the days of segregation. The place to be on Friday night was either Gollman's or Ward's Bar, both located on the corner of Virginia Avenue and Cochran Street. When anyone would ask, "Where are you going?," the answer was always "Down the street." (Blanchard House Museum of African-American History and Culture of Charlotte County.)

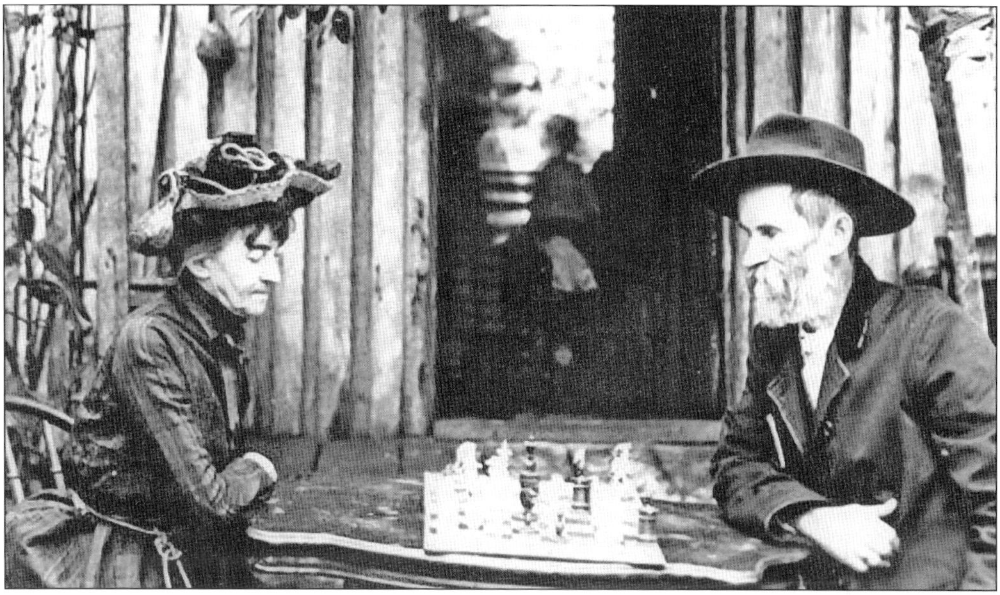

COL. ISAAC H. AND VIRGINIA TRABUE AT PUNTA GORDA, 1891. Colonel Trabue came from a notable family in Kentucky, as his grandfather was a general in the Revolutionary War. Trabue was a well-known chess player in Kentucky, and when he relocated to Florida in 1885, he took his pastime with him. Sight unseen, he purchased his first plot of land, which was 30 acres. In a deal with Henry Plant of the Southern Florida Railroad, he traded some of his land to Plant to have him extend the railroad into the new town, called Trabue. (Courtesy of Rollins College Archive.)

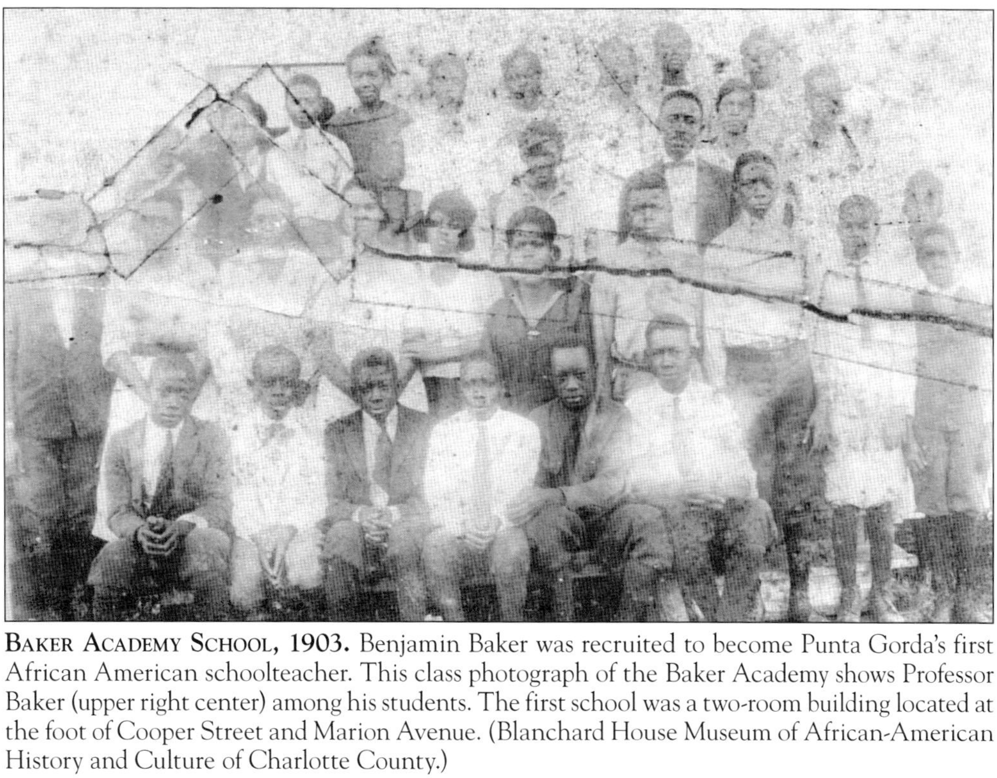

BAKER ACADEMY SCHOOL, 1903. Benjamin Baker was recruited to become Punta Gorda's first African American schoolteacher. This class photograph of the Baker Academy shows Professor Baker (upper right center) among his students. The first school was a two-room building located at the foot of Cooper Street and Marion Avenue. (Blanchard House Museum of African-American History and Culture of Charlotte County.)

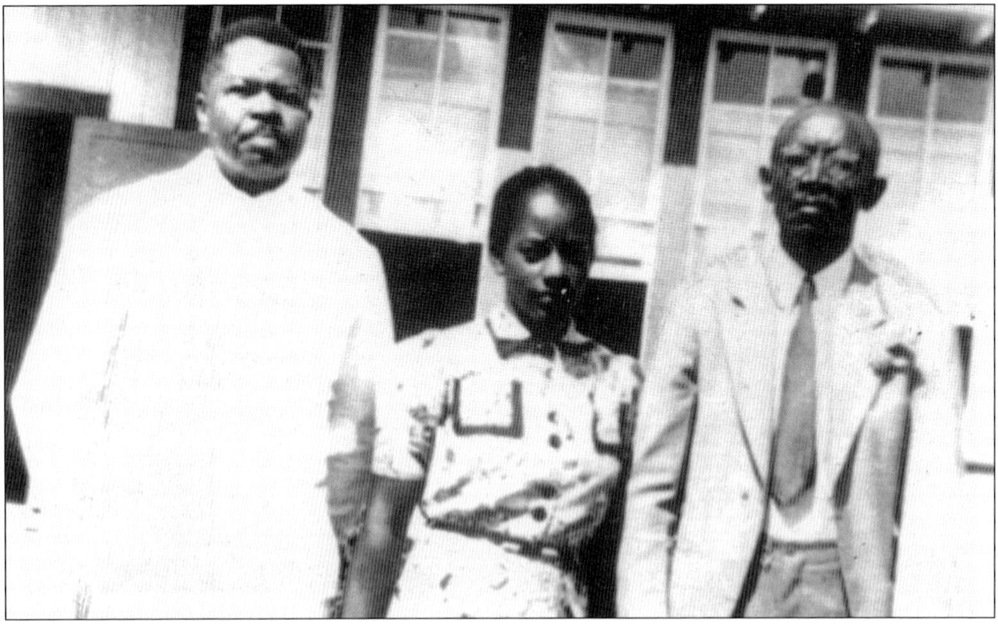

PRINCIPAL BENJAMIN J. Baker. Prof. Benjamin J. Baker (far right) was persuaded to come to Punta Gorda in 1903 to teach the "coloreds." Affectionately called "Fess" by his students, Benjamin taught for nearly 50 years and took personal interest in each and every student under his charge. The new Baker Center, dedicated in 2007, is Punta Gorda's third school named in his honor. (Blanchard House Museum of African-American History and Culture of Charlotte County.)

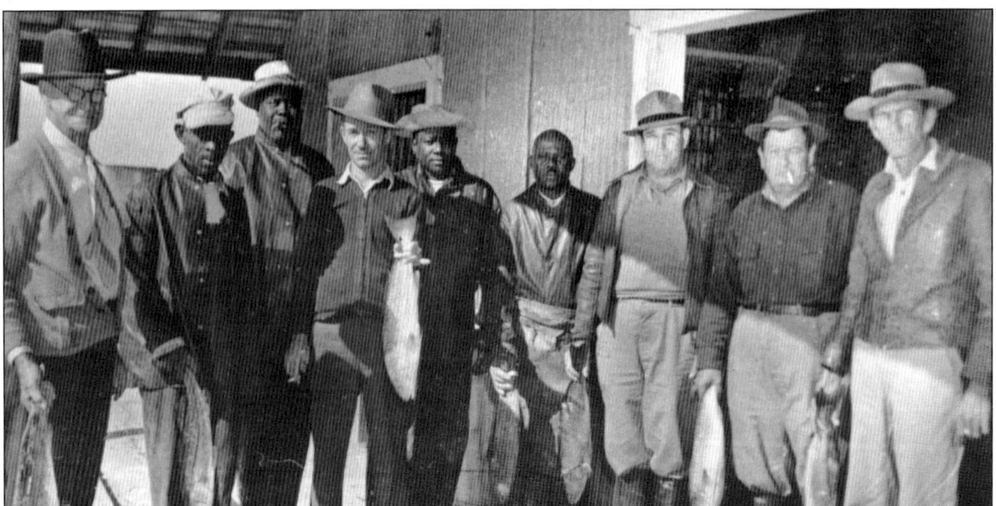

PUNTA GORDA FISH COMPANY WORKERS. Charlotte Harbor had been one of the most bountiful fishing grounds, first fished by the Cuban-Spanish Indians. Later the fish were commercially fished and shipped north to market. The Punta Gorda Fish Company, one of the largest fishing operations, was organized in 1897. However, a devastating fire broke out on the King Street Dock in June 1915 and temporarily stopped the Punta Gorda Fish Company. Men of the Punta Gorda Fish Company are, from left to right, Harry R. Dreggors, Andrew "Mullet" Owens, Tom Coleman, Harry R. Goulding, "Bum" Mansel Graham, Sammy Holmes, William H. Monson, Floyd Chadwick, and William E. Guthrie. (U. S. Cleveland Collection.)

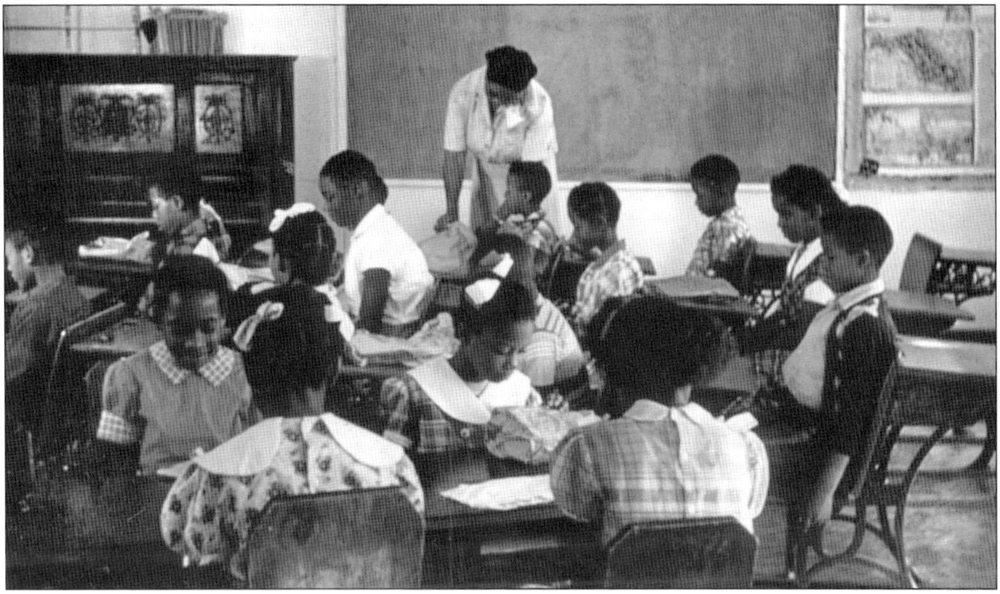

CLASSROOM AT THE BAKER ACADEMY. Pictured here is Nettie Mae Smith's classroom in the Baker Academy during the 1950s. The school added classes and eventually taught grades one through eight. Because of segregation, most local African American children had to attend Dunbar High School in Fort Myers. Baker Academy remained segregated until 1964, when Charlotte County Schools were integrated. (Blanchard House Museum of African-American History and Culture of Charlotte County.)

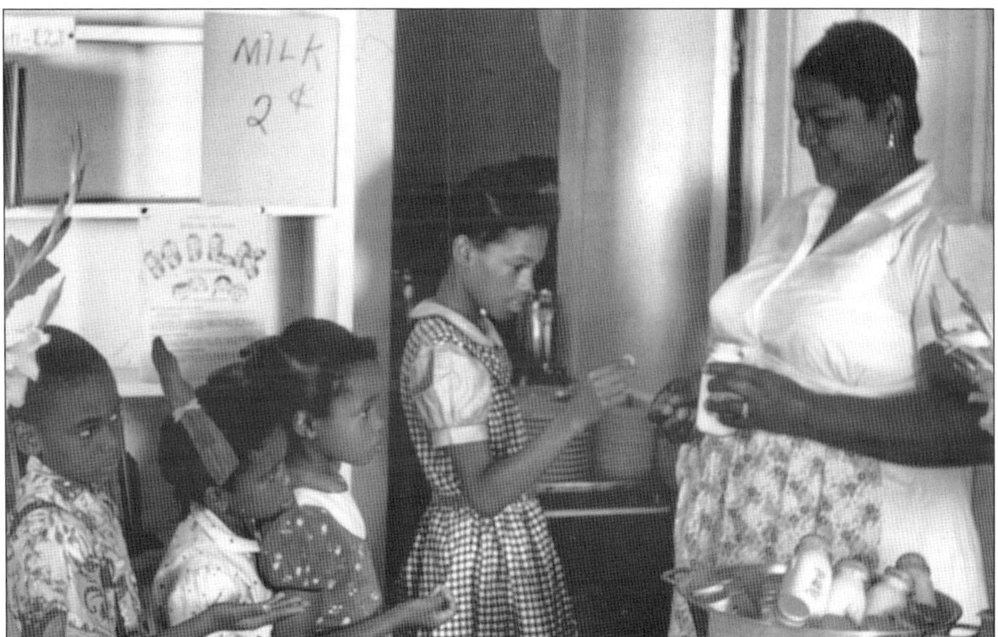

MARY GOODNIGHT AROUND 1955. At Punta Gorda's African American school, Baker Academy, lunch lady Mary Goodnight takes Martha Russell's 2¢ for a bottle of milk. The four-room school's library also functioned as the lunchroom. (Blanchard House Museum of African-American History and Culture of Charlotte County.)

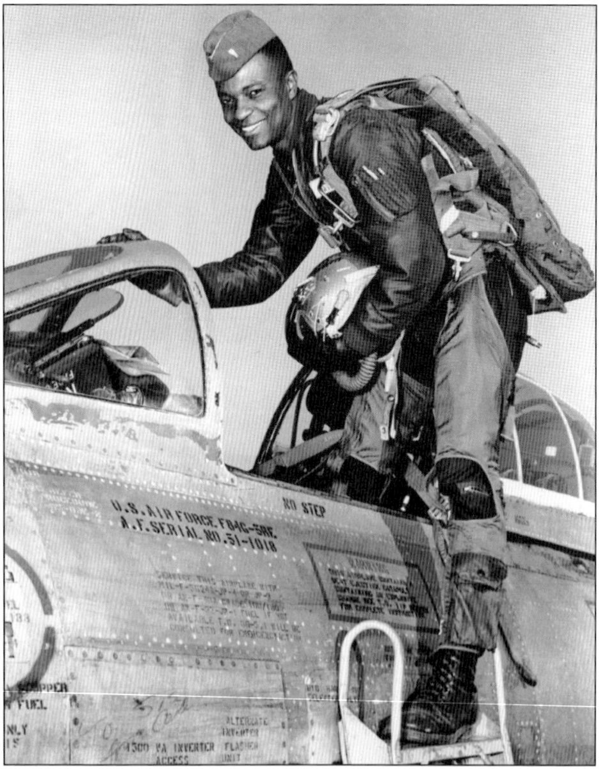

First Lt. Carl A. Bailey, USAF. Carl A. Bailey, the youngest son of Archie and Josephine Bailey's nine children, grew up in Punta Gorda and became one of the U.S. Air Force's first black jet pilots. Carl Bailey flew the F-84 Thunderjet during the Korean War. He was tragically killed in November 1957 in a car accident. Lt. Carl Bailey is buried in the historic African American cemetery named in his honor east of Punta Gorda on U.S. 17. (Blanchard House Museum of African-American History and Culture of Charlotte County.)

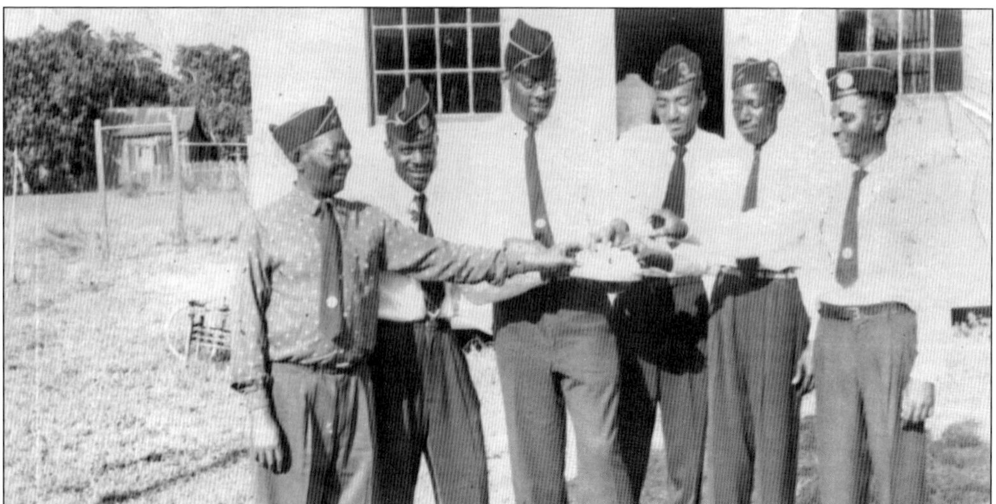

Punta Gorda's African American Post 186 American Legion. Punta Gorda's African Americans have served their country faithfully in every war. The veterans returning from service during World War II wanted to join the American Legion but because of segregation had to form their own post. The African American Leonard P. Fulford Post 186, named after a Punta Gorda African American soldier who died in France during World War I, was granted its charter on February 20, 1945. Members of the post are, from left to right, Lonnie Newkirk, Ernest Frederick, John Allen, Lloyd Thomas, John Doby, and unidentified in front of the recreation center on Dupont Street. (John H. Allen.)

Three

Industry

Due to the area's bountiful marine life, the waters of Charlotte Harbor were long known as a perfect fishing spot. Even today, Charlotte Harbor is noted as offering some of the world's best fishing. The area fishing began not just a sport but also an industry that actually started back with the Calusa Indians thousands of years ago. Upon the arrival of the Spaniards in the early 1500s, fishing continued as both a sport and a business, and tons of fish were harvested from the waters. The fish were dried and shipped by the Spaniards to Cuba. After the area became settled by Northerners in the late 1800s, area fishing companies were founded, such as the Punta Gorda Fish Company in 1897.

With the bustling fishing business, along came the need for ice. After all, the fish had to be packed in ice in order to be shipped. The Punta Gorda Ice Plant played a key role in the fishing and railroad industries from 1913 until 1933. Fishermen stored their catch in the fish companies' icehouses, where run boats picked up the harvest and carried it ashore. Shrimp ("pink gold") became an important industry to the area after World War II.

Fish wasn't the only commodity that was key to the area; cattle was a huge industry. Back in the early 1500s, Spanish explorer Ponce de León was the one who initially brought cattle into Florida. Later, as the Charlotte Harbor area became settled by the Northerners, they brought more cattle into the area. Cattle were shipped to Cuba via schooners for a handsome profit. During the Civil War, cattle were supplied to both the Confederate army and later the Union forces. Florida cattle were an important food source for the Confederate army during the American Civil War (1861–1865). The cattle were shipped to Columbus, Georgia, where a major trading post was located.

Florida's agricultural industry shipped its harvest north. This included oranges, lemons, mangoes, grapefruit, limes, guava, pineapples, and flowers. Phosphate was also mined from the rivers and shipped north.

The hotel industry and other tourist businesses were gaining momentum as Northern tourists would come to the area to fish for sport, enjoy the warm waters, and bask in the year-round Florida sunshine.

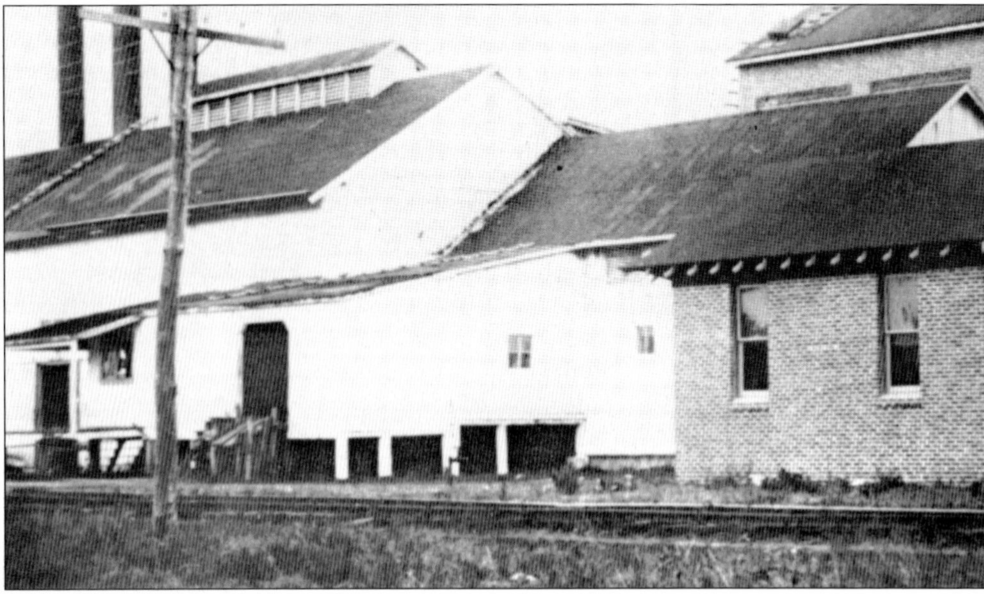

The Punta Gorda Ice Plant. The Punta Gorda Ice Plant, located at 408 Tamiami Trail, was built in 1913 and expanded in 1926. It was the first ice plant on the coast south of Tampa. The plant measures 41 feet by 41 feet and has brick walls that are 21 inches thick. The walls are lined with 6 inches of cork insulation. Ice was used to pack fish being shipped north on the railroad and via waterways. The fish were packed with ice in wooden boxes to keep them fresh. The plant was listed in 1990 on the National Register of Historic Places. (*Fact and Fable: Charlotte County.*)

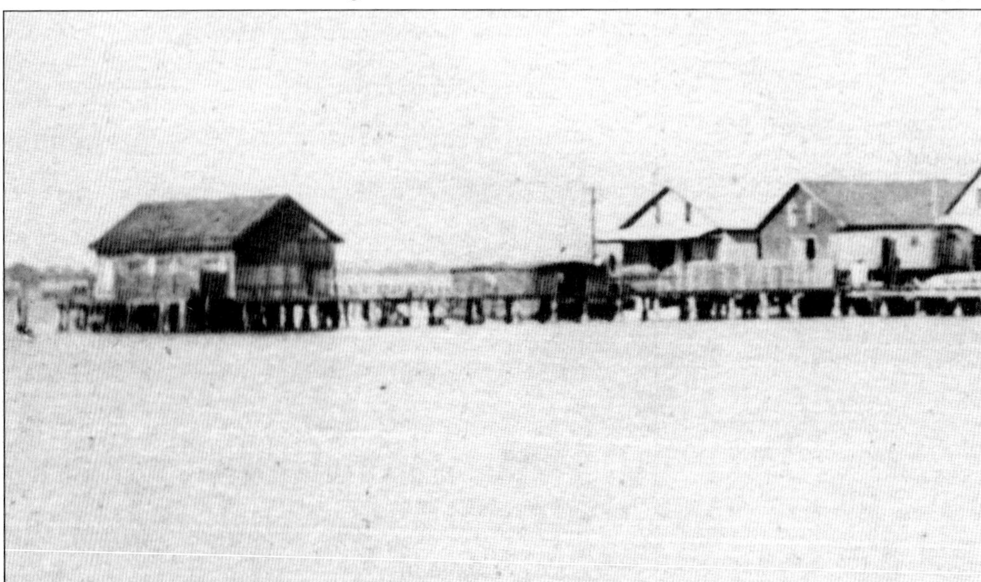

The Punta Gorda Fish Dock. When the Spaniards arrived in the early 1500s, tons of fish were harvested from the waters. After the area became settled by Northerners in the 1800s, area fishing companies were founded, such as the Punta Gorda Fish Company in 1897. This photograph of the Punta Gorda Fish Dock dates back to about 1905. The Punta Gorda Fish Company ceased operation in 1977. It was the last of the area's wholesale fish companies. (*Fact and Fable: Charlotte County.*)

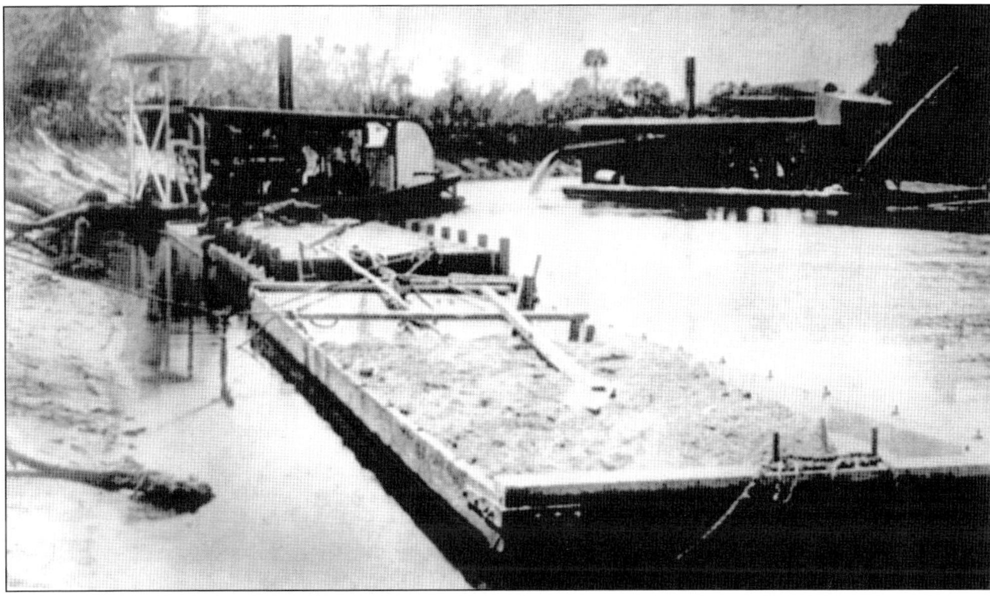

Phosphate Lighter on the Peace River. Phosphate was first discovered in the Peace River in 1860. The rich deposit of phosphate was rediscovered about 1880 by the Army Corps of Engineers' Capt. J. Francis LeBarron while he was surveying the Peace River for a planned canal project. It was not until 1887, when a private investor began purchasing land on both sides of the river near Arcadia, that mining operations began. The barge or "lighter" was a 60-70-foot flat-bottom wooden craft designed to move the mined phosphate down the river. (U. S. Cleveland Collection.)

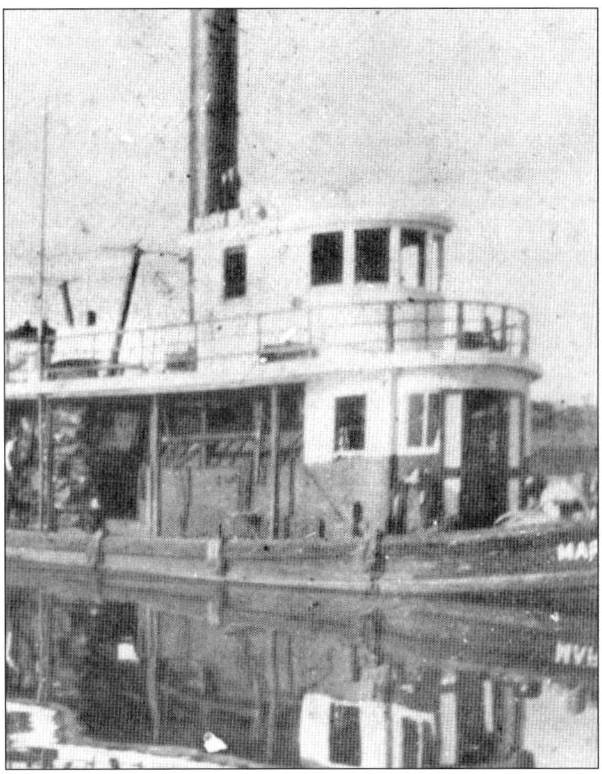

The Paddle-wheel Steamer *Mary Blue*. This early-1900s photograph shows the paddle-wheel steamer *Mary Blue* moving phosphate barges down the Peace River. The Florida phosphate industry was born in 1888, when Albertus Vogt found a fossilized mastodon jaw in a local riverbank near Dunellon, in Marion County. Upon discovery, he started the first mining company in Florida and named it Marion Phosphate Company. Phosphates come from a wide range of organic material and are extensively used in the agricultural industry as fertilizers. In 1892, Albert F. Dewey started Charlotte Harbor Lighterage and Stevedore Company with *Mary Blue*. In 1896, Florida Southern Railway had another paddle-wheel steamer, *St. Lucie*, that carried passengers and freight between Punta Gorda and Fort Myers. (*Fact and Fable: Charlotte County*.)

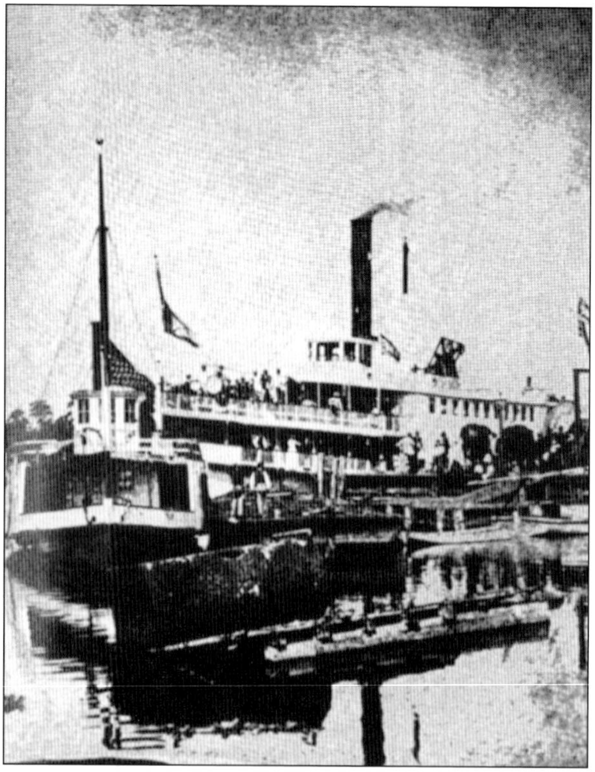

The Morgan Line. This 1885 photograph shows passengers aboard the Morgan Line, which operated out of Tampa and pulled into Florida docks. Northerners came down to the area to enjoy the warm weather, the sunshine, and the world-famous fishing. Tourism remains a growing industry in Florida to this day. (Punta Gorda Historical Society; Burgert Brothers Collection, Tampa Public Library.)

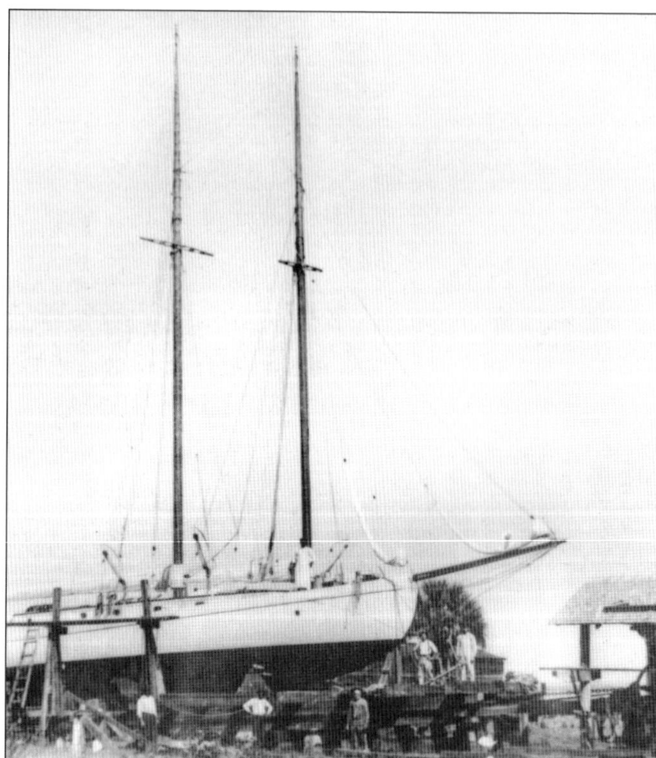

The Cleveland Marine Steam Ways. A ship is on the ways at the shipyard owned by George Brown, an African American shipbuilder and landowner. He was also one of Punta Gorda's early pioneers who originally came to the area to work for a phosphate mining company. George Brown opened his own shipyard, the Cleveland Marine Steam Ways, the largest shipyard in southwest Florida, in 1908. A respected citizen, Brown holds the distinction of being Florida's first equal opportunity employer. He hired both blacks and whites and gave equal pay for equal work. (Blanchard House Museum of African-American History and Culture of Charlotte County.)

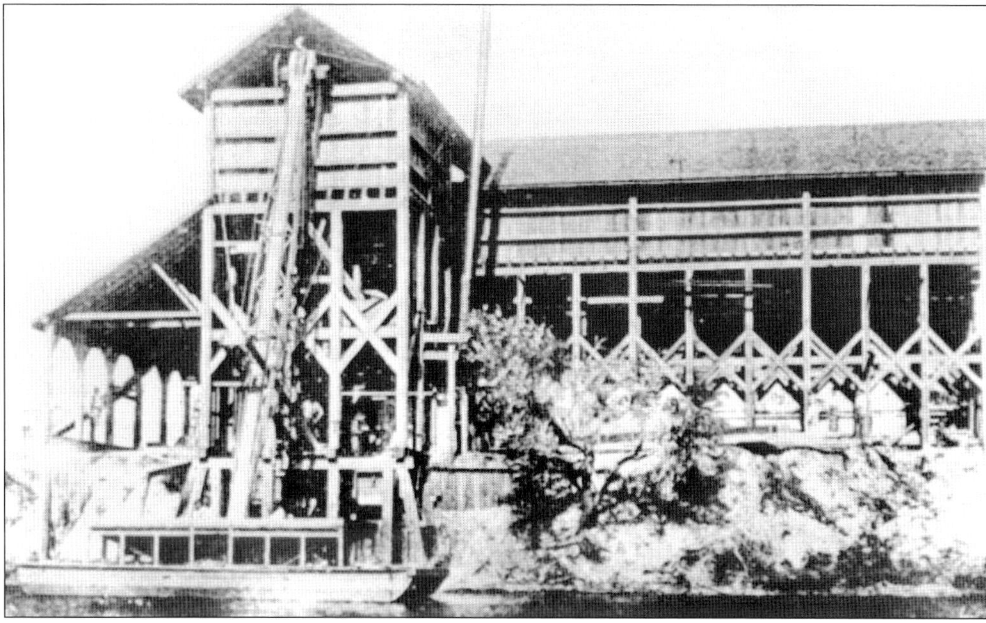

Peace River Phosphate Company Elevator, Drying Works, and Shipping Bin. Phosphate deposits were discovered in the 1890s near Florida's Peace River, and by 1907, the railroads and ships were transporting it. Sixty-foot phosphate lighters (flat bottomed boats used in loading or unloading a ship) were used to transport the phosphate down the Peace River. The lighters were built and maintained by the Cleveland Marine Steamship Company, which was owned by George Brown. (Florida Photographic Collection, the Florida Memory Project.)

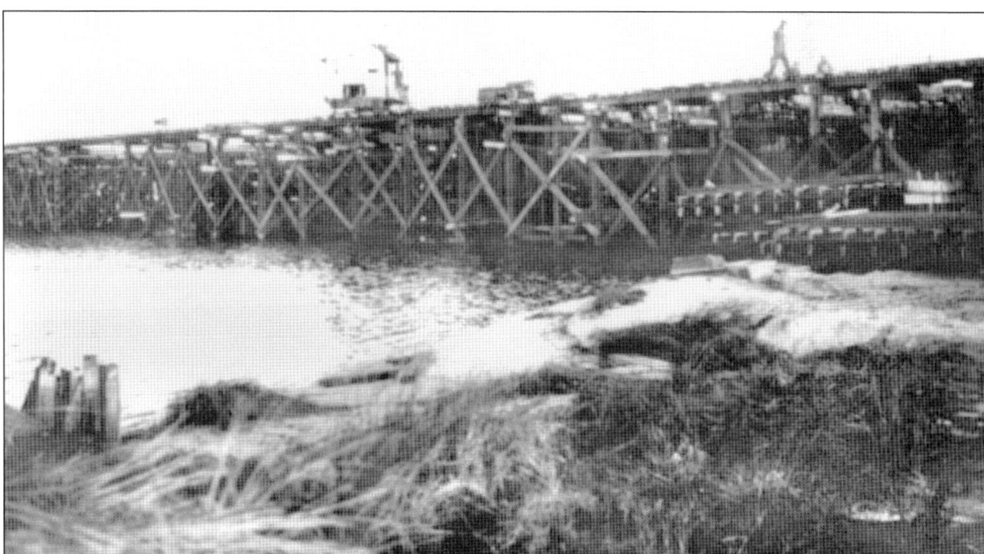

Building the Concrete Bridge. The Barron Collier Bridge was constructed of steel-reinforced concrete. The bridge was the width of two cars and had concrete railing on both sides. The cost of the bridge was just over $1 million. (Florida Photographic Collection, the Florida Memory Project.)

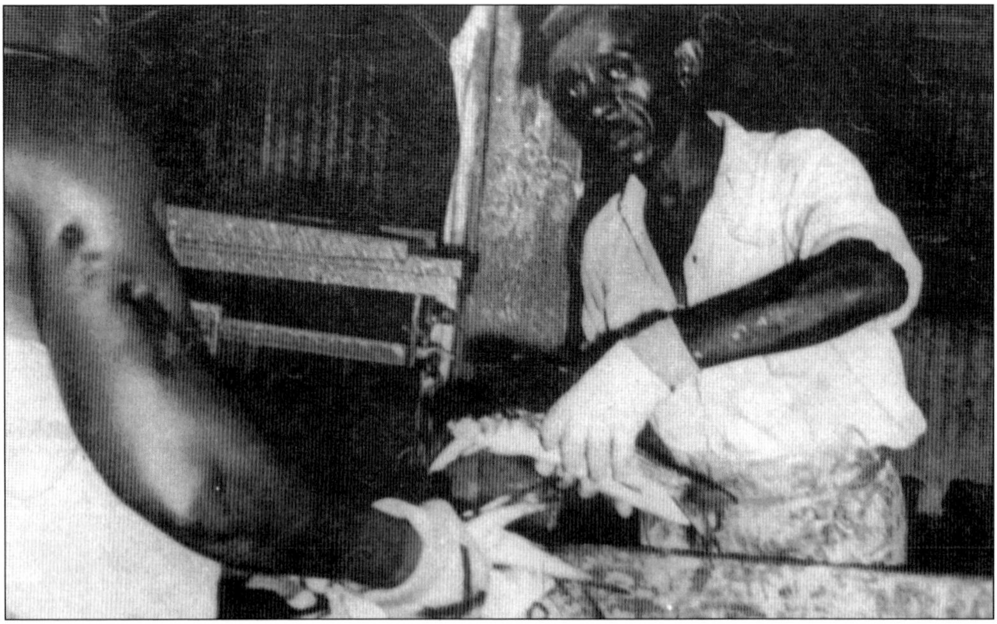

Andrew "Mullet" Owens of the Punta Gorda Fish Company. "Mullet" Owens worked for the Punta Gorda Fish Company for many years. The Punta Gorda Fish Company was started about 1900 by Eugene Knight and Harry Dreggors. It was located on the new railroad dock built at the foot of King Street. The Punta Gorda Fish Company ceased operations in 1977 after nearly 76 years. (Blanchard House Museum of African-American History and Culture of Charlotte County.)

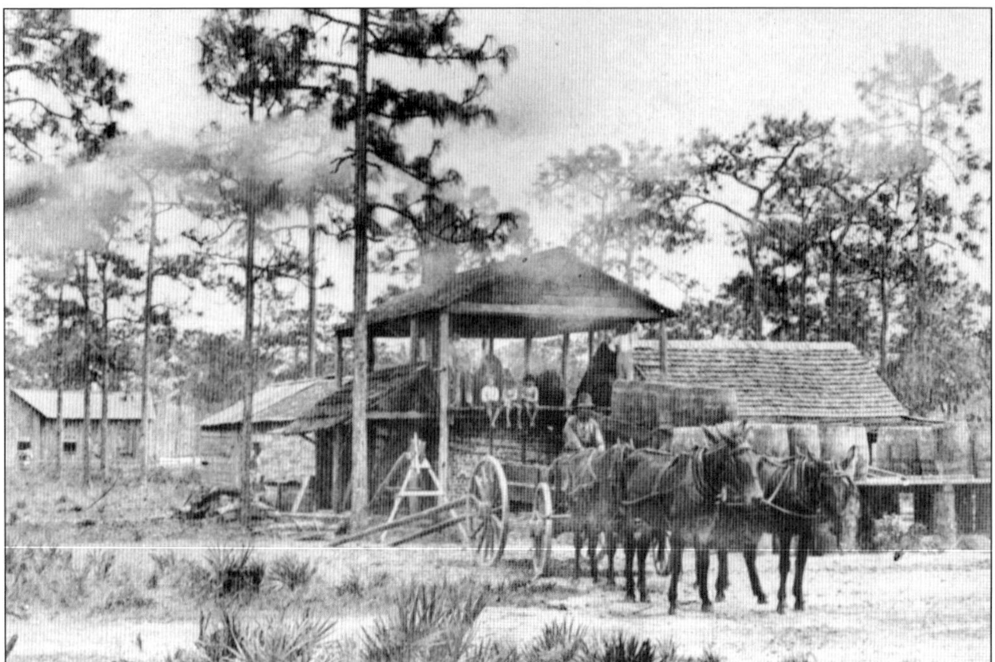

Early Turpentine Still. The distillation of turpentine was once a major industry in Charlotte County. One of the largest operations was located in the El Jobean pinelands, on the eastern shore of the Myakka River. It operated from the early 1910s to the 1920s. (U. S. Cleveland Collection.)

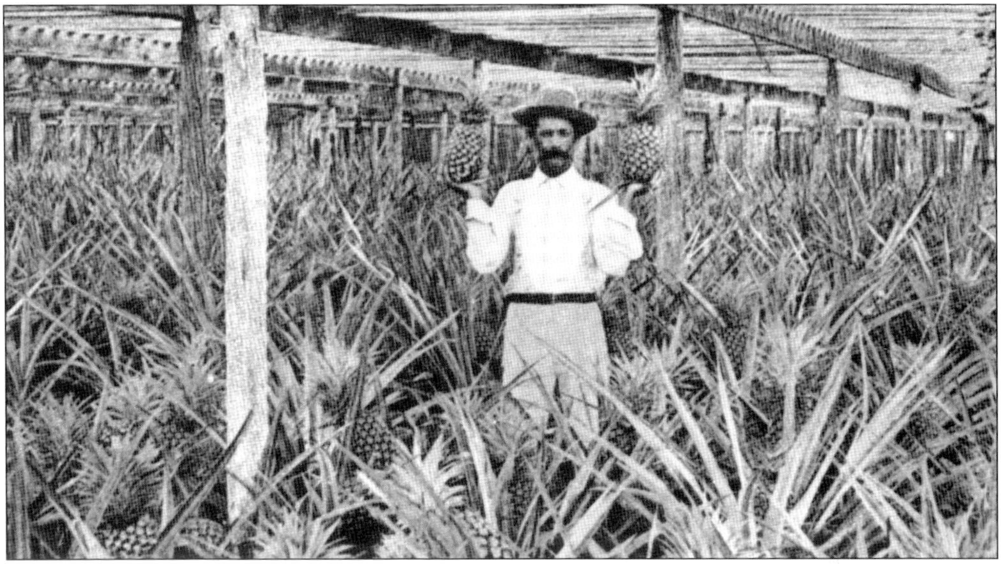

Punta Gorda Pineapples Grown under the Shade. Town founder Isaac Trabue was excited to discover that pineapples grew well in the area's soil. He set aside land in town (where the city hall annex is located) in the garden behind his home and near his office on Cross Street to grow pineapples. Pineapples were a profitable cash crop for Punta Gorda growers. In fact, the newspaper announced that over 40,000 pineapples were growing in the local Solana pineries. Unfortunately, the pineapple industry was wiped out with the freeze of March 1917. (U. S. Cleveland Collection.)

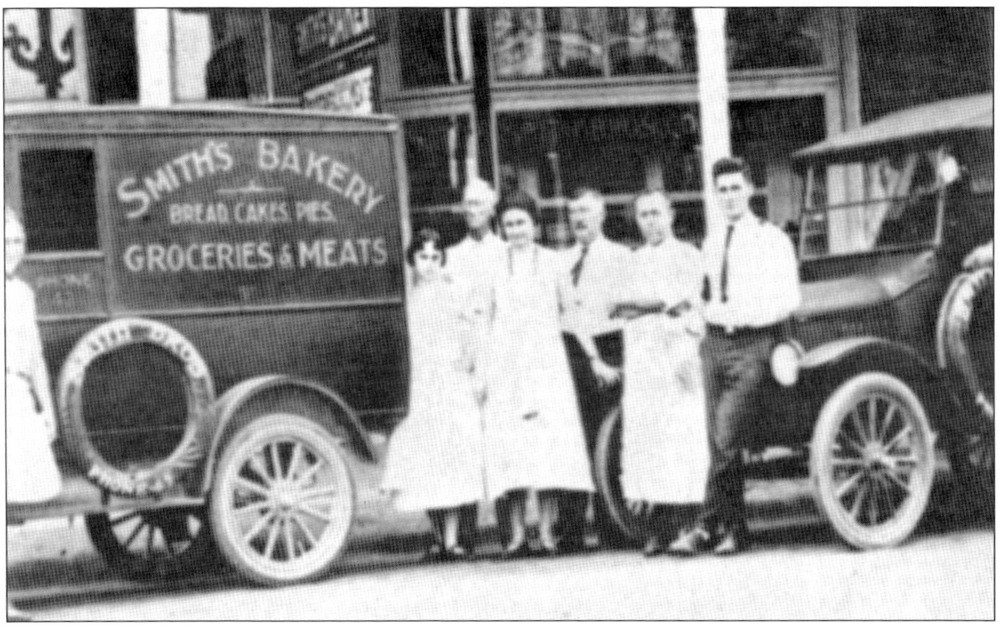

Smith's Bakery and Grocery. Smaller businesses also thrived with the growing population in Punta Gorda. As with most towns, local hardware stores, grocery stores, and bakeries can be found on the main streets. Bakeries like Smith's Bakery and Grocery made everything from scratch, including fresh bread baked daily. The bakery was owned by Henry Smith, who was also a proprietor of the Bayview Hotel. (*Fact and Fable: Charlotte County.*)

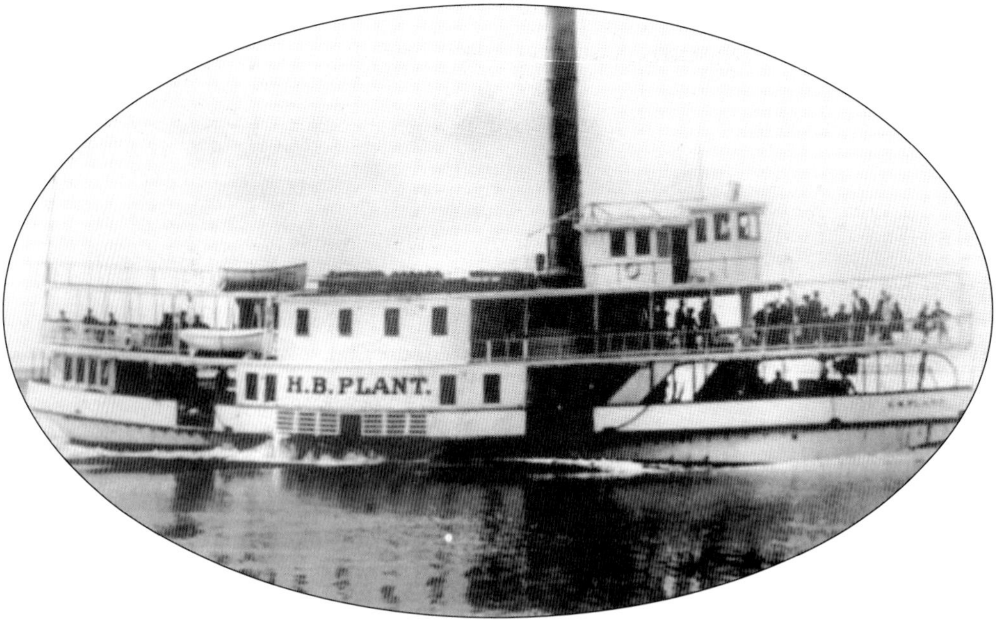

THE *H. B. PLANT*. A familiar sight in Charlotte Harbor was the steel-hulled side-wheeler steamer *H. B. Plant*. The ship was built in a Jacksonville shipyard in 1899 and made the Tampa–to–Manatee River run or Tampa–to–Punta Gorda run on a regular basis. The ship was built for the Plant Investment Line but was sold to the Favorite Line in 1912. The ship was lost when it burned at a Tampa pier in 1913. (Florida Photographic Collection, the Florida Memory Project.)

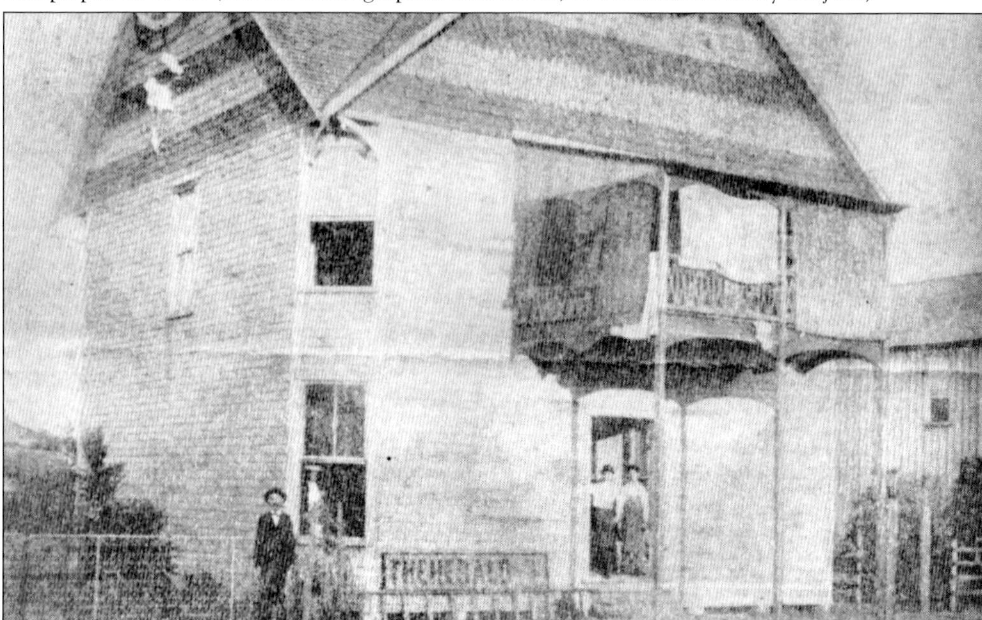

THE *HERALD*'S LOCATION IN PUNTA GORDA. The *Herald* was first published in 1893, and operation was located on the lower floor of a cigar factory at Cross Street and Retta Esplanade. Although its beginnings were humble, the paper, now known as the *Charlotte Sun-Herald*, has been in existence for over 100 years.

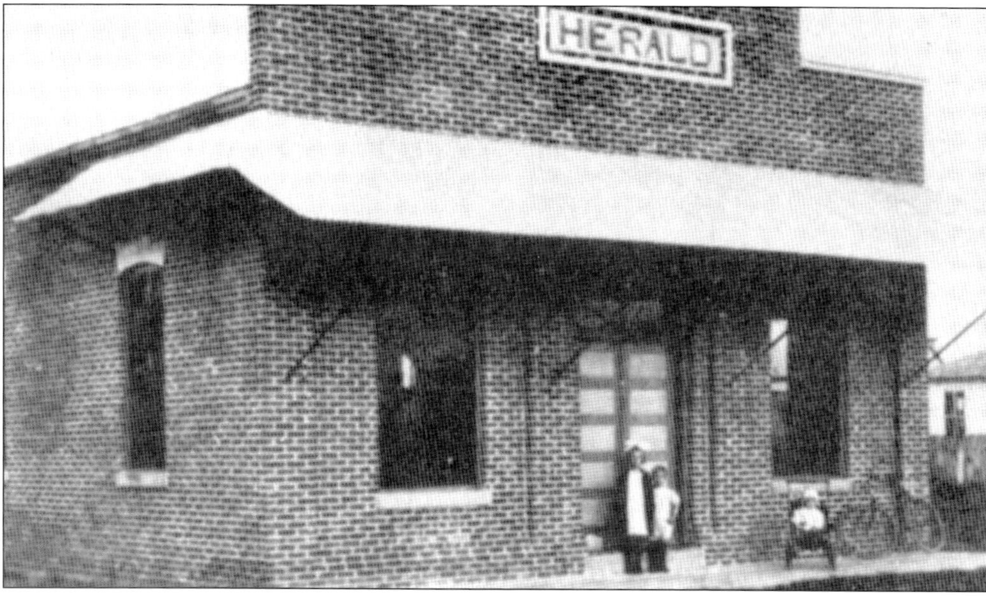

THE *HERALD* BUILDING IN PUNTA GORDA. After a fire broke out in the original building, the *Herald* building was rebuilt but was later moved to the corner of Marion Avenue and Taylor Street, which was used for this purpose for a few years. The move came after the publisher, Robert Kirby Seward, sold the newspaper to Adrian Pettus Jordan in 1901. The *Herald* building was constructed in 1913 and is still located on Taylor Street. (Punta Gorda Historical Society and *Fact and Fable: Charlotte County*.)

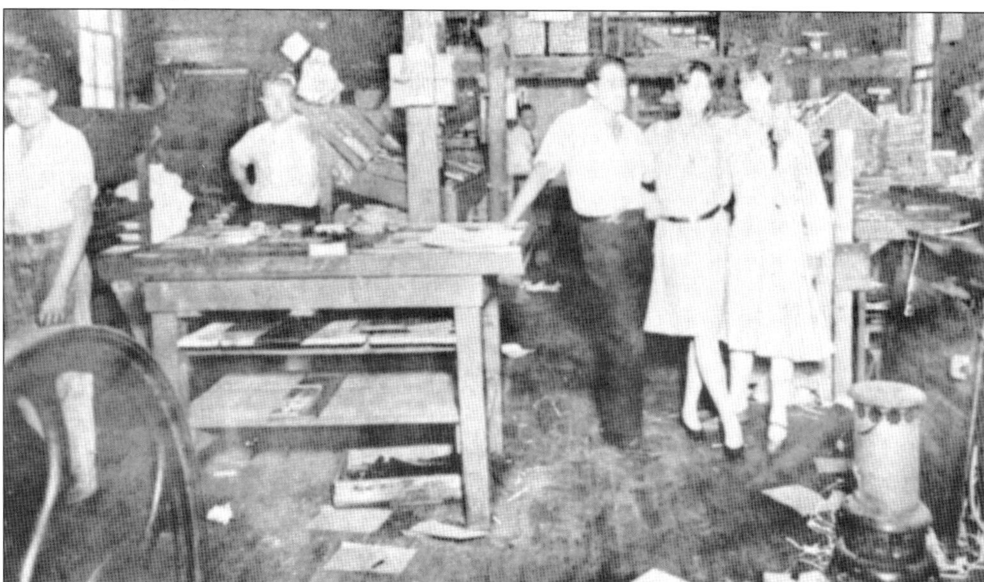

THE *HERALD* COMPOSING ROOM AROUND 1910. Newspapers, like the *Herald*, had composing rooms that had linecasting machines and other equipment. The equipment was used to typeset and assemble the pages of each day's newspaper. This photograph is from the *Herald*'s Marion Avenue and Taylor Street location some time after 1901. The building was two stories and was constructed by publisher Adrian Pettus Jordan. The equipment was located on the second floor, and Jordan lived on the first floor. (*Fact and Fable: Charlotte County*.)

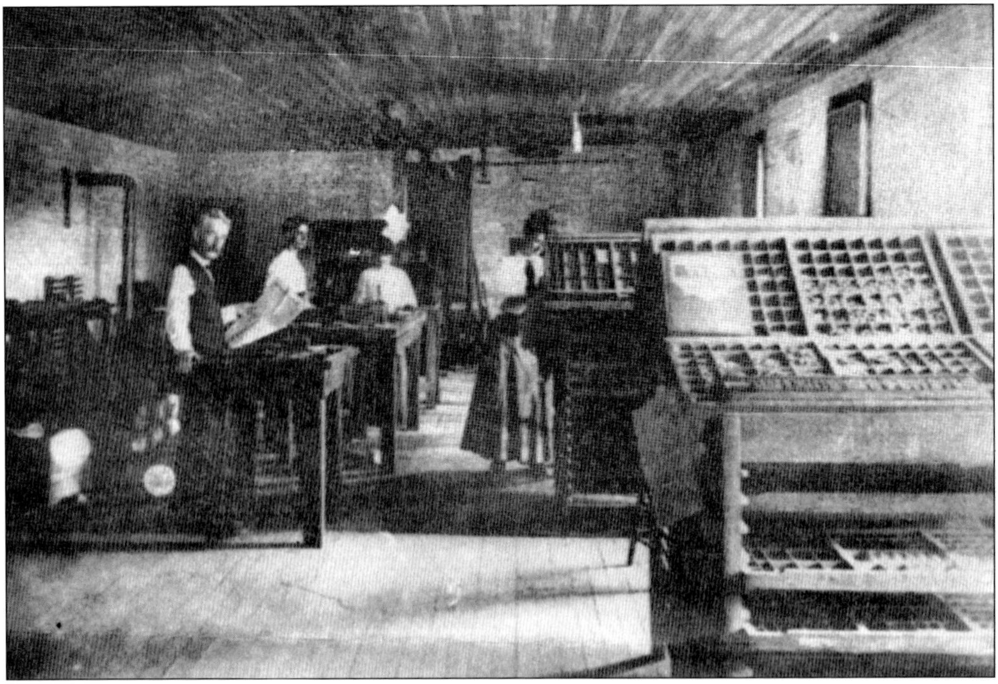

HERALD WORKERS SETTING TYPE. Editor Adrian P. Jordan stands on the far left of the composing room, located on the second floor of the *Herald* building on Marion Avenue and Taylor Street.

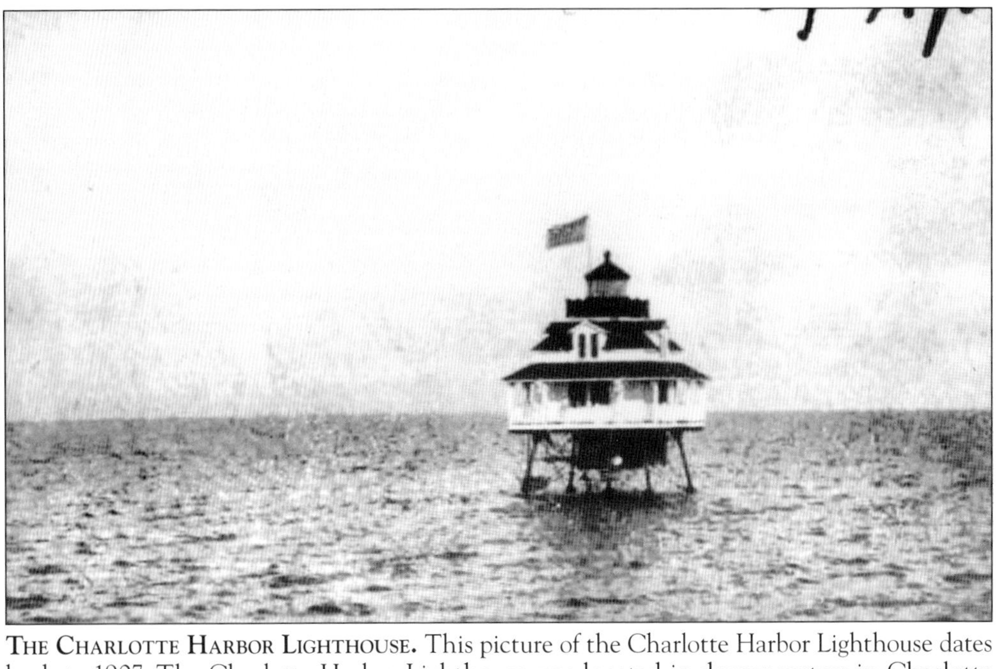

THE CHARLOTTE HARBOR LIGHTHOUSE. This picture of the Charlotte Harbor Lighthouse dates back to 1907. The Charlotte Harbor Lighthouse was located in deeper waters in Charlotte Harbor. The purpose of the lighthouse was to guide ships to the railroad docks in Punta Gorda. The lighthouse was demolished in 1943; however, the iron pilings stood until 1975. (Punta Gorda Historic Railroad Depot and Antique Mall, Linda Wilson collection.)

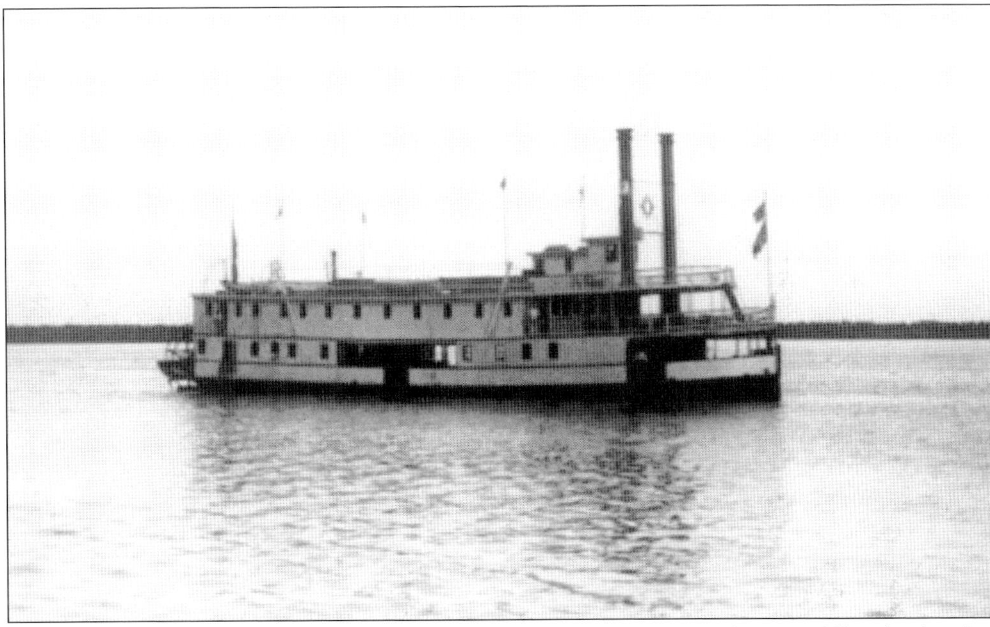

The *St. Lucie* Pulling into Punta Gorda. The *St. Lucie* was a large paddle wheeler that regularly plied the waters between Punta Gorda and Fort Myers. The ship was 120 feet long, had a beam of 24 feet, and was able to carry 40 tons, yet only drew 3 feet of water. The *St. Lucie* operated until 1904, when she was moved to Tampa. (Florida Photographic Collection, the Florida Memory Project.)

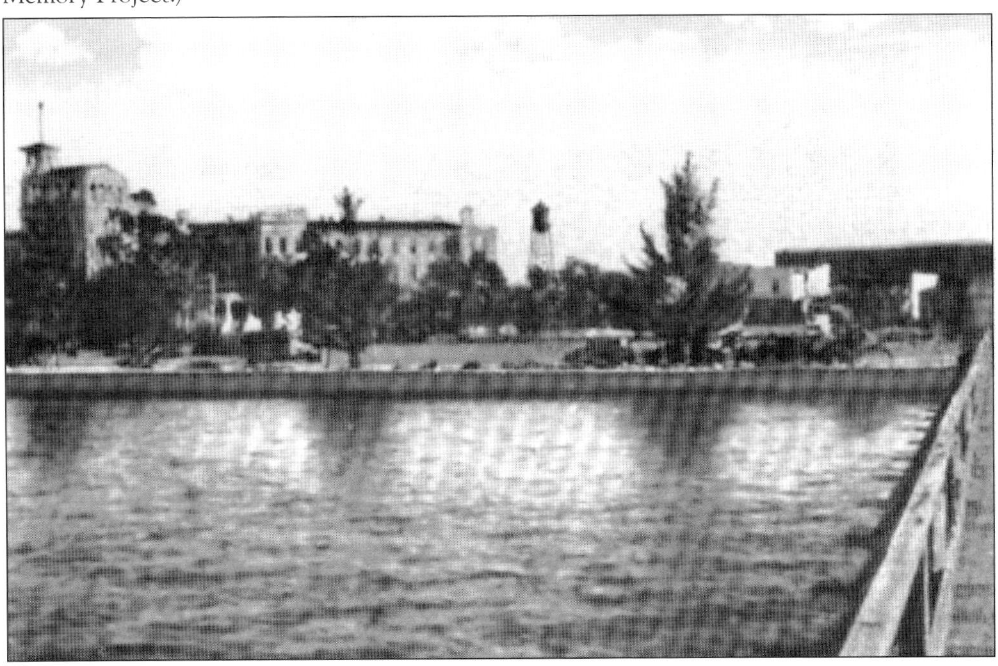

Hotel Charlotte Harbor as Seen from the City Dock. This image shows Hotel Charlotte Harbor from the city dock. A water tower was located near King Street, and the weather bureau tower was located at the foot of the city dock, where storm signals were displayed. (Florida Photographic Collection, the Florida Memory Project.)

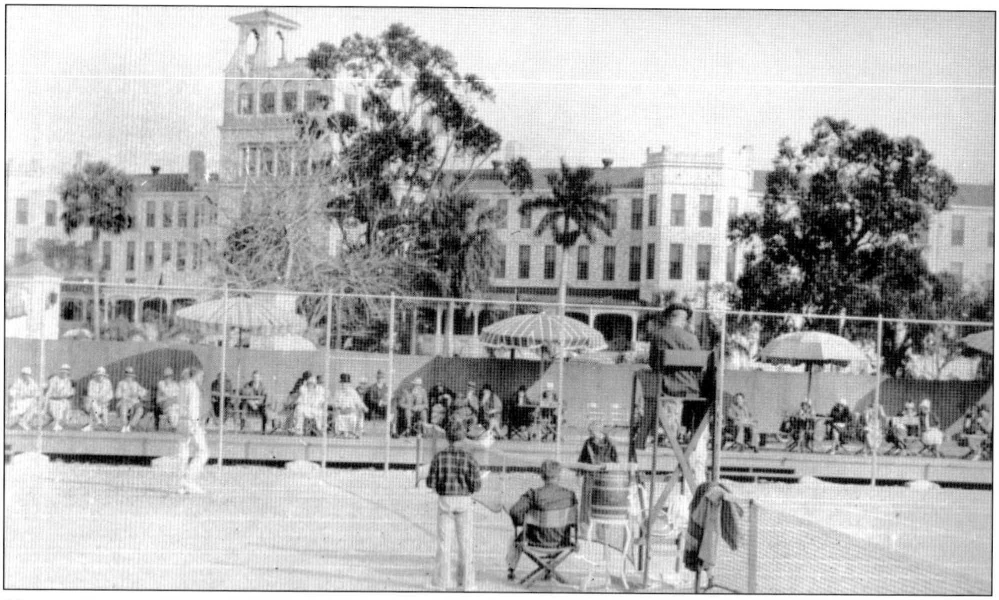

Hotel Punta Gorda's Tennis Courts. This image shows the tennis courts outside of the 150-room Hotel Punta Gorda, built in 1886 by Henry B. Plant, the railroad baron, in an attempt to get visitors down to the area and increase railroad travel. This luxurious hotel was the first of its kind built on the West Coast of Florida. Some of the hotel's famous guests included the Edisons, the Fords, and the Firestones. Nationwide tennis tournaments with tennis stars like "Big Bill" Tilden were held at the tennis court.

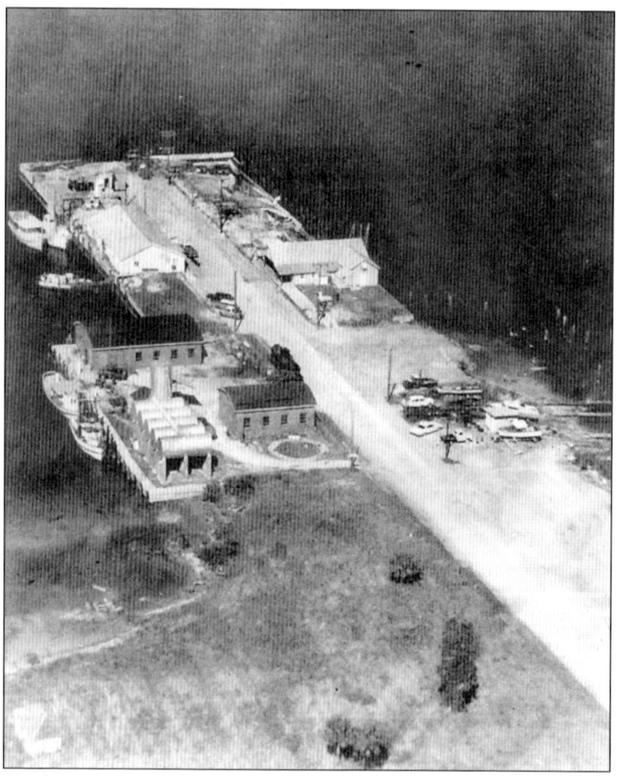

Punta Gorda's Municipal Dock. This aerial view of Punta Gorda's Municipal Dock was taken shortly after the municipal fish dock fire of 1939. The dock was the location of the Punta Gorda and West Coat Fishing Companies, the Watercraft Boat Way, the Gulf Shore Sea Food Company, and the Gulf Oil Company's tanks and office. Luckily, in 1922, Punta Gorda had purchased its first fire truck. After the 1927 grand reopening of Hotel Charlotte Harbor, the hotel's owner, Barron Collier, requested that the municipal railroad dock be demolished, and so a new one was built at Maud Street. (Richard May.)

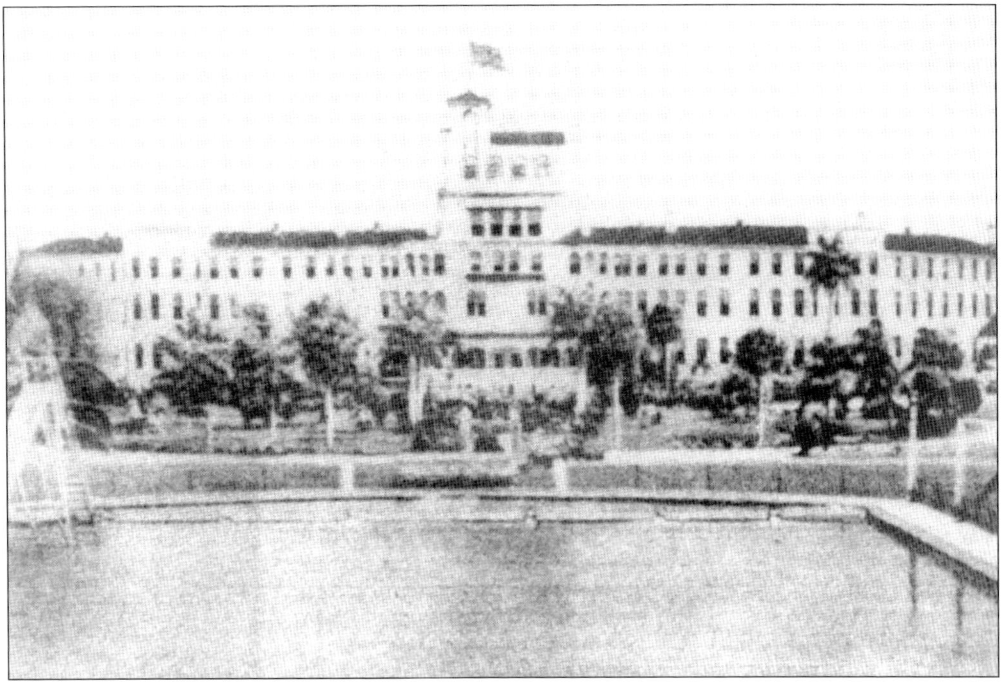

Hotel Charlotte Harbor. In 1959, the magnificent Hotel Charlotte Harbor, then known as the Charlotte Harbor Spa, was gone within hours after a fire broke out on August 14, around 2:30 in the morning. The hotel was a total loss, and an investigation deemed the fire suspicious.

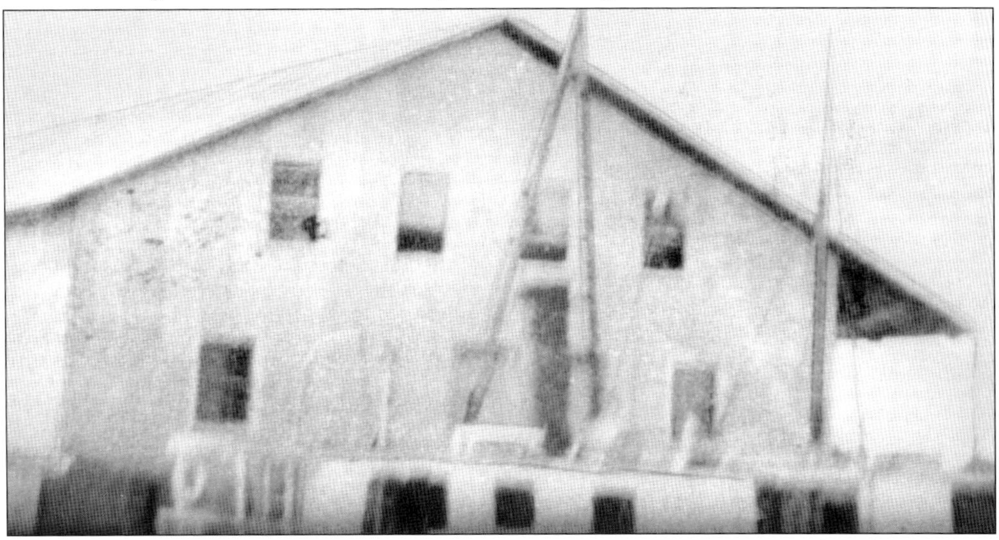

Punta Gorda Fish Dock around 1935. Boats unloaded at the Punta Gorda Fish Company and the West Coast Fish Company at the Punta Gorda Fish Dock. The boats collected fish from icehouses. Once unloaded, the fish traveled on the train in refrigerated boxcars. The fish dock was the third home of the fish companies. The fish companies were moved off the Long Dock because of the railway's abandonment of the dock in 1897. They were then moved from the King Street Pier by the City of Punta Gorda in order to build a bridge across Charlotte Harbor. The bridge was part of the Tamiami Trail. Punta Gorda then built the fish dock and this metal building that housed the fish companies.

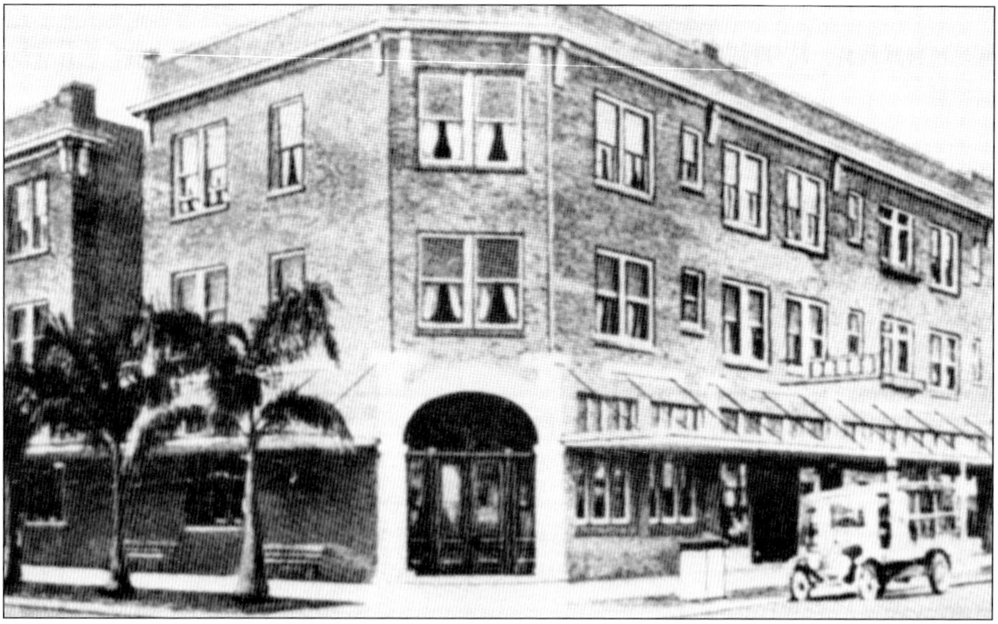

CHARLOTTE BAY HOTEL AROUND 1925. Hotel Punta Gorda wasn't the only hotel in the area. Tourism was big, so there were more hotels, such as the Charlotte Bay Hotel, later called the Princess Hotel. It was renamed after the new owner, H. Rae, purchased the property around 1940. Also on the corner was a bank, a drugstore, a barbershop, the Punta Gorda Dry Goods, and the Western Union.

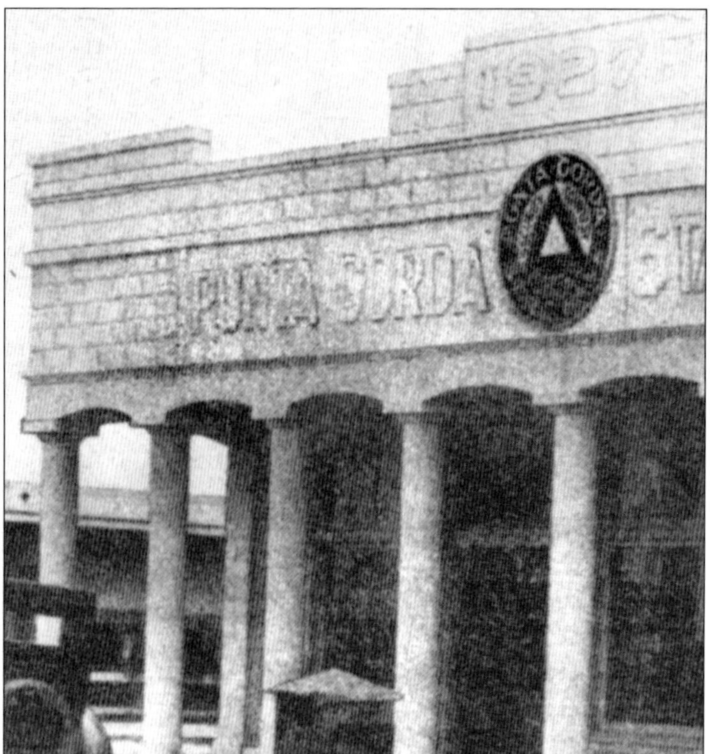

PUNTA GORDA STATE BANK. In 1930, the Punta Gorda State Bank was one of only three banks in the area to survive the stock market crash. Barron G. Collier was credited for helping to ensure that the bank did not crash. He was one of the bank's directors. Because of the land boom in Florida during the 1920s, Punta Gorda State Bank prospered and so was in good financial shape when the crash took place. Of course, along with the stock market crash in 1929 came the crash of the Great Florida Land Boom. (*Ceremonial Journal*; Charlotte Harbor Area Historical Society.)

Four

BUILDINGS

Punta Gorda was the country's first incorporated city and, to this day, is the only incorporated city in Charlotte County. Charlotte County was formed in 1921 right after DeSoto County was split into five counties: DeSoto, Glades, Hardee, Highlands, and Charlotte. Many early buildings date back to the early 1900s, when Punta Gorda was being rapidly developed by land developers, homesteaders, cattle ranchers, farmers, and fishermen—all coming down to the southernmost end of the rail line to start a new life and make some money. This era has been referred to as the Great Florida Land Boom, as many speculators came to Florida to make a mint buying buildings, businesses, and land. Some of the more famous buildings were the waterside hotels frequented by Northerners and famous people like Theodore Roosevelt, Henry Ford, Thomas A. Edison, Winston Churchill, and the Vanderbilts. The Princess Hotel and the regal Hotel Punta Gorda were two of the more famous hotels in the area. They were deluxe hotels that offered many fine amenities. For instance, the Hotel Punta Gorda hosted formal evening dances with a live orchestra. Other buildings were constructed specifically for the area's industry, such as the 1913 Punta Gorda Ice Plant and the *Herald* newspaper. Some of the buildings are Spanish Mission style, with white stucco walls and red tile or flat roofs, such as the 1928 Punta Gorda Historic Railroad Depot, while others are Colonial style with white woodwork and impressive round pillars, such as the Charlotte County Courthouse. When it came to home styles, many were Florida Cracker style, constructed with wooden frames, metal roofs, and raised floors. Large porches were also popular in the early 19th century as well, as people used their porches to stay friendly with their neighbors and cool off in the evenings, especially after hot summer days. English cottage and English Tudor styles, with their steep roofs, brick or stucco frames, and round-top doorways, were also some of the popular home styles, many of which were adorned with lush, tropical gardens and tall palms.

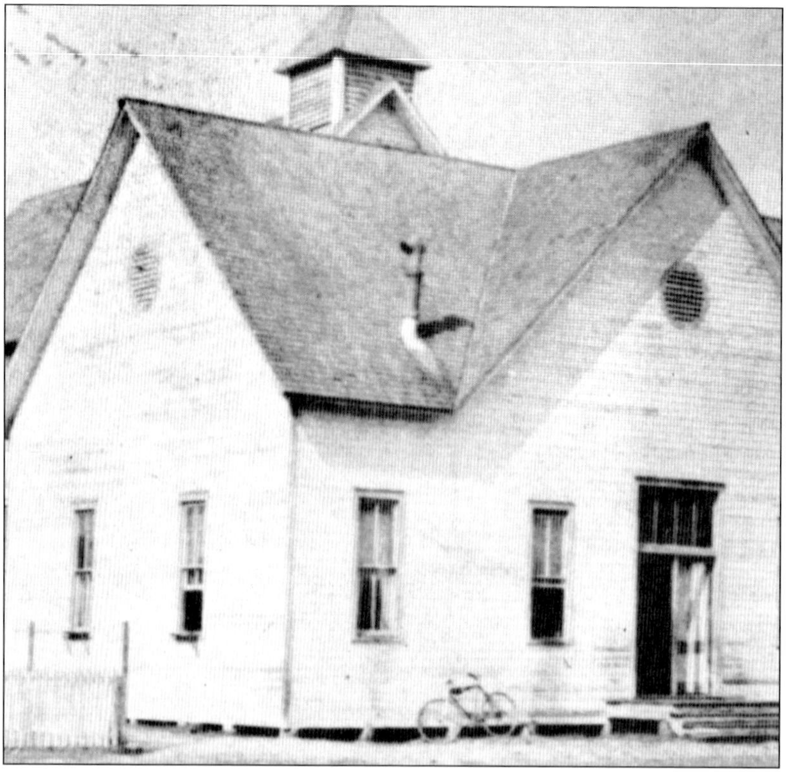

Punta Gorda High School around 1908. When the school first opened in 1896, Punta Gorda High School had only about 150 students. The school was later expanded in the early 1900s and a second floor was added on for grades 9 through 12. The school had a wooden frame and a steep roof. This was the only high school in the county until the 1970s. (*Fact and Fable: Charlotte County*.)

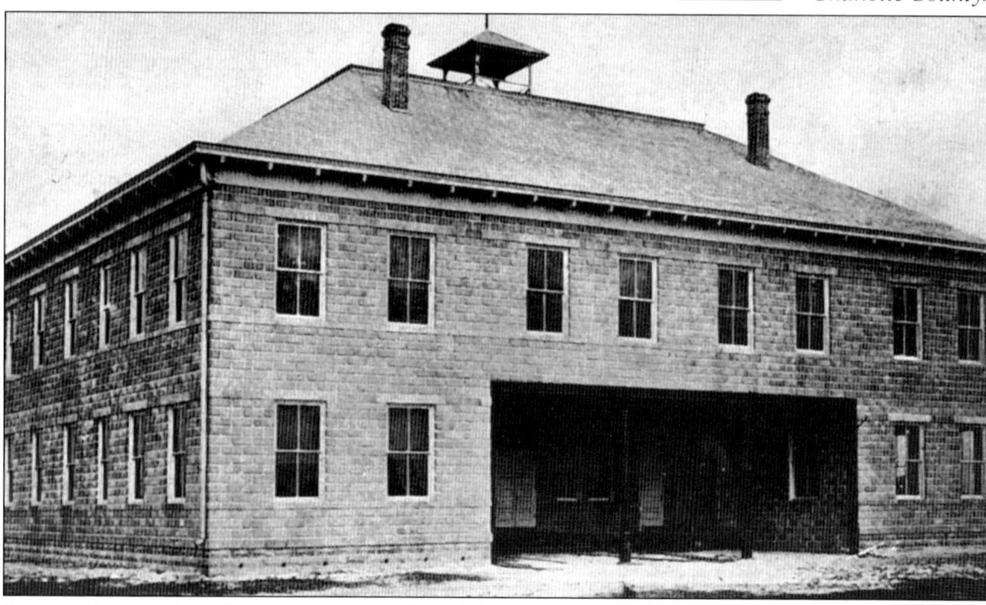

Punta Gorda High School around 1912. This early-1900s photograph shows the Punta Gorda High School that used to be located on Taylor Street and Charlotte Avenue. Due to a growing number of students, the school was no longer large enough. A new site was donated by Gov. Albert W. Gilchrist, and the new high school was opened in 1912. This building was made with a longer lasting material: brick. Brick could better withstand termites and inclement weather. (Punta Gorda Historic Railroad Depot and Antique Mall, Linda Wilson collection.)

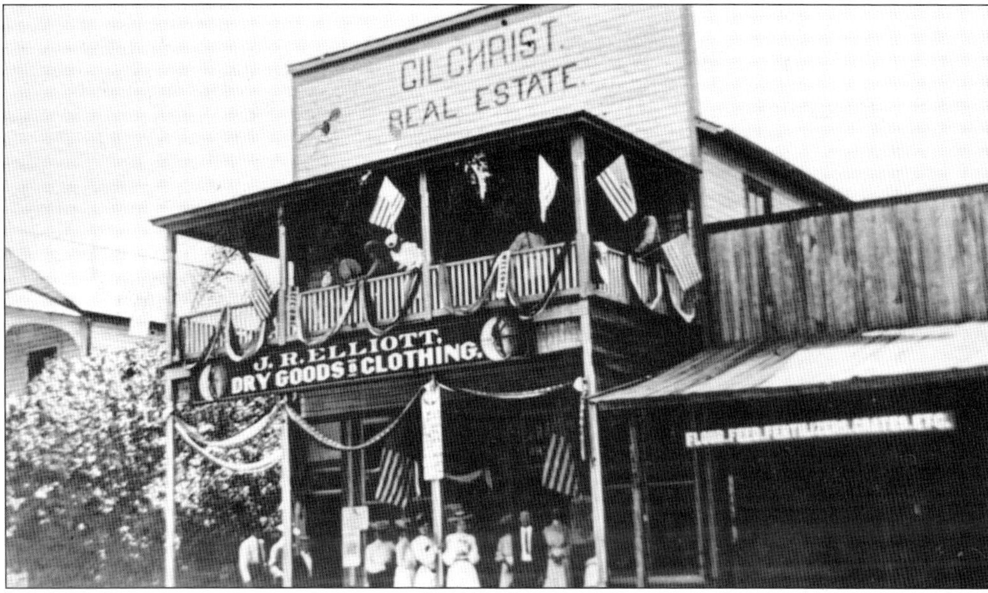

THE 1903 OFFICE OF ALBERT GILCHRIST. Albert Gilchrist came to Punta Gorda as the surveyor for the Florida Southern Railroad. He decided to stay in the area and became an early businessman of Punta Gorda. He sold real estate, owned an orange grove, and was elected to the Florida House of Representatives. In 1908, he was elected the governor of Florida. His office was upstairs, and the downstairs was rented to J. R. Elliot Dry Goods. The building was located on Marion Avenue. (U. S. Cleveland Collection.)

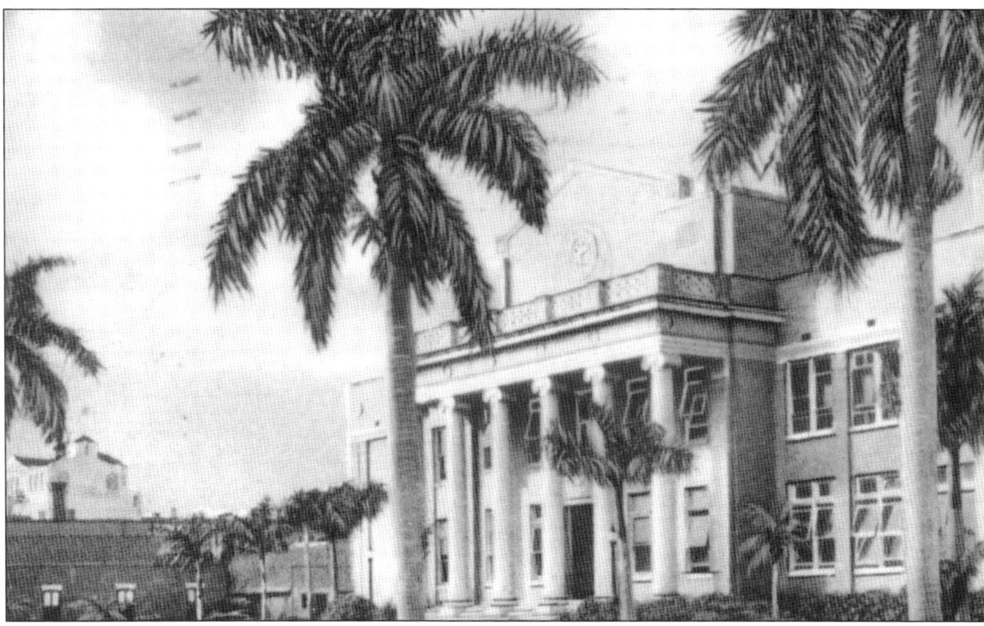

THE CHARLOTTE COUNTY COURTHOUSE. The Charlotte County Courthouse was built between 1927 and 1928 and located at 227 Taylor Street. It was a two-story yellow brick building. The courthouse was occupied by the sheriff, school superintendent, clerk of the court, tax collector, tax appraiser, supervisor of elections, county judge, and even the county jail. The building was renovated in 2008.

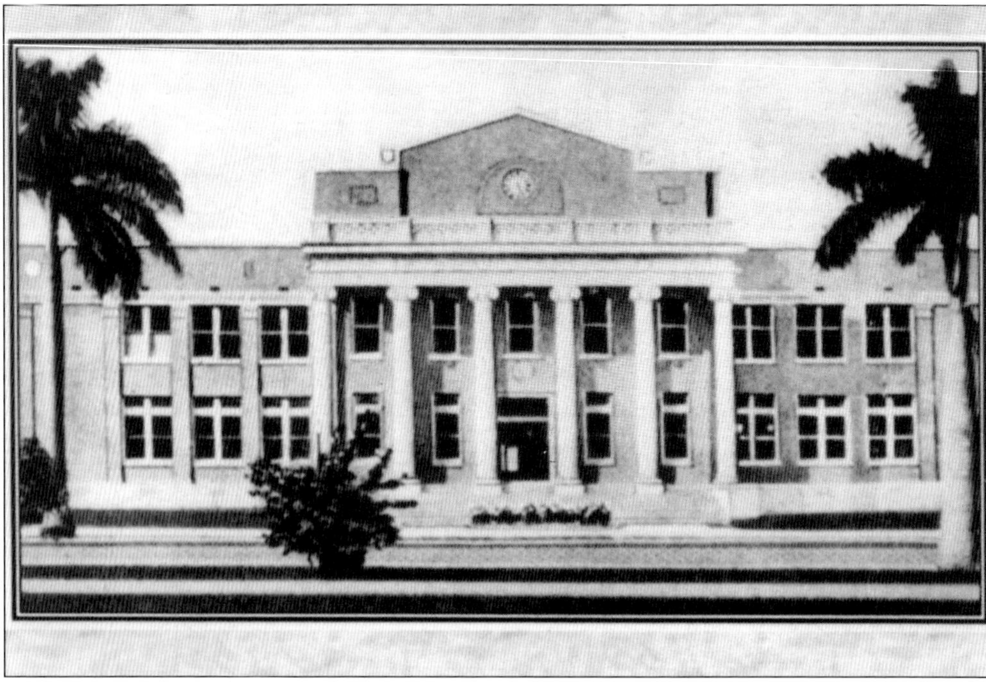

The Charlotte County Courthouse, Front View. This image depicts the front of the courthouse. It features Roman and Greek architecture for a stately appearance. Before the courthouse was built, the county government was conducted in rented offices.

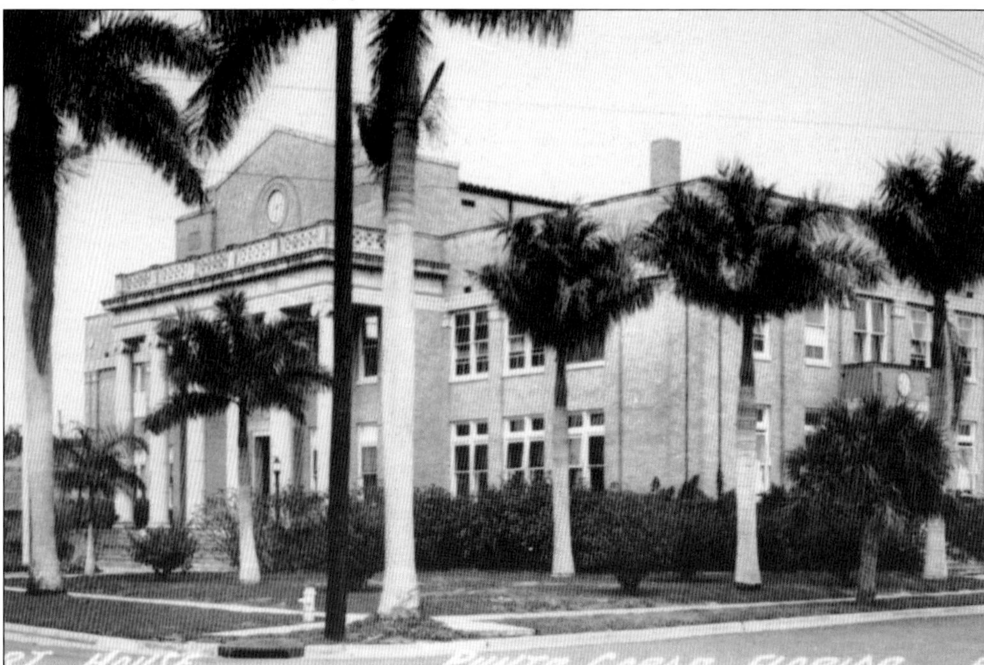

The County's New Courthouse. Two lots on Taylor Street were purchased from George Brown, African American proprietor of the Cleveland Marine Steam Ways, to build the Charlotte County Courthouse. The purchase price was $25,000.

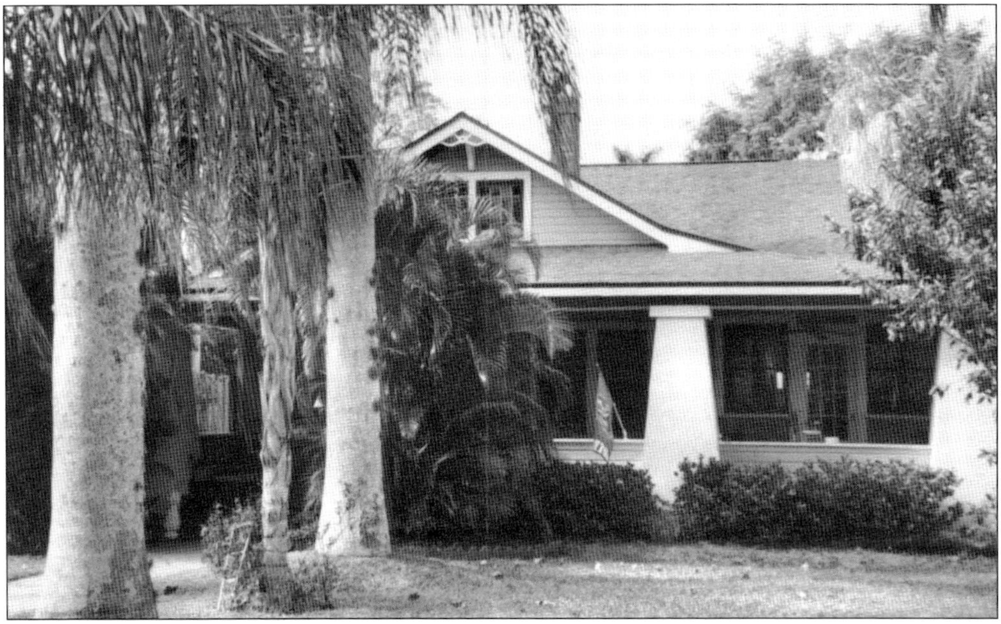

THE MOBLEY HOUSE. The Mobley House was built in 1922 by real estate agent William H. Johnson. It is located at 604 West Marion Avenue. The classic bungalow wooden home was made with locally cut pine and cypress and boasts tapering piers that support the porch roof. Wallace E. Mobley was the earliest known owner, and he, along with his brother, B. Hugh, owned and operated the Seminole Pharmacy. Mrs. Mobley (Madie) was a schoolteacher.

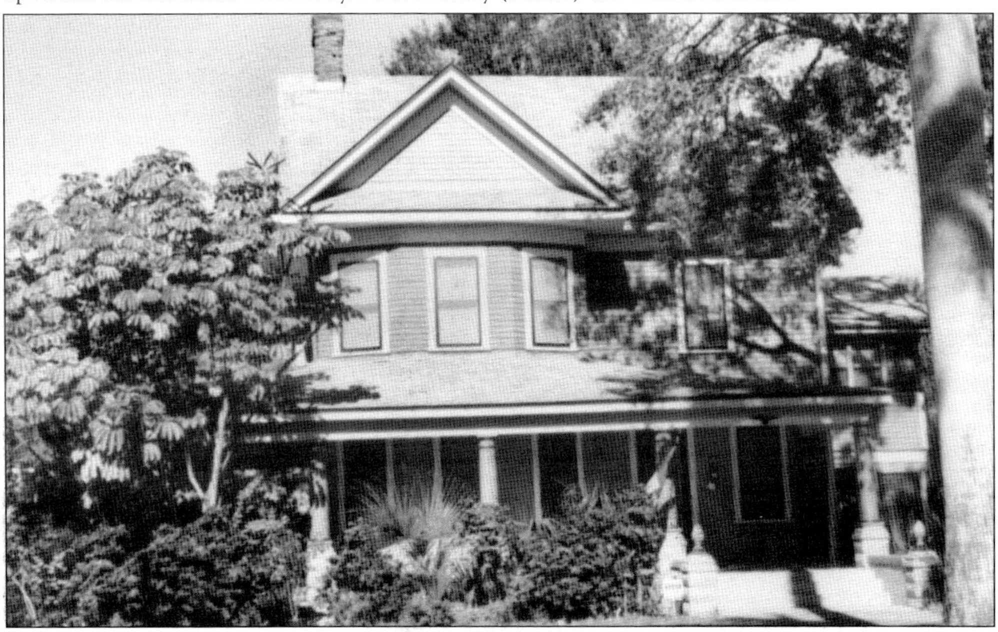

THE HANCOCK HOUSE. The Hancock House was built around 1902 and is located at 412 West Marion Avenue. Attorney John Hancock and his wife, Emma, lived in this 12-room, two-story frame house for many years. They were active members of the First Methodist Church. The porch features columns, bay windows, and a front gable located above the porch. Inside, the home features fireplaces, heart-pine floors, and French doors.

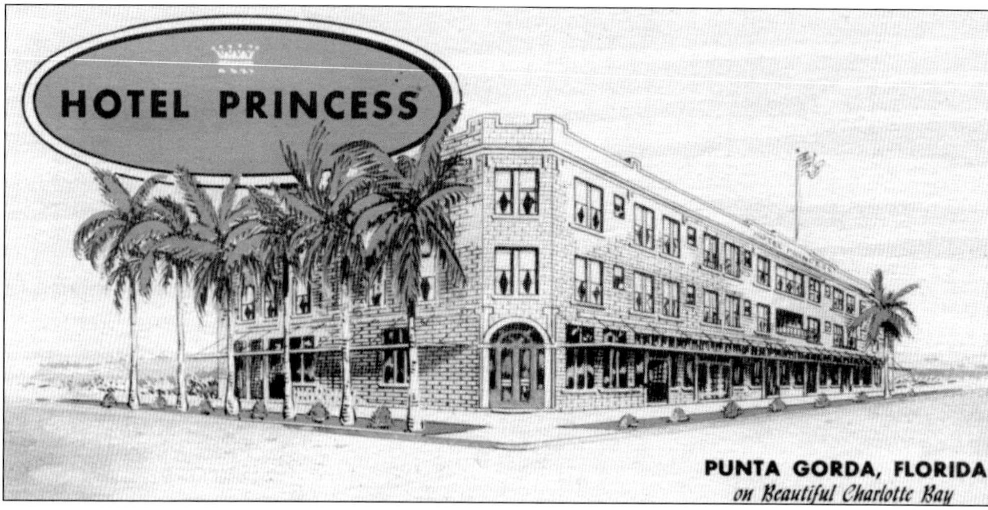

Hotel Princess. The Hotel Princess, a three-story hotel on Charlotte Harbor, offered rooms for wealthy visitors. It was originally call the Charlotte Bay Hotel.

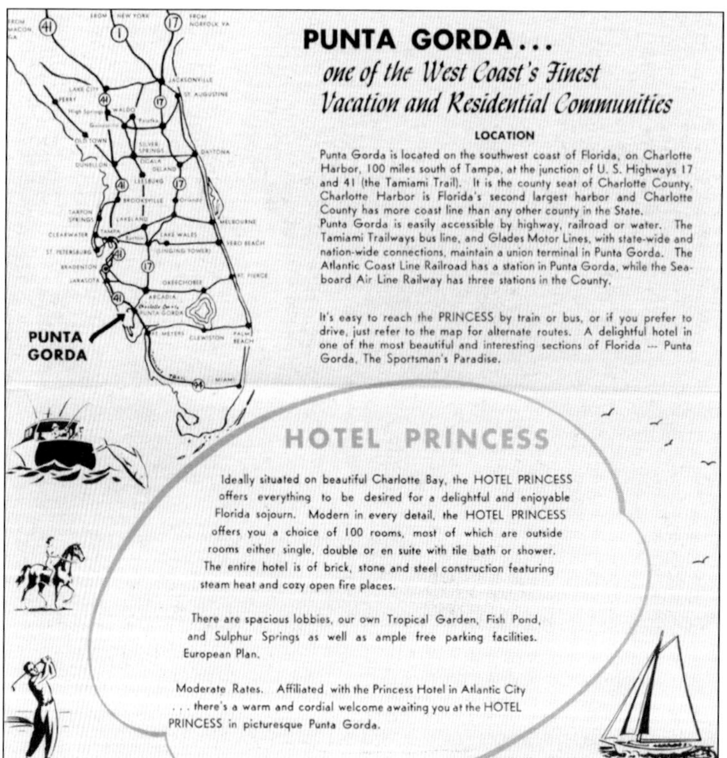

Hotel Princess Brochure. The Hotel Princess featured 100 rooms, tropical gardens, a fish pond, and sulfur springs. The brochure refers to the Punta Gorda area as "Sportsmen's Paradise."

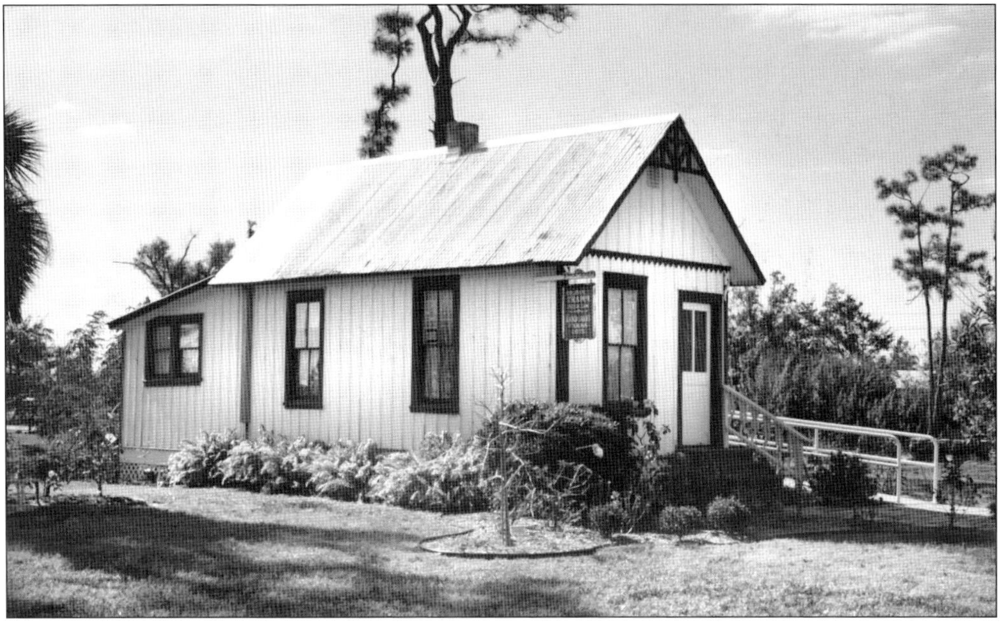

TRABUE'S LAND SALES OFFICE. Col. Isaac Trabue's original land sales office, the oldest building (1886) in Punta Gorda, was moved by Old Punta Gorda, Inc., from its original Cross Street location to the corner of East Marion Avenue and Nesbit Street for restoration. Today the building is on display at the Punta Gorda History Park on Shreve Street. (Photograph by Scot Shively; Blanchard House Museum of African-American History and Culture of Charlotte County.)

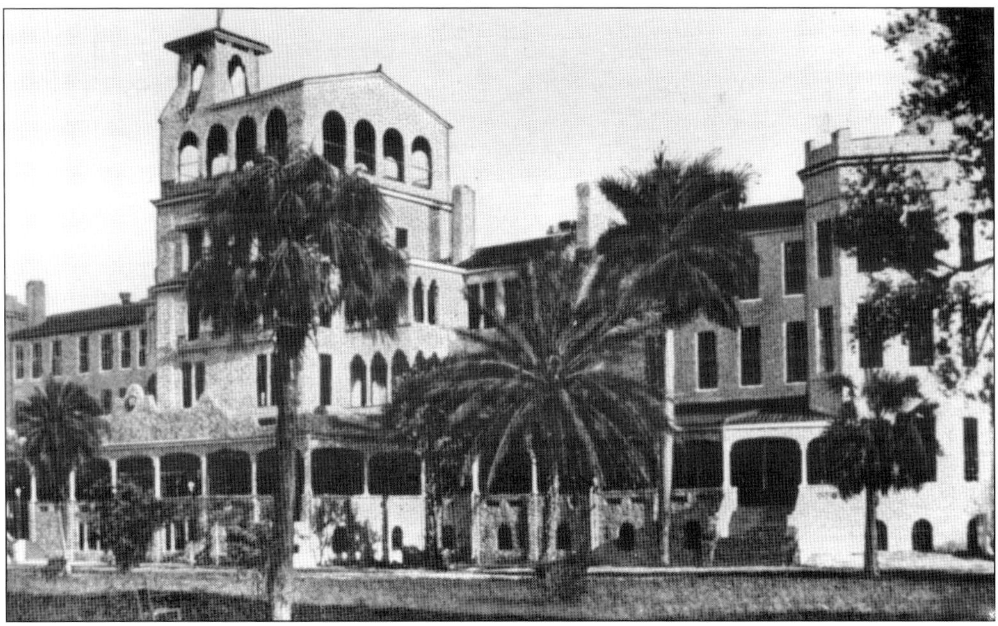

HOTEL CHARLOTTE HARBOR. Hotel Charlotte Harbor offered an 18-hole golf course and moving picture shows and featured the hotel's own orchestra. There was also plenty of fishing, sunbathing, and swimming for guests. The hotel burned to the ground in 1959 as a result of a suspicious fire. The grand hotel rested on the banks of the Charlotte Harbor, named for Queen Charlotte, the wife of King George III.

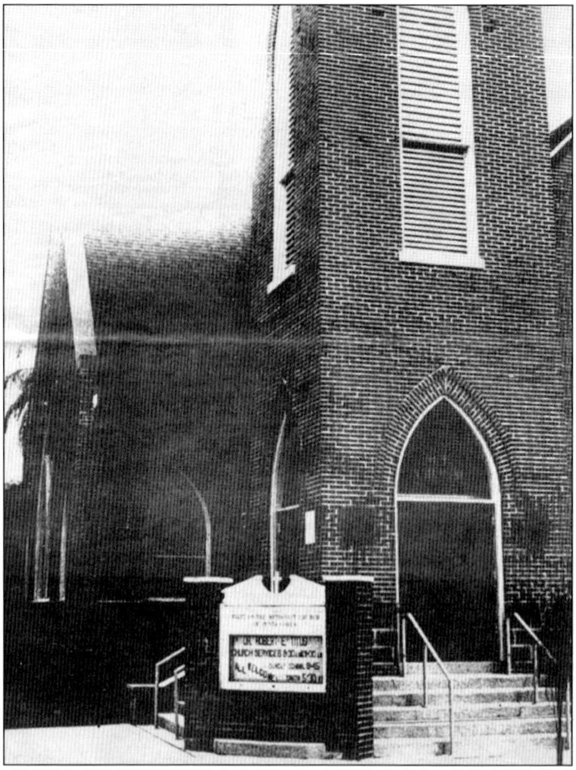

The First United Methodist Church. The First United Methodist Church was built in 1915 and was estimated to have cost $10,000 to complete. Earlier services were held in the Community Hall built by Col. Isaac Trabue in 1887. It is the city's oldest congregation.

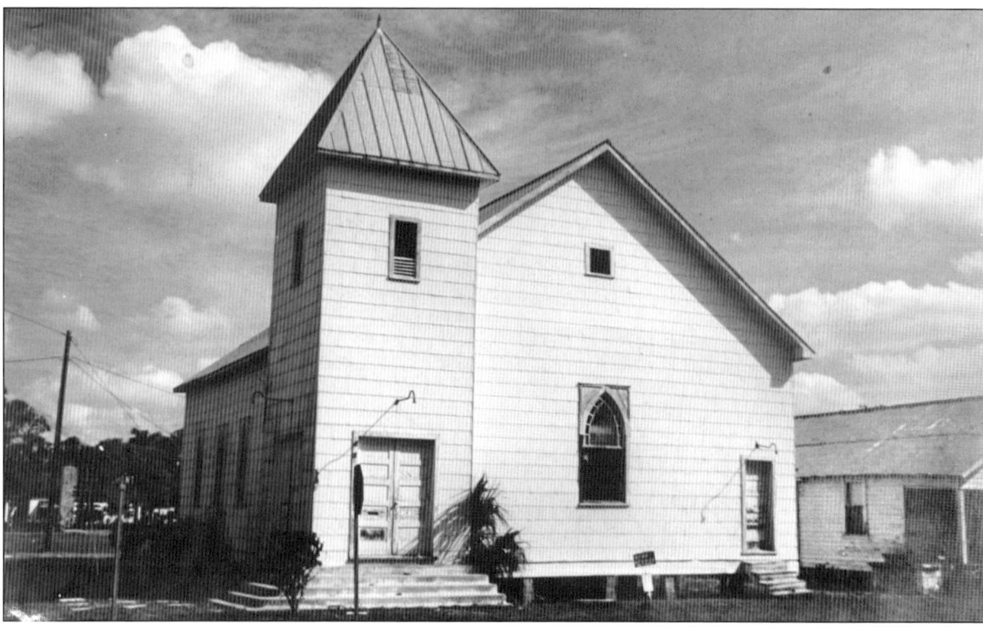

St. Mark Missionary Baptist Church. St. Mark Missionary Baptist Church is located at 402 Dupont Street. The church was founded in the late 1880s by Punta Gorda's Dan Smith. Smith was an African American pioneer, area businessman, and civic leader. He named the church and was ordained as its first deacon. The church is still used today. (Blanchard House Museum of African-American History and Culture of Charlotte County.)

Church of the Good Shepherd. The history of the church dates back to 1886, when Virginia Trabue, wife of Col. Isaac Trabue, requested that Bishop William Gray, the missionary bishop of South Florida, make arrangements for Episcopal services in the town. Early church services were held in the Community Church until 1893, when Bishop Gray met with the church community to establish a church mission and select property for the building. Albert Walter Gilchrist donated land for the church on the corner of West Virginia Street and Cross Street. Gilchrist became governor of Florida in 1909. (*Fact and Fable: Charlotte County.*)

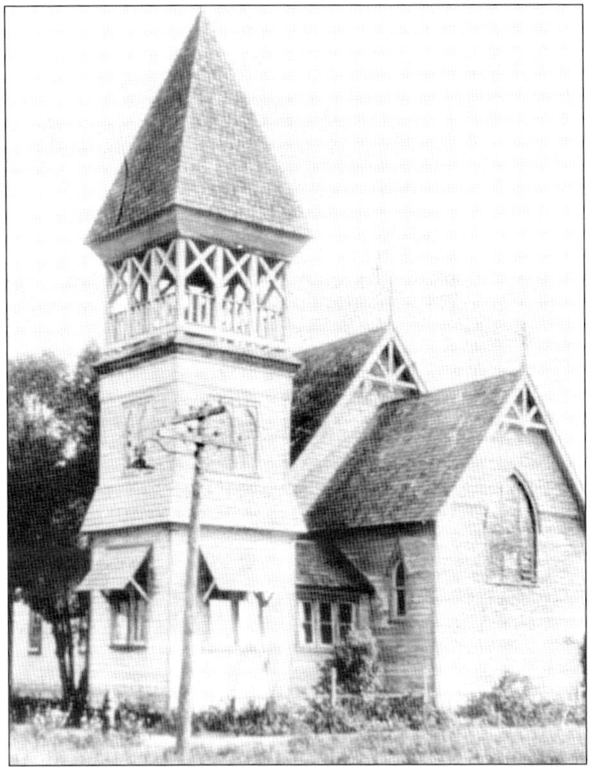

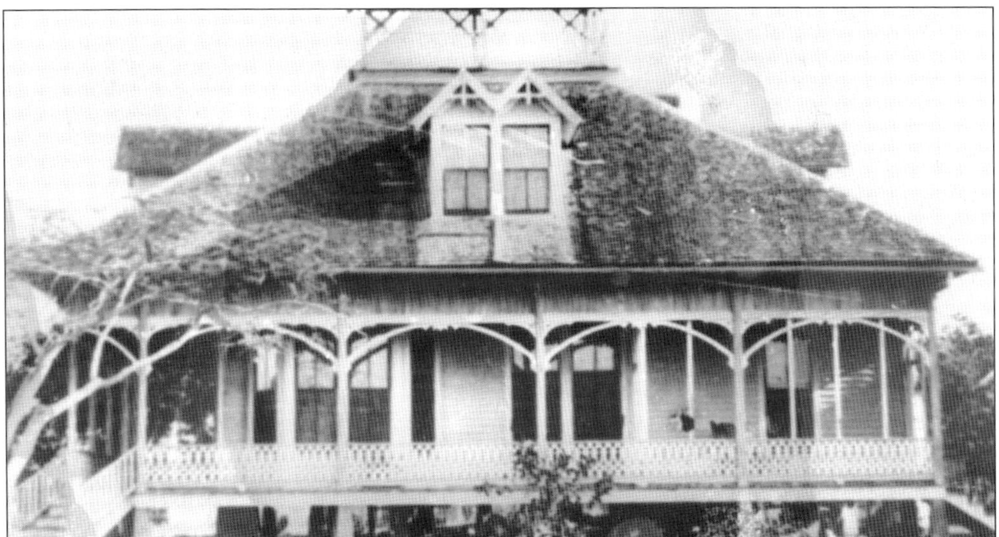

The Sandlin House. This home was built in 1890 by James L. Sandlin. The wooden house features a widow's walk, a popular addition to coastal homes created to observe vessels at sea. The name comes from wives of mariners, who would patiently watch for their spouses' return. Sandlin had numerous business interests with cattle, lumber, and produce, but he focused mainly on real estate. He also had some dealings with J. P. Morgan. James L. Sandlin was one of Punta Gorda's first city aldermen. He later became mayor of Punta Gorda. (Punta Gorda Historical Society, Linda Wilson collection.)

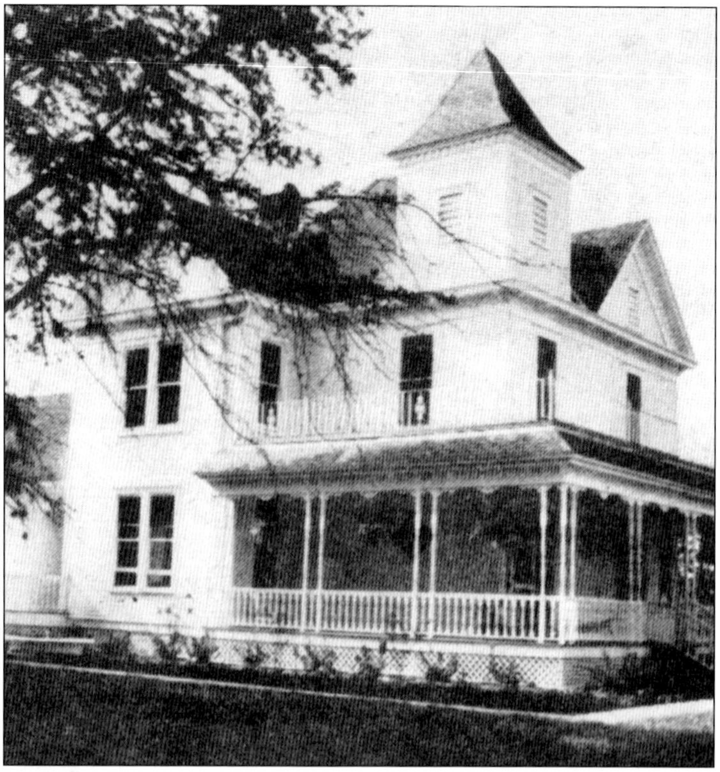

The A. C. Freeman House. The A. C. Freeman House is a two-story frame Victorian home that was built in 1903 and was originally located on East Marion Avenue. It was built for a cost of less than $900. It is considered Carpenter Queen Anne style and features a square tower on the northeast corner and a wraparound first-story porch. It is the only remaining Victorian home of its kind in Charlotte County. It is now located at 639 East Hargreaves Avenue. The home was listed on the National Register of Historic Places in 1987.

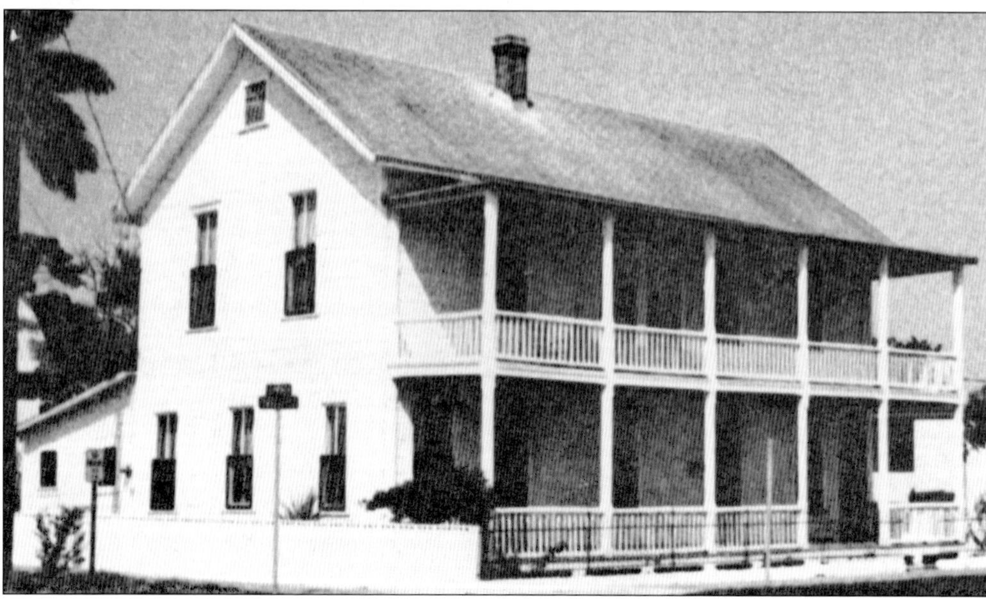

The Hector Building. In 1887, thirty-four men, four of whom were African American, met at Hector's Billiard Parlor and Drugstore to discuss incorporation of the city. They drafted a city charter and changed the name from Trabue to Punta Gorda. Afterward, a group of the signers walked all night to the county seat located at Pine Level, which was 23 miles away, just to register the document. Hector's house is a two-story wooden frame house. Originally a drugstore was located on the first floor, and upstairs was a billiard hall.

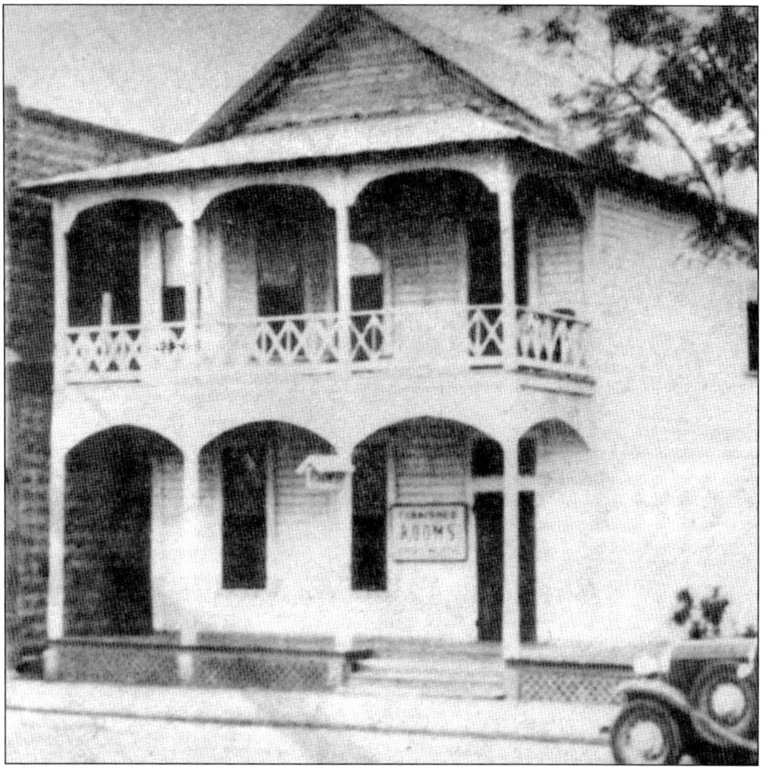

THE GOLDSTEIN HOUSE. This two-story wooden home was owned by Ephriam Goldstein, an accomplished musician, and housed Ephriam, his son, Harry, and his wife, Fredericak. The family was one of the earlier settlers to the town then known as Trabue. The Goldstein House was built in one day in 1886 by the same carpenters who built the new Hotel Punta Gorda. The building was dismantled in 1968. (Charlotte Harbor Area Historical Society.)

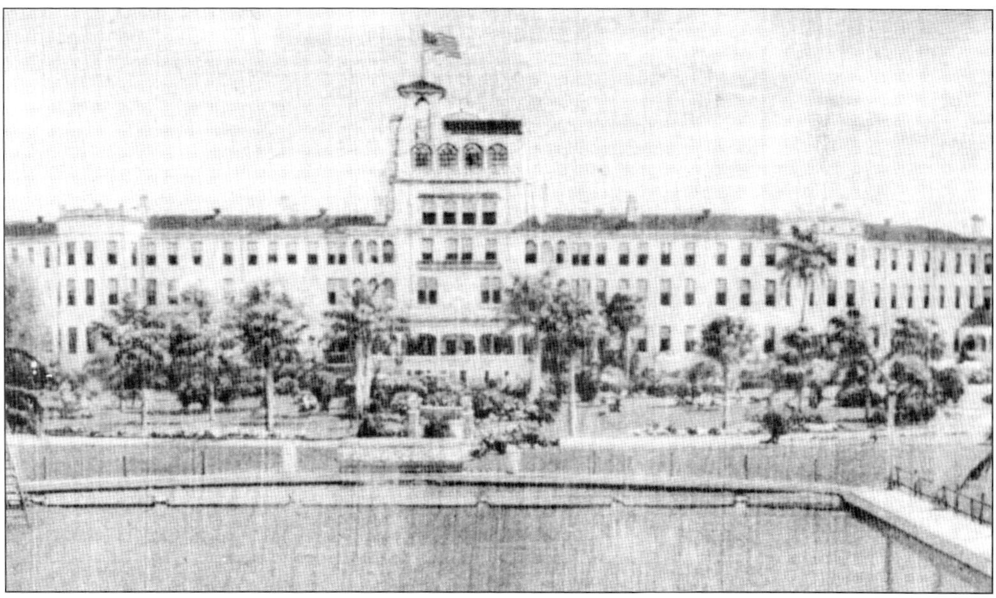

HOTEL CHARLOTTE HARBOR'S SWIMMING POOL. The grand swimming pool at the Hotel Charlotte Harbor is pictured here. As one of the area's finest hotels, located right on the harbor, the hotel would attract famous people and dignitaries, such as Pres. Theodore Roosevelt and his vice president, Charles W. Fairbanks. In 1916, Pres. Teddy Roosevelt, it was said, caught a 15-foot great white shark while visiting Punta Gorda, although other accounts consider this a fish tale. He also caught a large manta ray, the "devil fish."

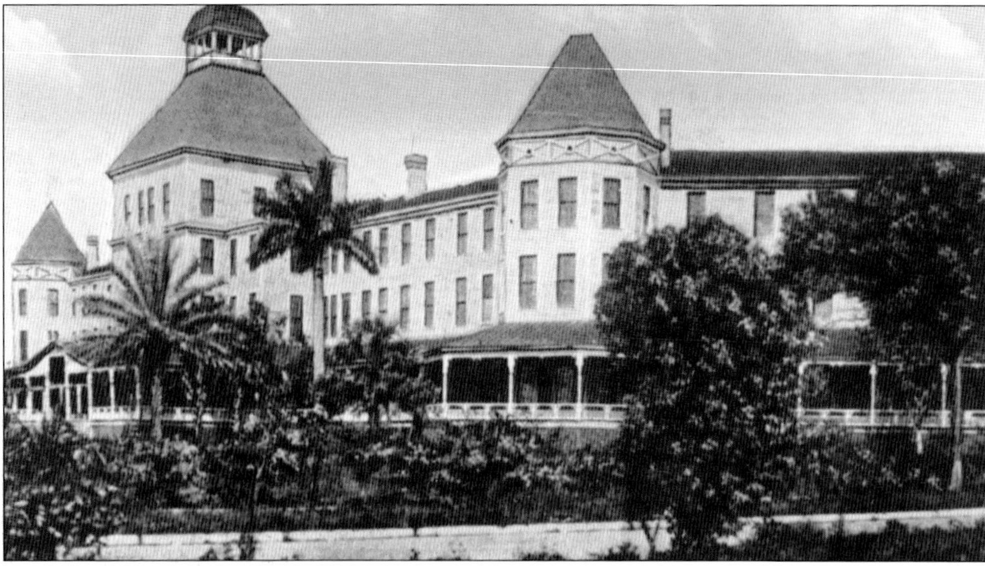

HOTEL PUNTA GORDA. Here is another view of Hotel Punta Gorda, which was for a time partly owned by Cornelius Vanderbilt. The hotel catered to the upper class. Hotel visitors would sometimes stay for months during the wintertime, as many of them enjoyed the year-round sun, boating, and the fishing—especially for tarpon. However, in 1894, tragedy struck. Caldwell Colt, heir to the Samuel Colt Arms Manufacturing Company's business and fortune, drowned while vacationing at Hotel Punta Gorda. His distraught mother donated the money to build the new Good Shepherd Episcopal Church in her beloved son's memory.

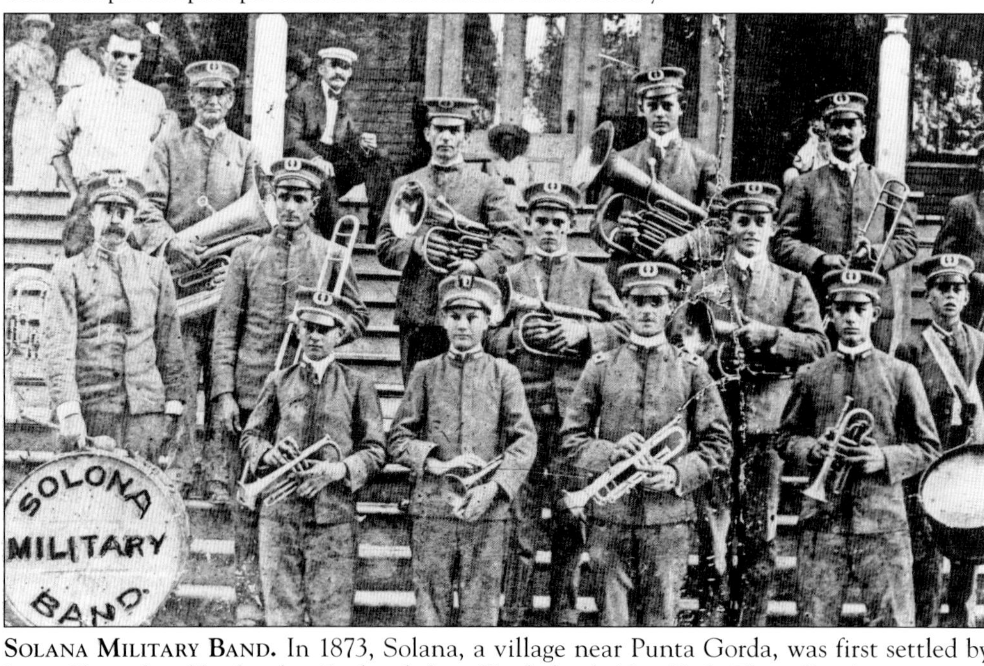

SOLANA MILITARY BAND. In 1873, Solana, a village near Punta Gorda, was first settled by Jarvis Howard and his brother Frederick from Kinderhook, New York. The village's name was a combination of Sol (for the sun) and Anna (for Frederick Howard's wife). The Solana Military Band was a very popular local musical troupe that entertained early visitors to Punta Gorda. The band was photographed on the steps of Hotel Punta Gorda.

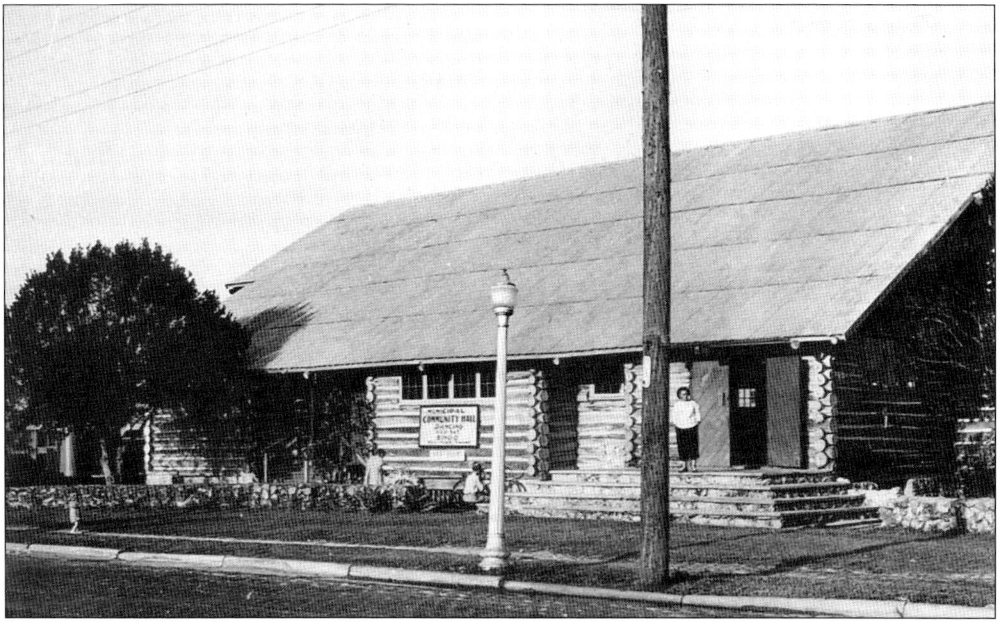

MUNICIPAL COMMUNITY HALL. The Municipal Community Hall also featured a trailer park where vacationers would come to stay. The "tin can" trailer park, as it was referred to, was once located in what was Laishley Park. The trailer park was later moved by the city of Punta Gorda to Buttonwood Park, where it still stands today. (Punta Gorda Historic Railroad Depot and Antique Mall, Linda Wilson collection.)

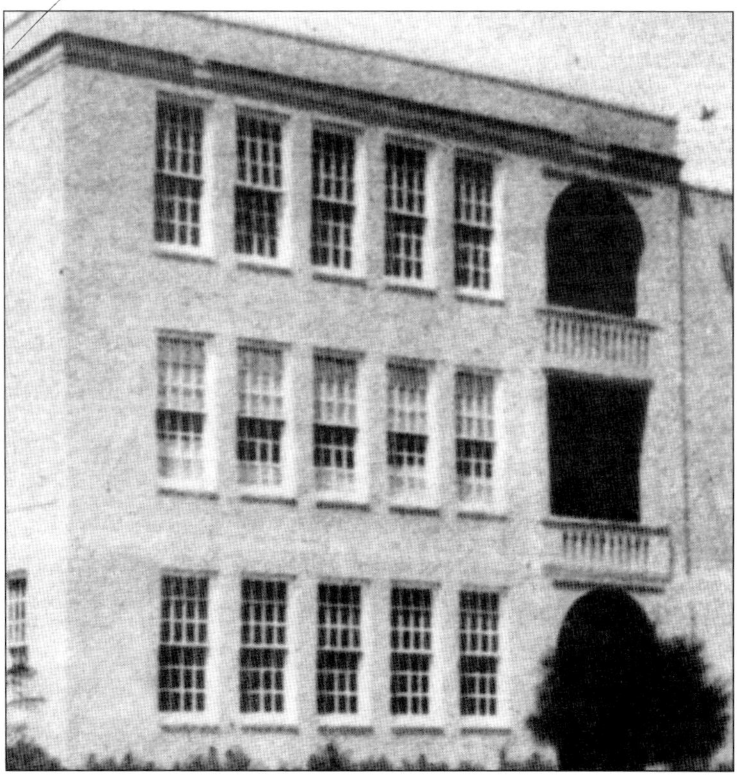

CHARLOTTE HIGH SCHOOL AROUND 1935. The three-story Charlotte High School is located at 1250 Cooper Street. The first students attended the school in 1927. Because busing from rural areas increased the enrollment, this larger school was constructed. The building was added to the National Register of Historic Places in 1990. The original school was held in a community hall back in 1888. By 1896, a larger school was built on Goldstein Street and later another one on Taylor Street in 1911.

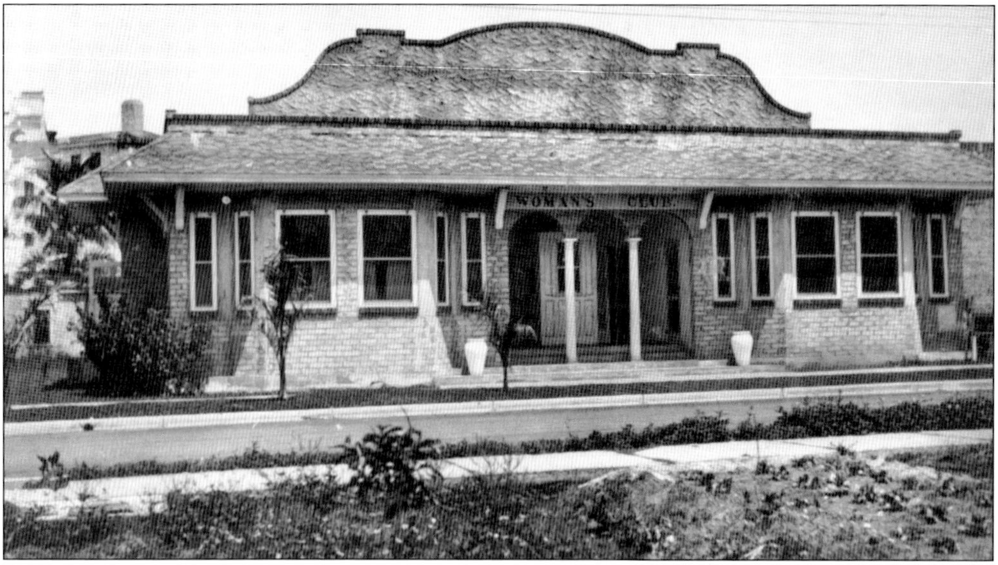

The Woman's Club Building. The Woman's Club Building was constructed in 1927 on land donated by Judge William Fenmore Cooper of Cook County, Illinois. The building's architecture is considered Mediterranean Revival, a style noted for arched entrances, columns, and other classical details. The building is similar in style to the Punta Gorda Railroad Depot, built in 1928. On April 5, 1991, the building was added to the National Register of Historic Places. In 2000, the Punta Gorda Woman's Club transferred the building's deed to the Punta Gorda Historical Society.

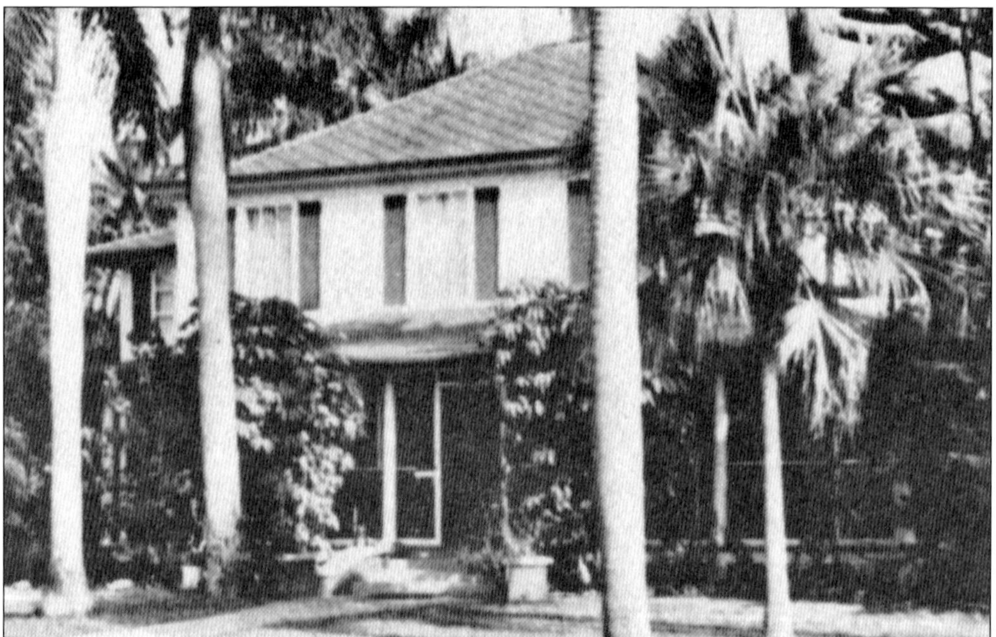

Sallie Jones's House. As a young child, Sallie Jones came to Punta Gorda, where she grew up and graduated from Charlotte High School. She attended Florida Southern College and earned her teaching degree. She later returned to Punta Gorda and taught English, history, and science. Sallie Jones was elected Charlotte County's first woman school superintendent in 1937, and she served for 16 years. Jones was Florida's first school superintendent. (*Fact and Fable: Charlotte County.*)

Five

Neighborhoods

During the early years, Punta Gorda was a mix of various classes who all lived and worked together. Although the Hotel Punta Gorda, later known as Hotel Charlotte Harbor, was at one point partly owned by upper-class Cornelius Vanderbilt, Punta Gorda was for the most part a rugged frontier town, not unlike many others back then. However, in the early 1900s, Punta Gorda transformed itself into the county seat of Charlotte County, a county formed in 1921 after DeSoto County was divided into five counties. During that same year, the first bridge was constructed along the new Tamiami Trail that connected Punta Gorda with Charlotte Harbor. (The name Tamiami comes from the phrase "Tampa to Miami.") Due to the area's growth and the poor construction of the first bridge, it was replaced by the Barron Collier Bridge in 1931 and later by the current bridge that crosses the Peace River. In 1926, Punta Gorda installed brick streets, a statement that showed the area's progress from horses to automobiles as means of transportation. The area's development followed the shorelines of Charlotte Harbor, the Peace River, the Myakka River, Lemon Bay, and the Gulf of Mexico. The shoreline development was a result of the railroads' and ships' access to the area. Once the highway system came into place, Punta Gorda also developed along the highway U.S. 41.

Punta Gorda is situated between Retta Esplanade to the north and Virginia Avenue to the south. It is between U.S. 41 South on the west and Wood Street on the east. Marion Avenue and Taylor Street, located in the heart of Punta Gorda, have always been key streets to many of Punta Gorda's businesses.

Punta Gorda's residential areas feature many brick streets that are beautifully lined with huge old royal palms that date back to the early years. In fact, in 1900, Albert Gilchrist donated royal palm trees that still line Marion Avenue. In 1905, a fire destroyed most of downtown; hence, Punta Gorda Council ordered all new business structures be constructed with bricks or concrete. Tin roofs also become a popular choice at this time. Many of the old Florida homes that feature tin roofs and wide verandas still stand today. Hurricane Donna blew into the area in 1960, and in 2004, along came Hurricane Charley, so strong building construction is imperative.

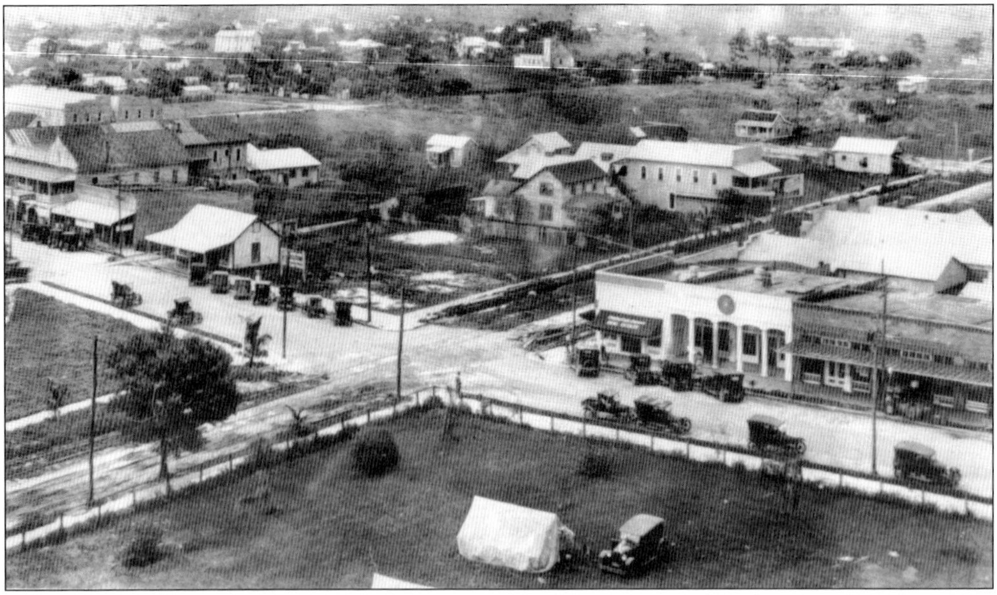

Intersection of Marion Avenue and King Street, 1920s. The photograph, taken from Hotel Punta Gorda, shows the Punta Gorda State Bank (white building just right of center, with black circle) on Marion Avenue. The bank, opened in 1917, took over the old Punta Gorda Bank's deposits.

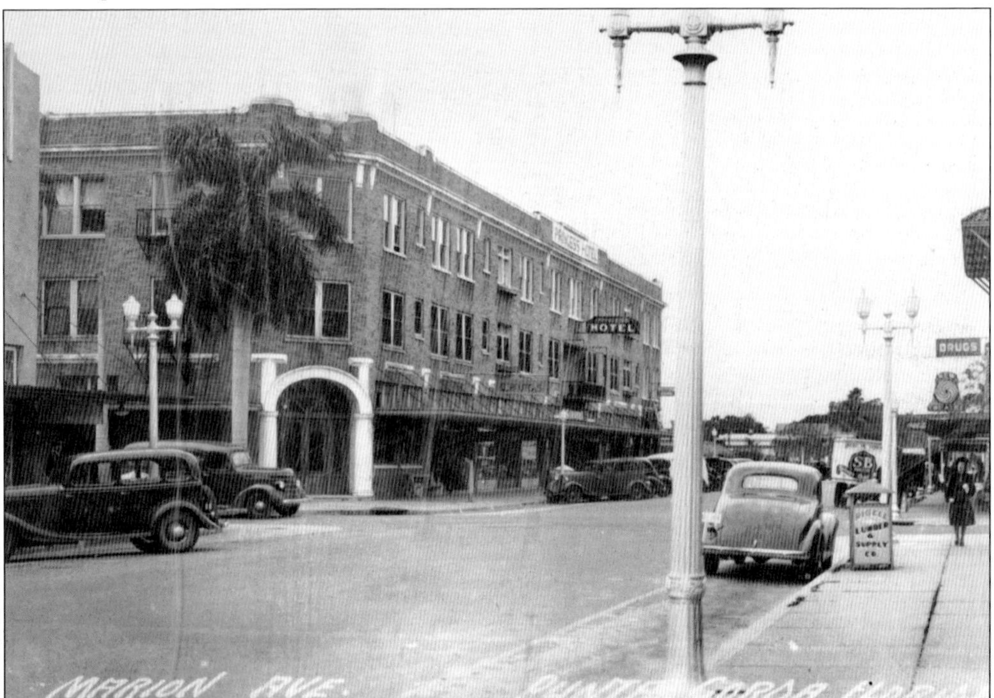

The Charlotte Bay Hotel around 1925. The Charlotte Bay Hotel was located on the corner of Marion Avenue and Taylor Street. This was a prime business corner in the city. The Fidelity Trust Company, a subsidiary of the First National Bank of Punta Gorda, was also in the building, along with a drugstore.

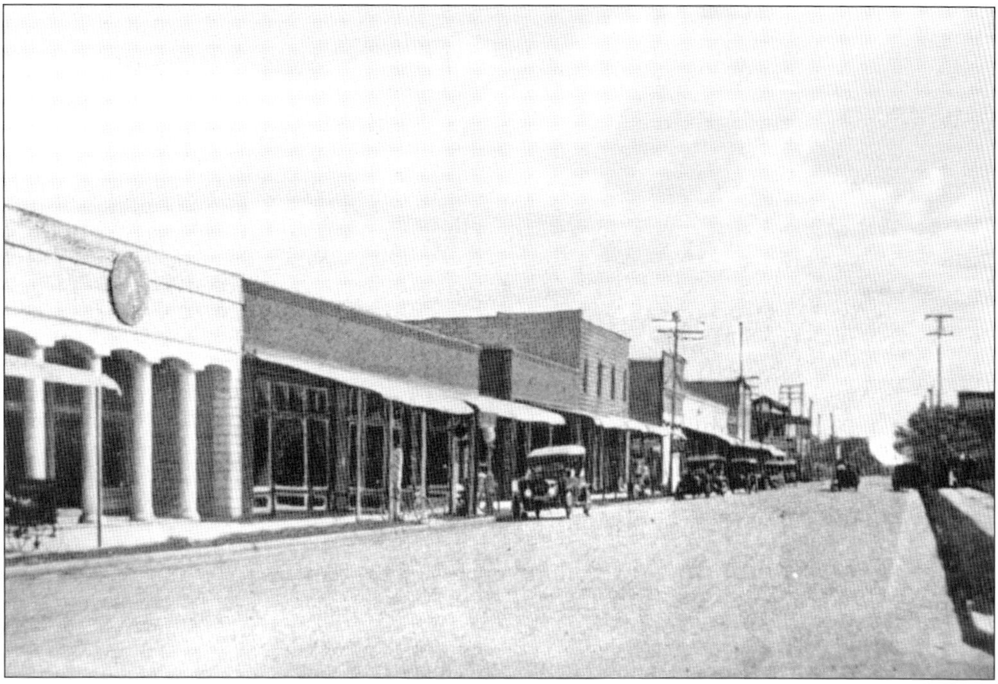

PUNTA GORDA BANKING. The bank is one of a few in Punta Gorda that gave residents and businesses a place to get a loan or save their money. During the land boom in the early 1920s, no doubt the banks were also booming.

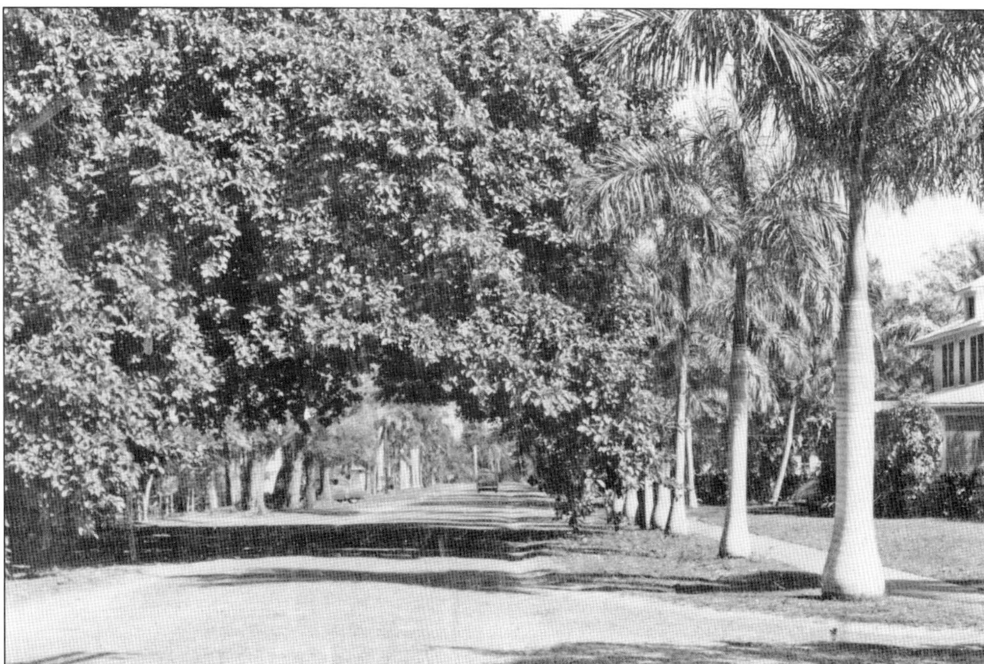

TREES LINING A CITY STREET. Punta Gorda's residential area features many brick streets that are lined with old royal palms and present a canopy of shade. The trees provide both beauty and much-needed shade to keep everything cooler, especially back before air-conditioning was a staple.

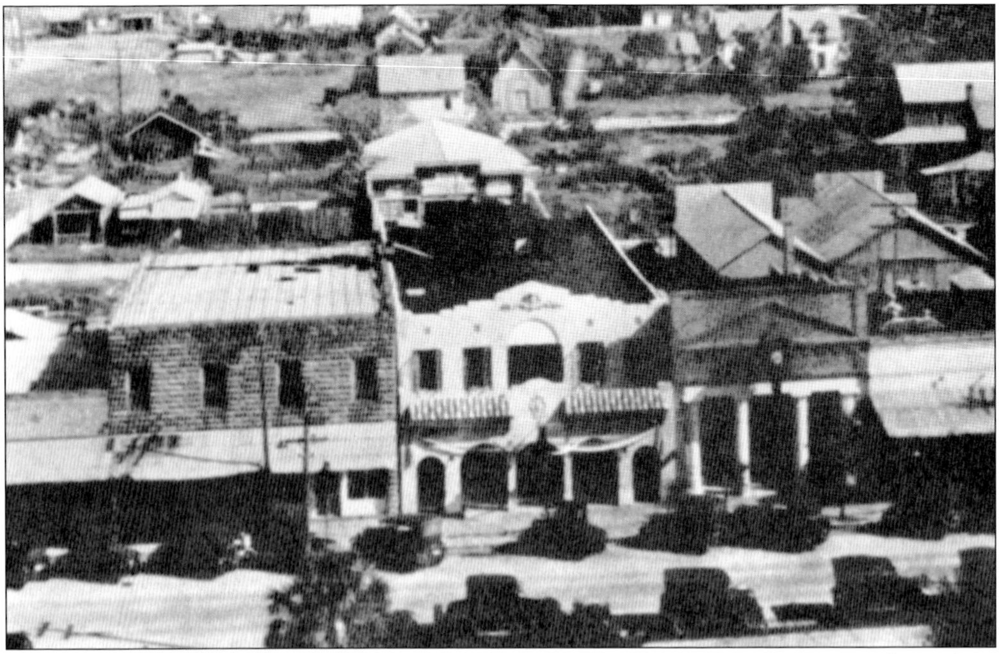

Marion Avenue as Seen from the Hotel Charlotte Harbor. Marion Avenue is shown here between Taylor Street and U.S. 41. The photograph looks south and shows the main business district of Punta Gorda. The photograph was taken from Hotel Punta Gorda. (*Ceremonial Journal*, Punta Gorda Historical Society.)

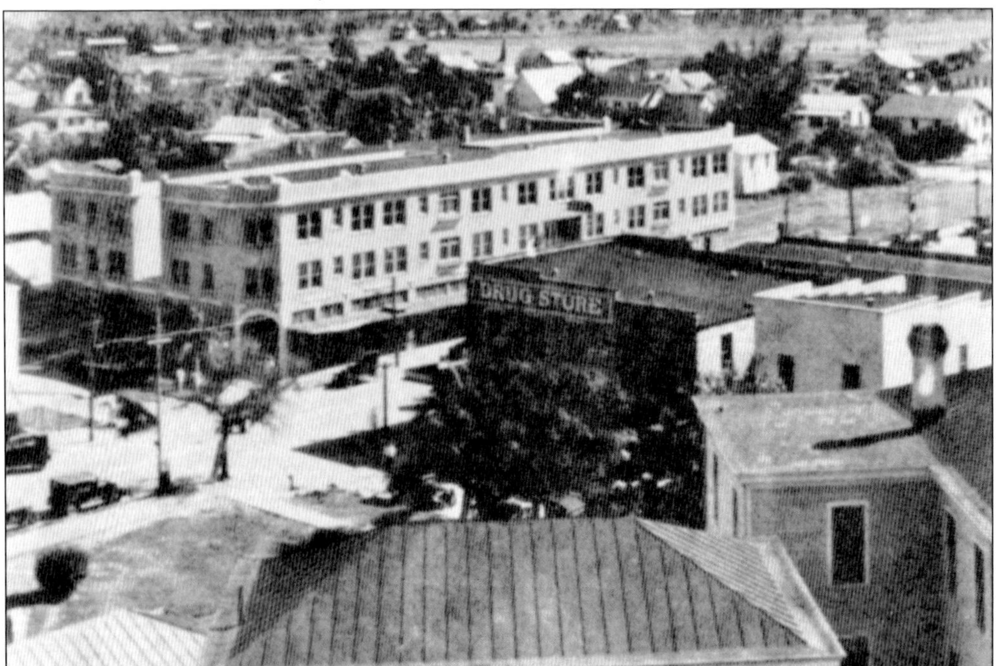

Charlotte Bay Hotel. The Charlotte Bay Hotel was a three-story hotel located on the corner of Marion Avenue and Taylor Street. It was one of many hotels in the area, thanks to the large tourism industry. Across the street was the Plaza Theater.

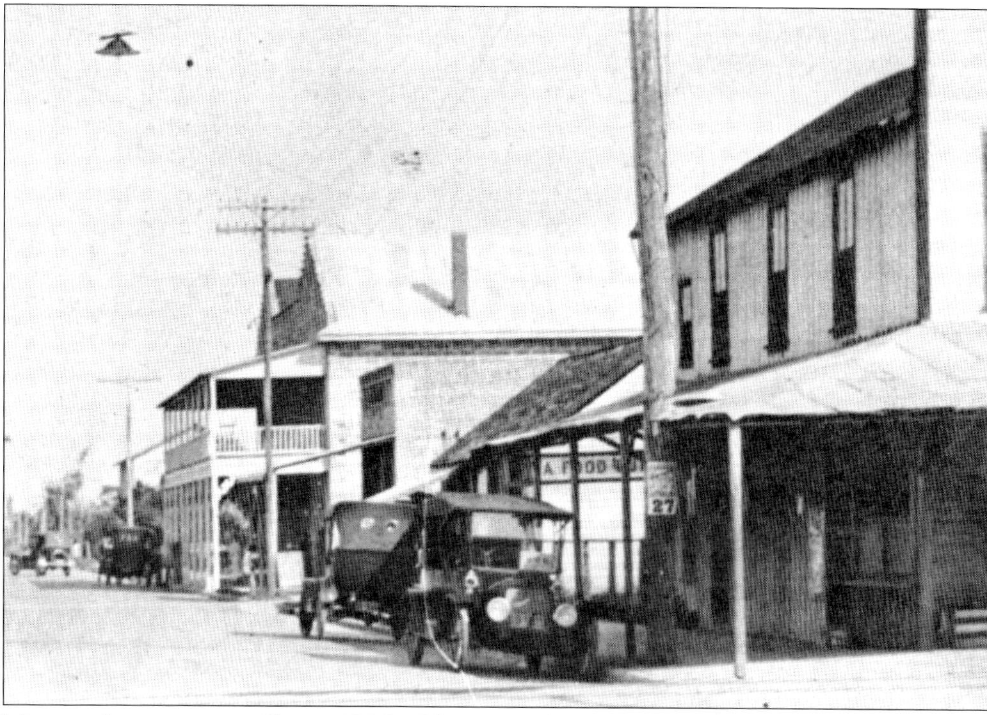

MARION AVENUE IN THE EARLY 1920S. This view of Marion Street shows off some of the many businesses that lined the city's bustling community.

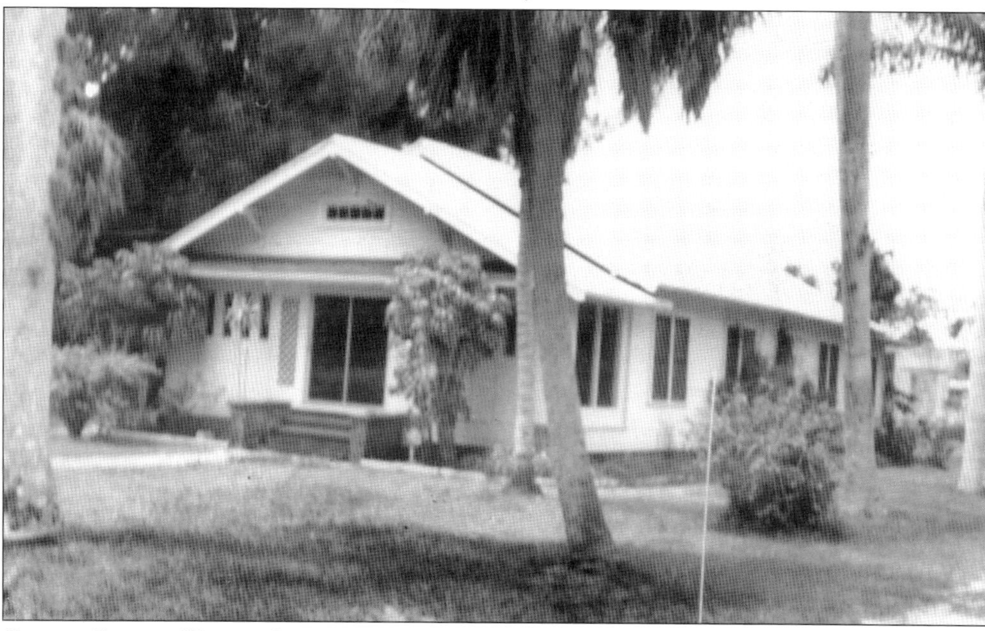

GEORGE BROWN HOUSE, CLEVELAND, FLORIDA. George Brown wound up moving his shipyard operation to property fronting Peace River that he purchased in nearby Cleveland, Florida. He rented a bungalow-style house next the shipyard until he purchased additional acreage and the house in 1916. Today the house is privately owned and remains much the way it was when George and his wife, Tommie Brown, lived there. (Bernice A. Russell Collection.)

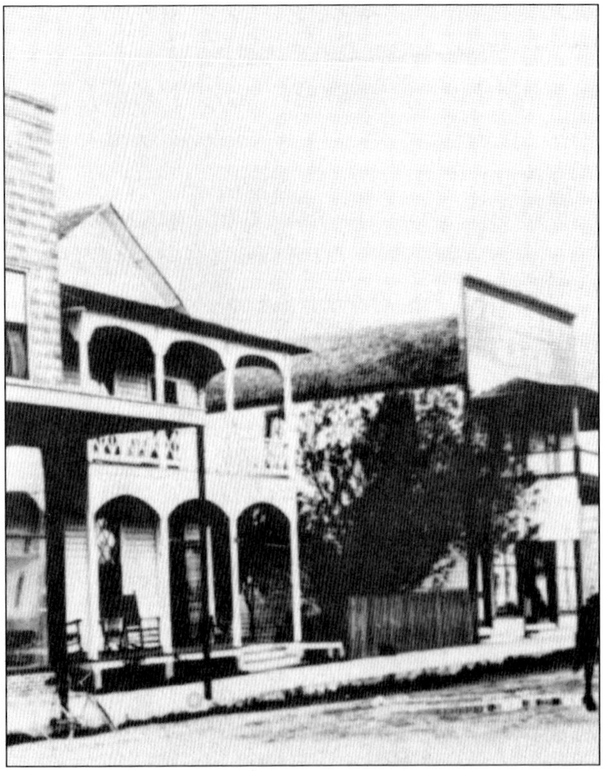

GOLDSTEIN'S HOUSE. Marion Street boasted many businesses and even some homes, like this two-story white frame home. This home was once owned by Ephriam Goldstein. He was the owner of a furniture store, Goldsteins, that was located next to his home.

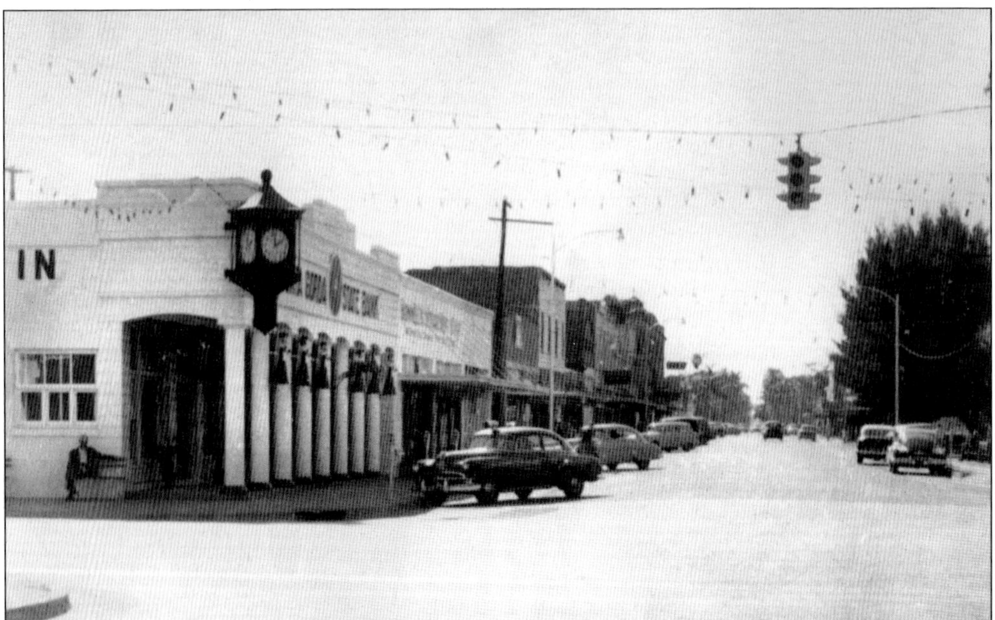

PUNTA GORDA STATE BANK. The original public clock was hung over the First National Bank entrance. Once the bank failed, the clock was moved to the Punta Gorda State Bank at the southwest corner of King Street and Marion Avenue, as shown here. The clock's chimes ring on the half hour and on the hour.

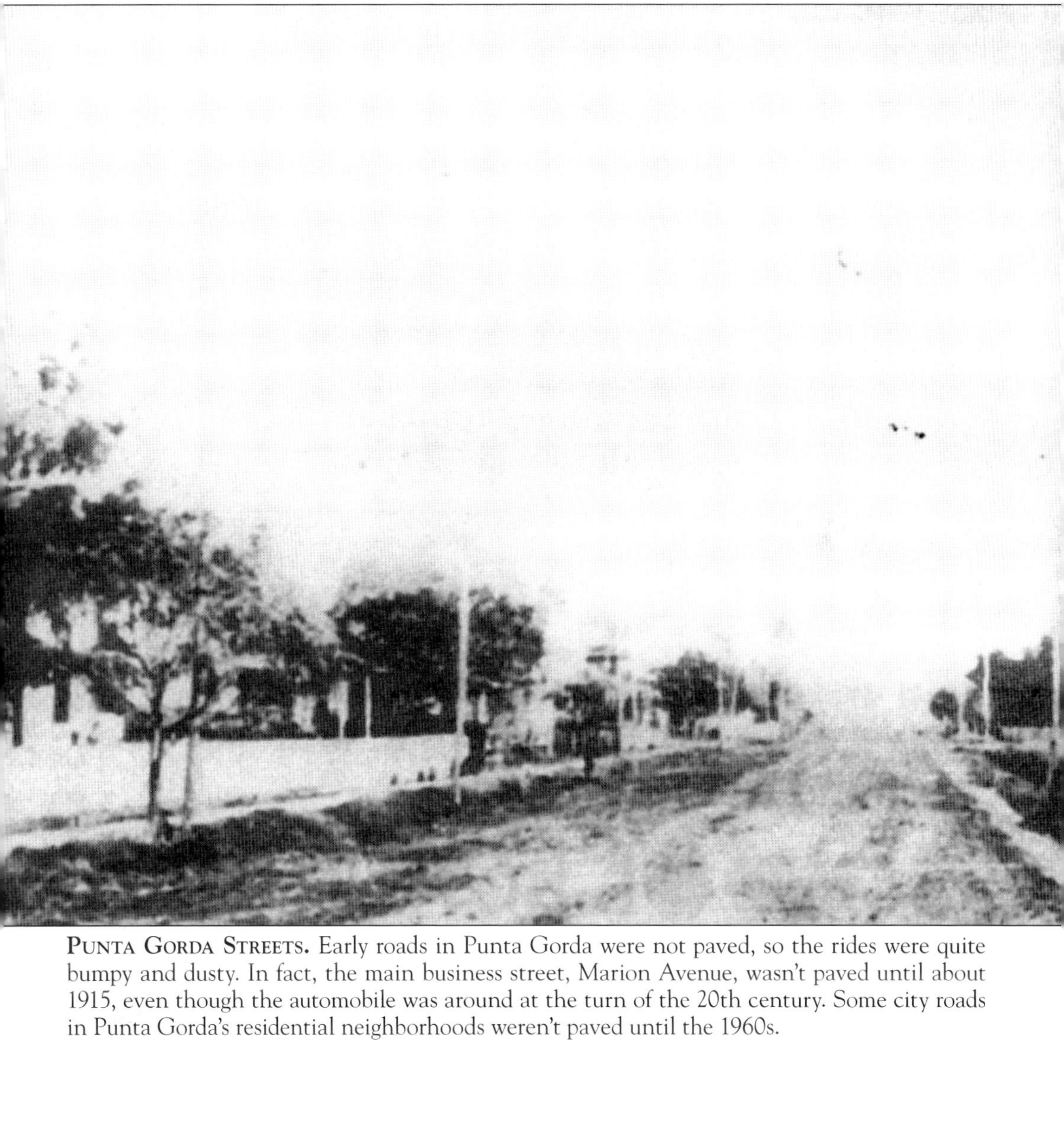

PUNTA GORDA STREETS. Early roads in Punta Gorda were not paved, so the rides were quite bumpy and dusty. In fact, the main business street, Marion Avenue, wasn't paved until about 1915, even though the automobile was around at the turn of the 20th century. Some city roads in Punta Gorda's residential neighborhoods weren't paved until the 1960s.

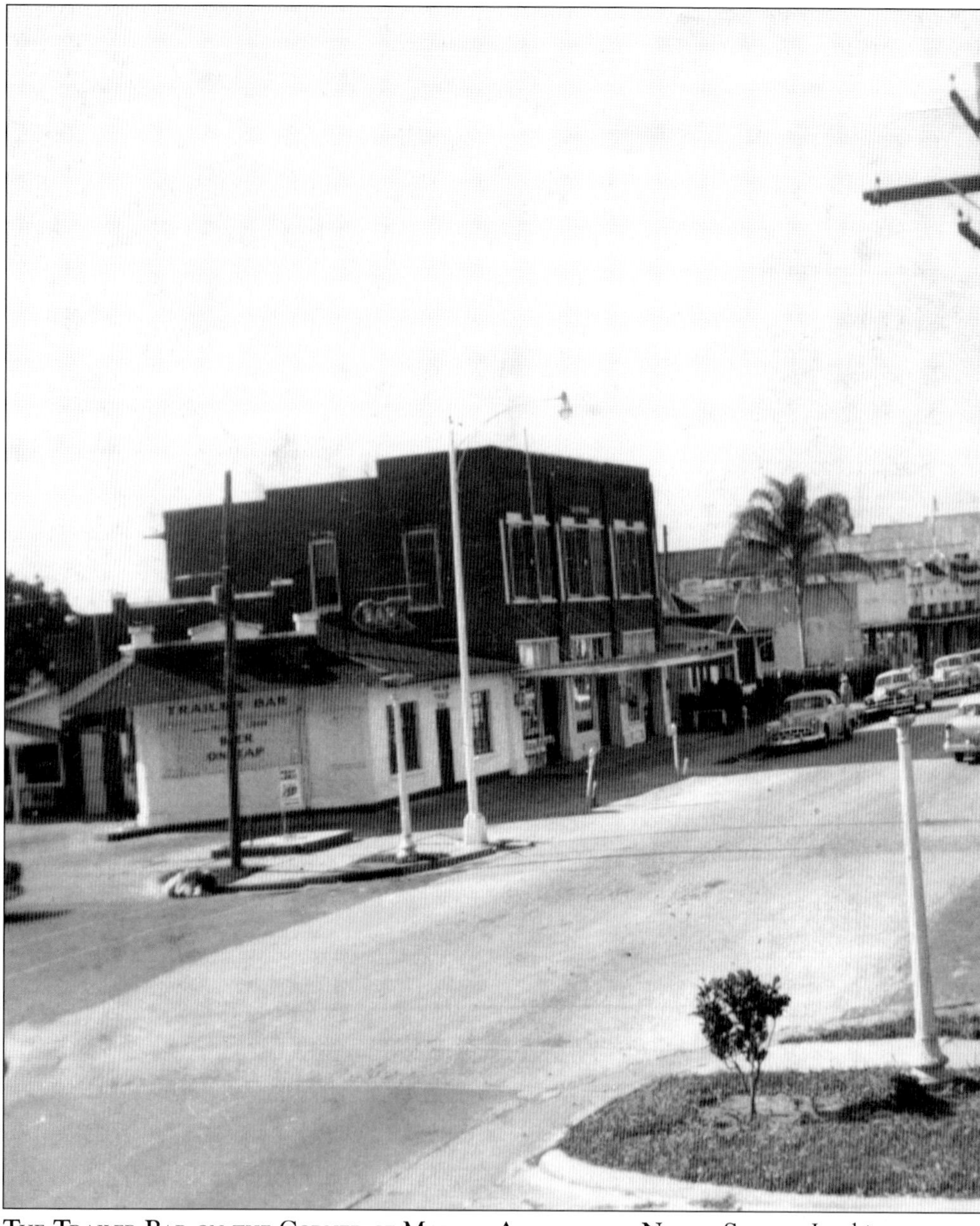

The Trailer Bar on the Corner of Marion Avenue and Nesbit Street. Looking west on east Marion Avenue, readers can see the Trailer Bar. It was a popular watering hole for the "tin can tourists" staying at Punta Gorda's Municipal Trailer Park. The photograph was taken on December 15, 1955.

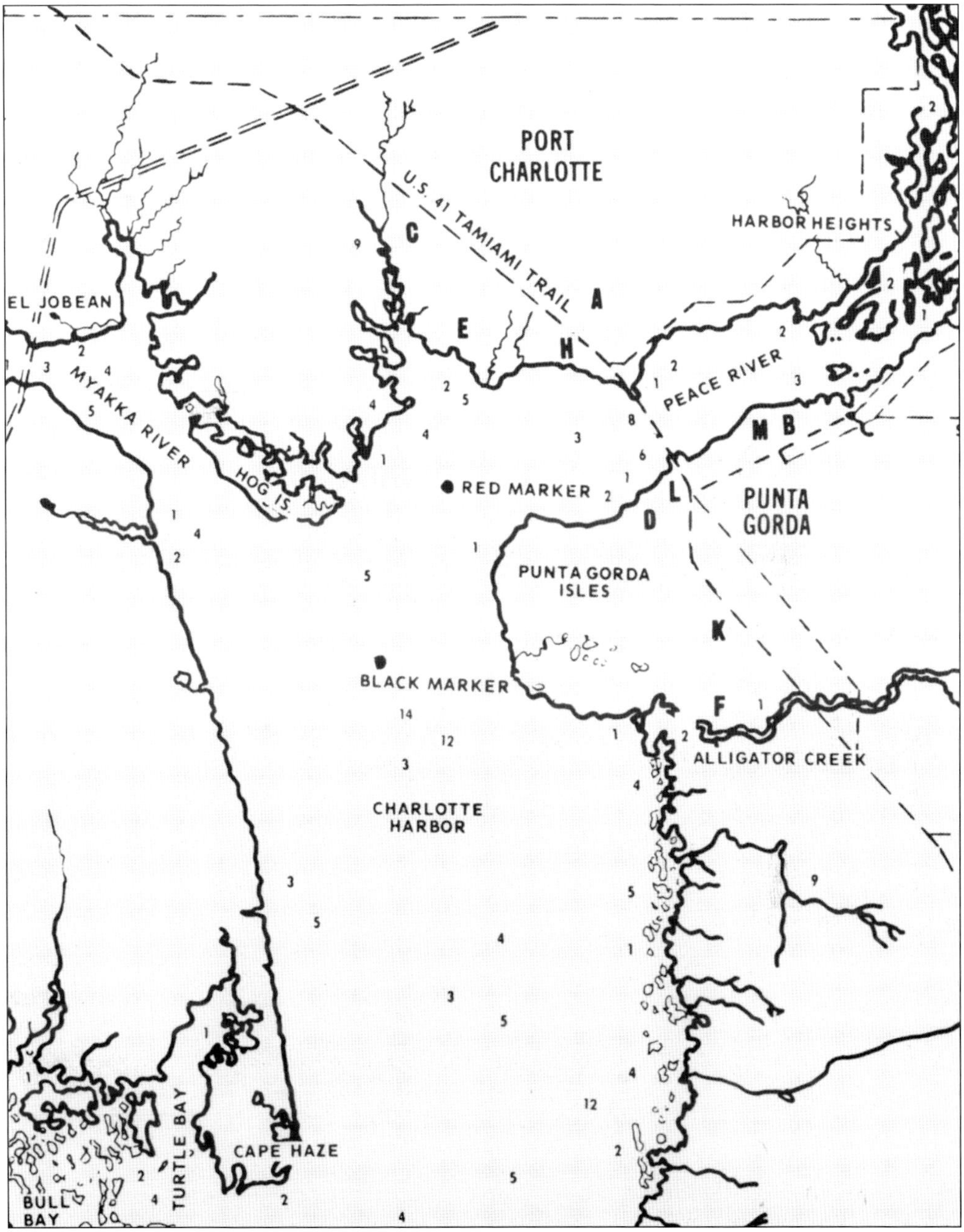

CHARLOTTE HARBOR CHART. Charlotte Harbor is a natural inlet of the Gulf of Mexico located in Southwest Florida. It is fed freshwater by the Peace River, Caloosahatchee River, and the Myakka River. The harbor is about 25 miles long and 5 miles wide and has an average depth of just over 7 feet.

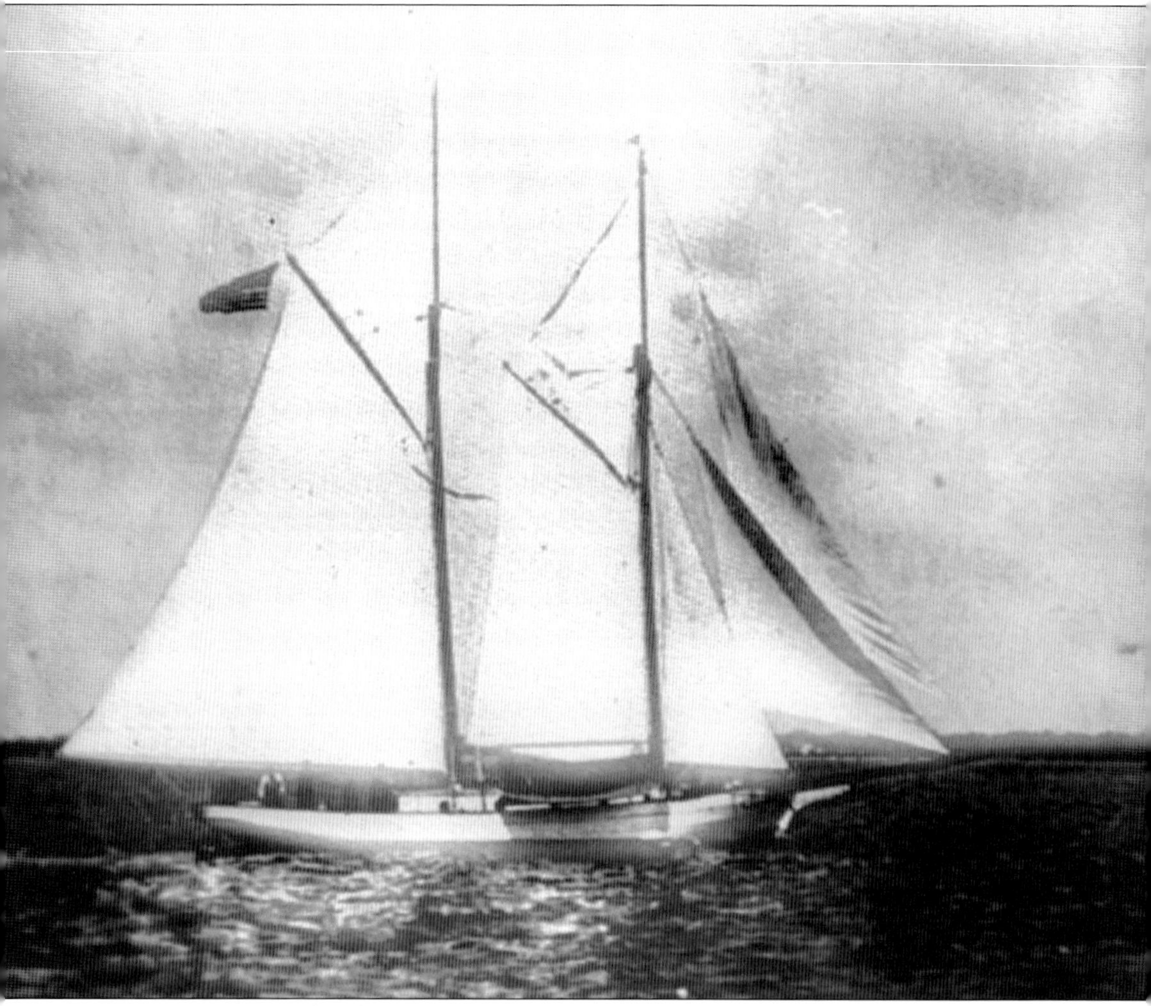

THE *IFIS* SAILBOAT. The *Ifis* was originally built in Freeport, Long Island, in 1886; however, in 1908, it was rebuilt at George Brown's shipyard in Cleveland, Florida, a town north of Punta Gorda that is also located in Charlotte County. With a 45-foot length, 14.6-foot width, and a 2,200-square-foot sail, the *Ifis* was large enough for a family to live on. The tradition of fishing, as well as living, on a sailboat started as early as the rest of the settlement off the waters of Charlotte Harbor. The harbor is about 30 miles in length and 10 in width. It is easily accessible from the Gulf of Mexico. (Florida Photographic Collection, the Florida Memory Project.)

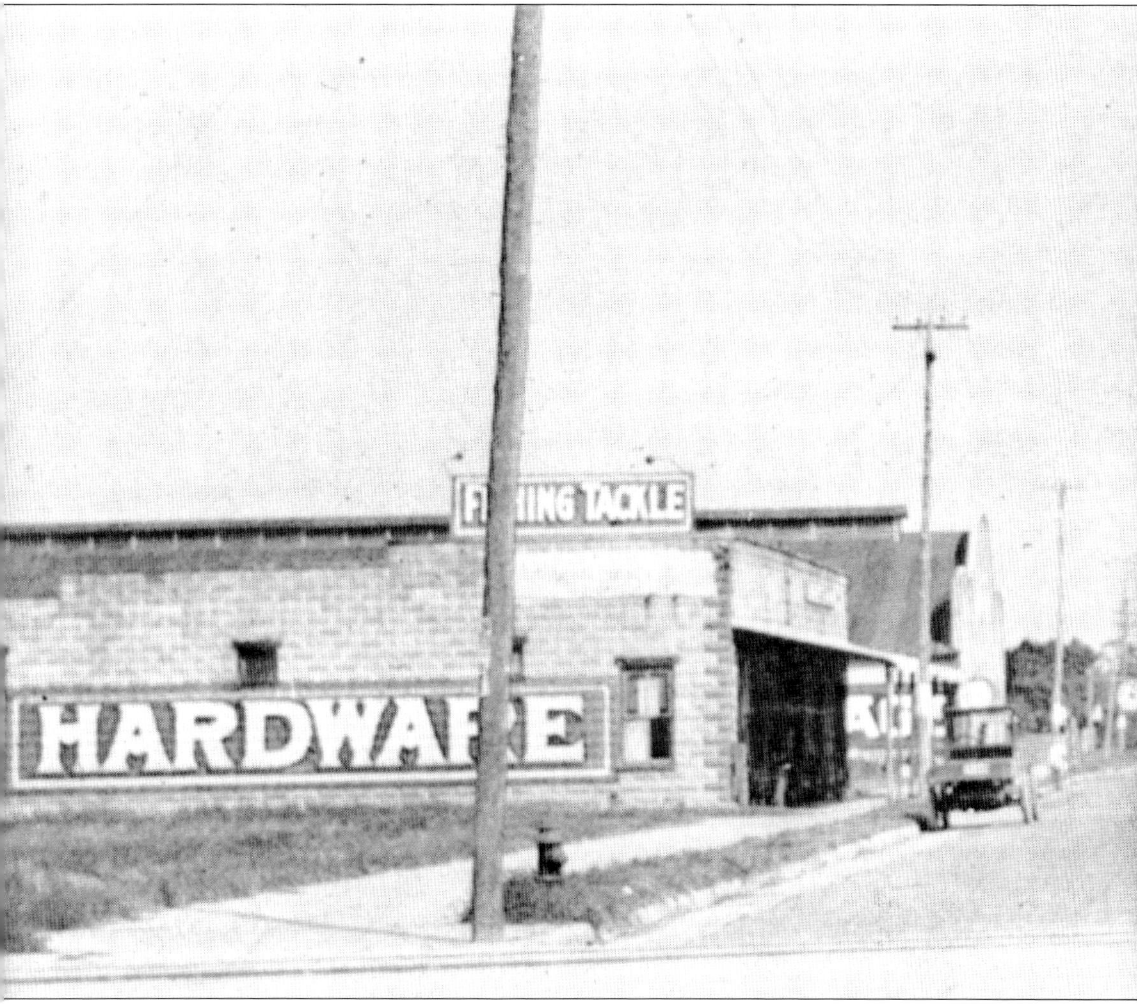

HARDWARE STORE ON MARION AVENUE. Punta Gorda Hardware Company was one of the main businesses along Marion Avenue. The October 14, 1904, edition of the *Punta Gorda Herald* listed C. L. Fries as the store manager. The business was the location for hardware, crockery, paints, oils, varnishes and ship chandlery, builder's supplies, harnesses, and household and kitchen furniture. The store was also the main supplier of coffins and burial cases. (*Fact and Fable: Charlotte County.*)

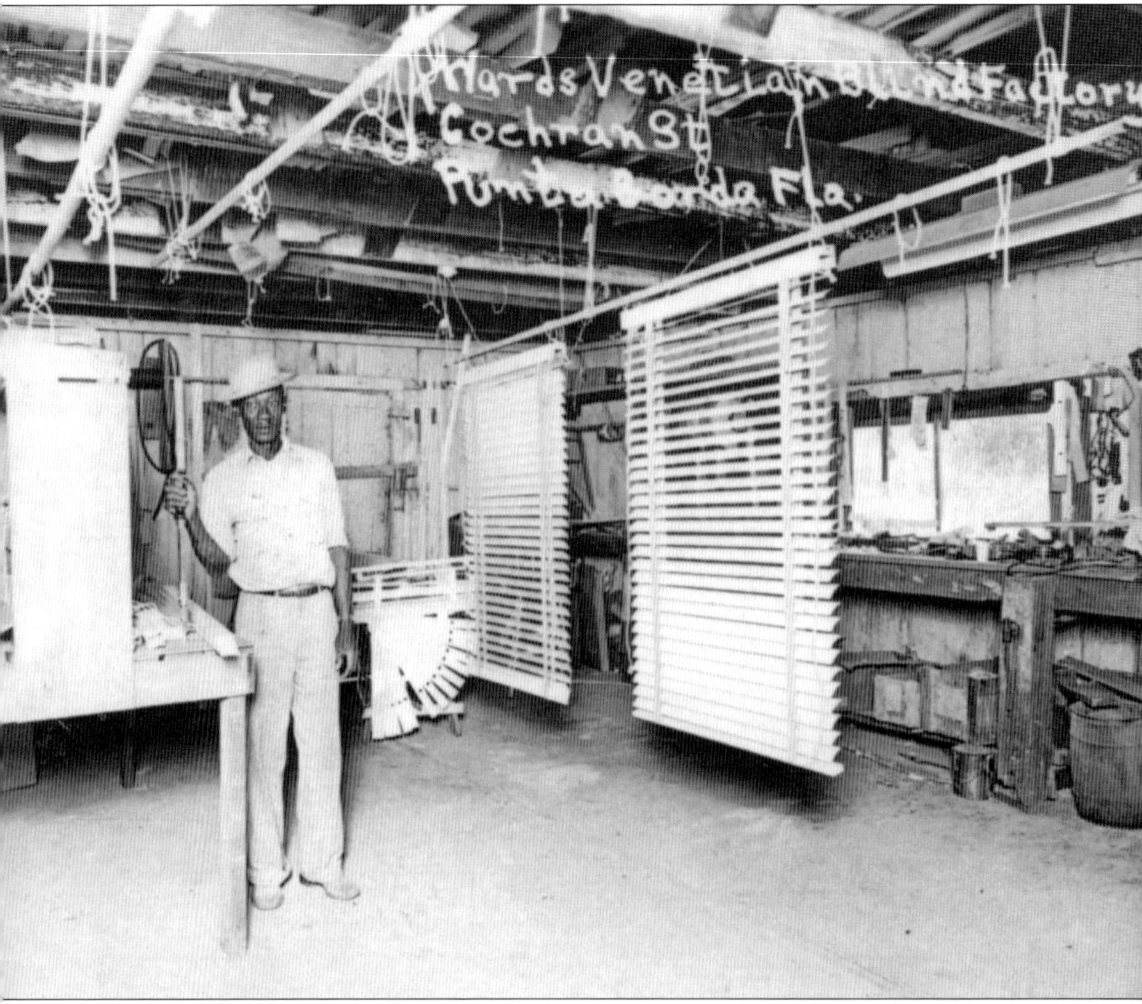

Charlotte County Blind Factory. Renalder Ward was the owner and operator of Charlotte County Blind Factory, makers of Venetian blinds located on the corner of Cochran Street (now Martin Luther King Jr. Boulevard) and Fitzhugh Avenue. (Blanchard House Museum of African-American History and Culture of Charlotte County.)

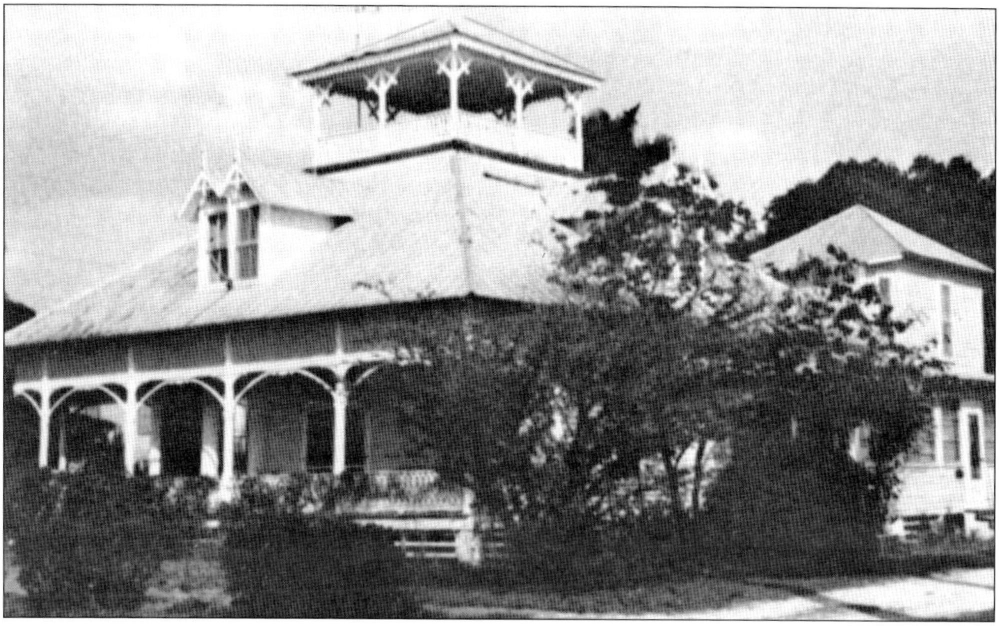

The Sandlin House. The Sandlin House is located on Retta Esplanade, a prominent Punta Gorda street. Along with having many business interests, James L. Sandlin was the president of the Punta Gorda Pilot Commission. He also donated the land for the Indian Springs Cemetery, which lies along the banks of the Alligator Creek in Punta Gorda. James L. Sandlin was married to Mary Seward, who was from a local pioneer family.

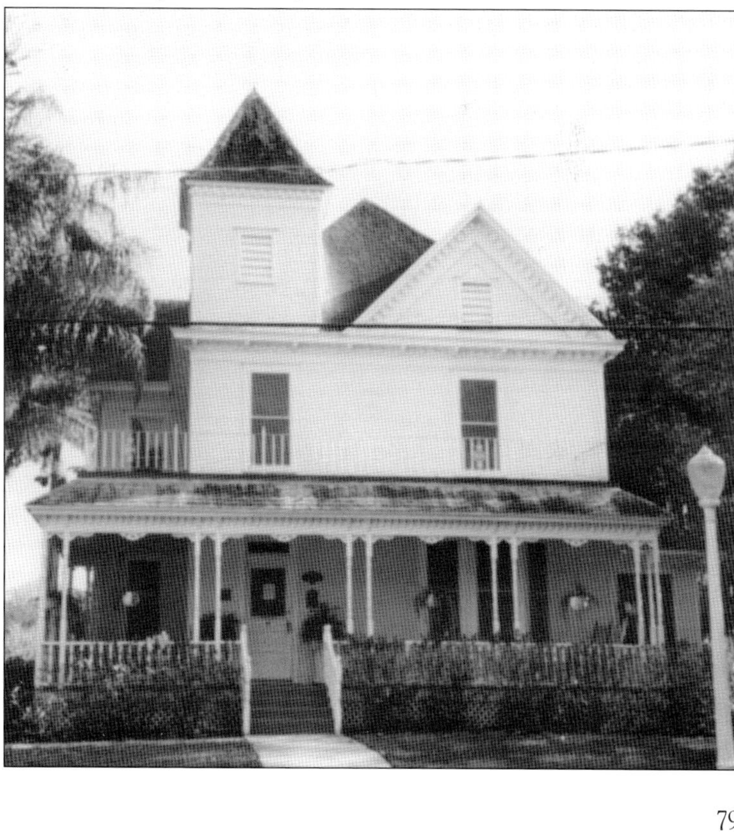

The A. C. Freedman House. In 1889, Augustus C. Freeman moved from Jasper County, Georgia, to Punta Gorda to work for the Florida Southern Railroad. He opened a hardware store that also sold caskets. Additionally, Freeman served as a city tax collector. He was also mayor of Punta Gorda and a county commissioner of DeSoto County (from the Punta Gorda district), as well as a DeSoto County sheriff from 1905 to 1913.

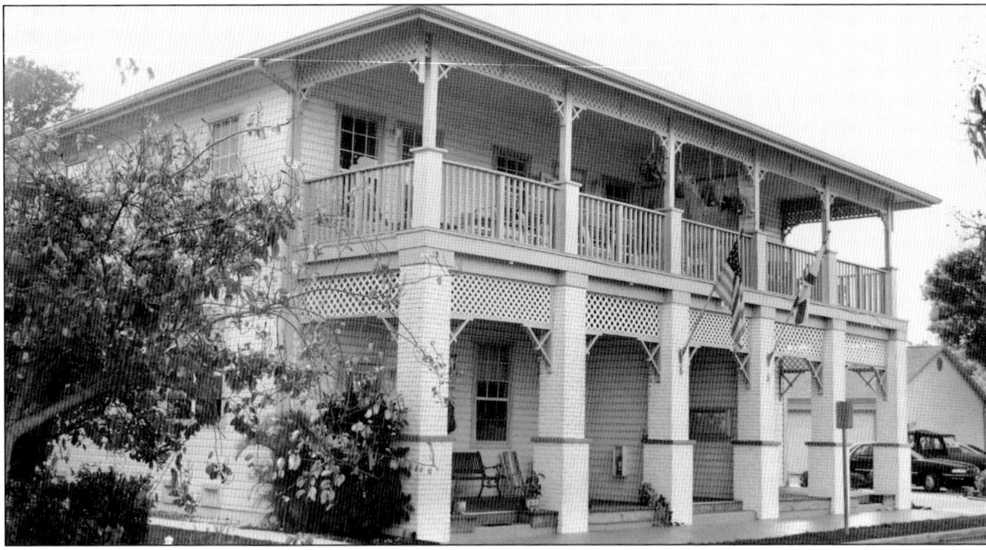

Early Schoolhouse. Punta Gorda's first public school was located in a community building where the First Methodist Church is located. The first building constructed to be a school was on Goldstein Street. Built in the 1890s, the one-room frame structure accommodated the lower grades and was operated by the City of Punta Gorda. In 1902, the school was enlarged and a second floor was added. In September 1902, the enrollment totaled 226, which included 20 above sixth grade. The next year, 1903, junior high was added, and in 1905, it became Punta Gorda High School, with a 12th grade class graduating in 1906. By 1909, it was apparent that a new school was needed. A site was donated by Gov. Albert W. Gilchrist on the corner of Taylor Street and Charlotte Avenue. The new high school opened in 1912. (Photograph by Scot Shively; Blanchard House Museum of African-American History and Culture of Charlotte County.)

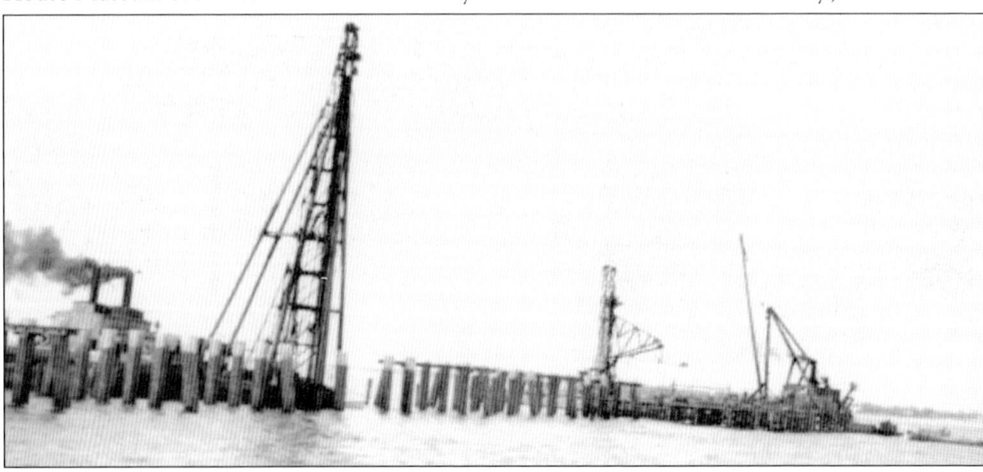

Charlotte Harbor Bridge. The first bridge built to span the harbor was named the Charlotte Harbor Bridge. Construction began in 1915 and was not finished until 1921. This was due to many delays but mainly because buildings (and materials) were hard to come by during World War I. A bridge dedication and public fish fry was held on the Fourth of July 1921. Estimates are that at least 6,000 guests attended the event. The bridge was narrow, only 14.5 feet wide, and had a speed limit of only 15 miles per hour. After only five years in service, sections of the concrete began falling off because of beach sand and saltwater utilized in the concrete. (Florida Photographic Collection, the Florida Memory Project.)

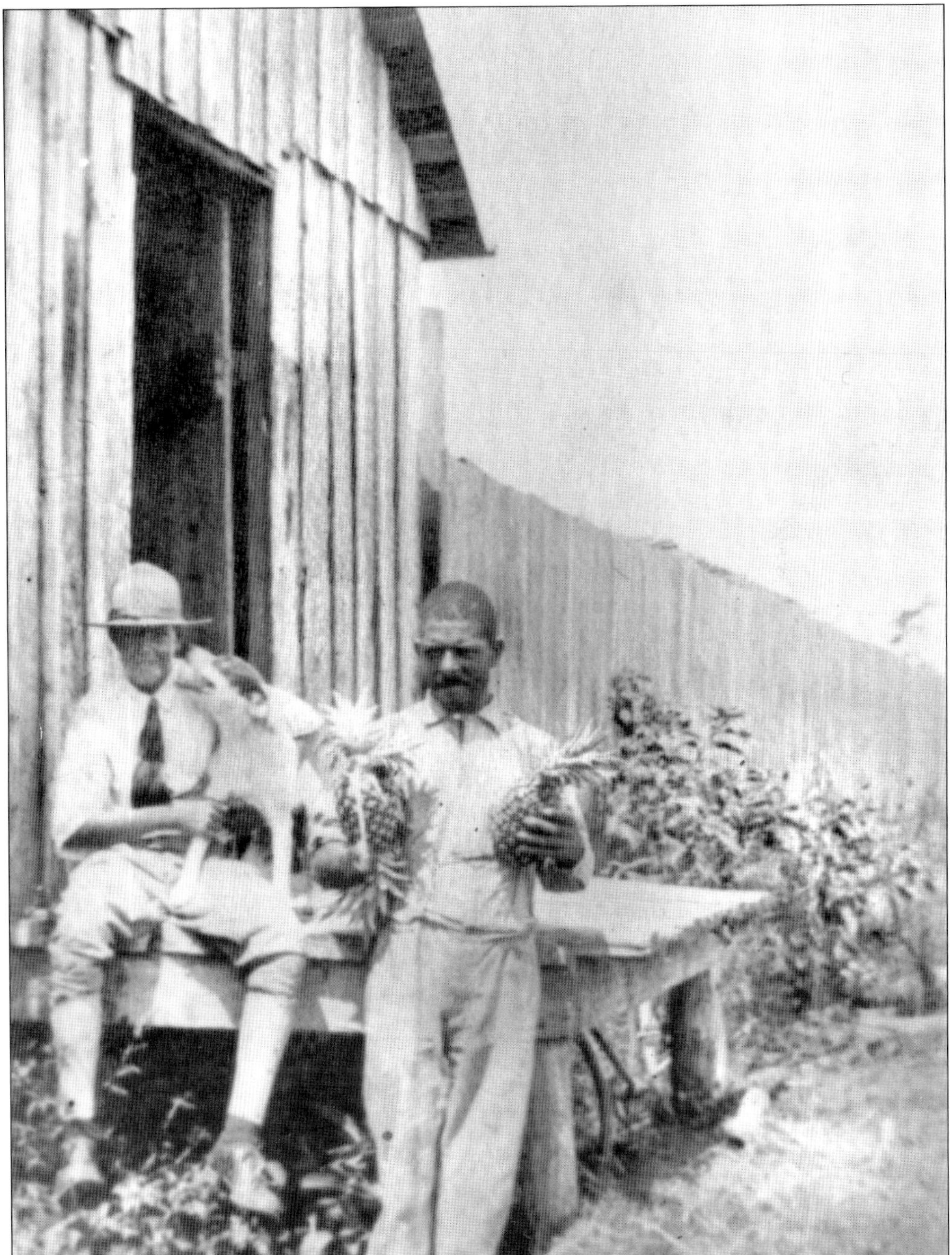

Byron Rhode and Cleve Mays. Cleve Mays, the one-handed pineapple packer, poses with two smooth-skinned Cayenne pineapples. Behind him, Byron Rhode holds Rev. B. F. Oswald's dog, Max. The photograph was taken at a Solana pineapple packinghouse in 1915. (Blanchard House Museum of African-American History and Culture of Charlotte County.)

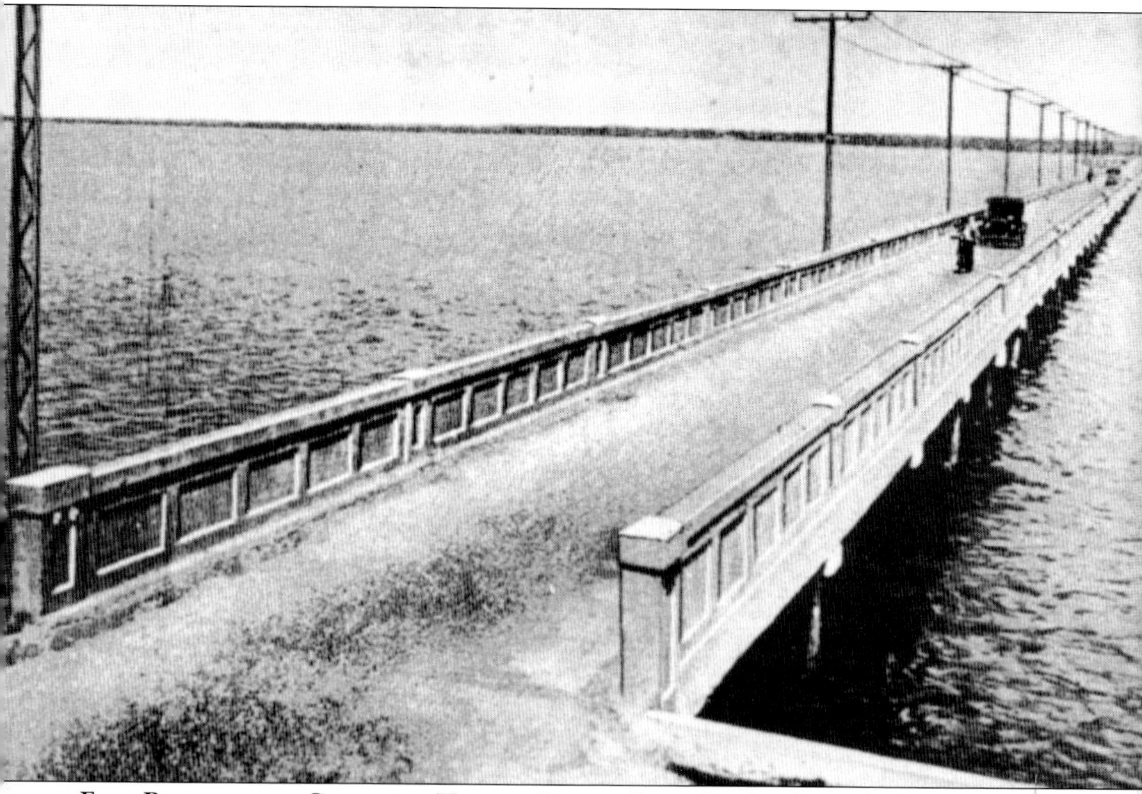

FIRST BRIDGE ACROSS CHARLOTTE HARBOR. Because Punta Gorda is located right on the waters of Charlotte Harbor, close to where the Peace River flows in, the area fishing and tourist industry were booming from the early days. The fishing was fantastic, and the Charlotte Harbor waters were picturesque. This early photograph shows the Tamiami Trial crossing Charlotte Harbor in the distance. The bridge was constructed in 1921 and linked Punta Gorda to Port Charlotte. (Punta Gorda Historic Railroad Depot and Antique Mall, Linda Wilson collection.)

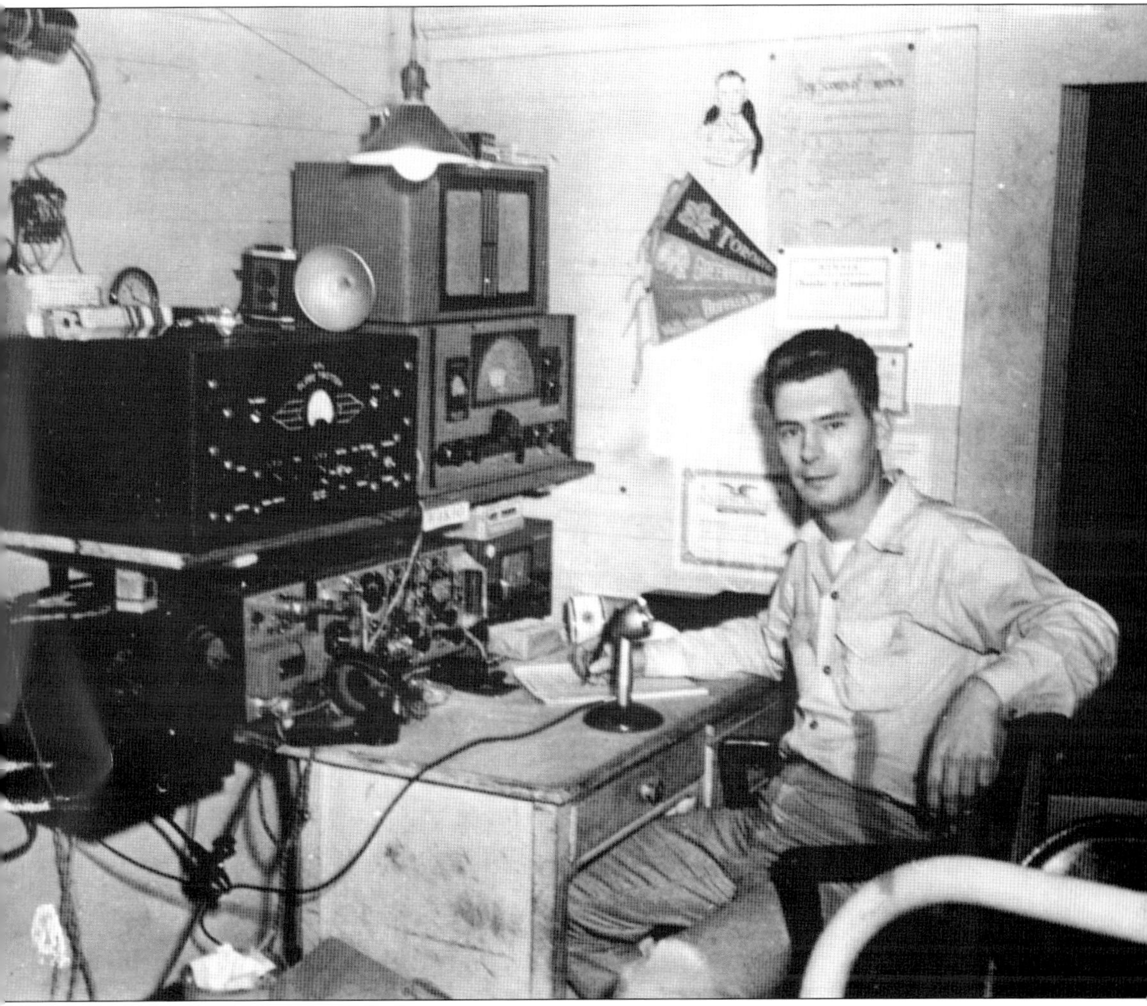

U. S. CLEVELAND AT HIS RADIO STATION AROUND 1949. A native of Punta Gorda, U. S. Cleveland was a Tarpon football player at Charlotte High School and also a Boy Scout. He is shown here in his shortwave radio room, W4K10, at his Punta Gorda home. In World War II, Cleveland was a Signal Corps officer in a secret radio project that undermined Hitler's missions on D-Day. (U. S. Cleveland Collection.)

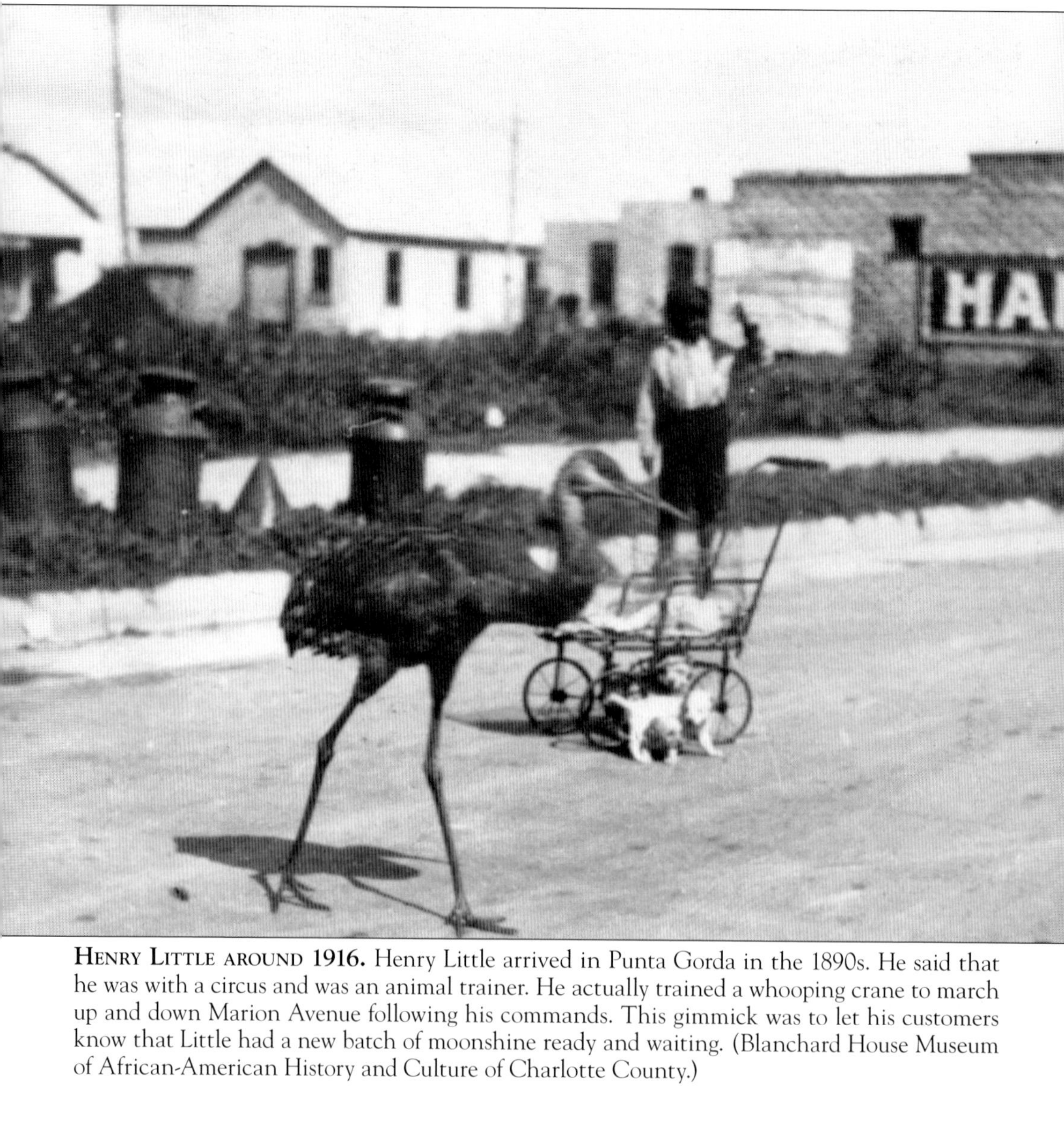

Henry Little around 1916. Henry Little arrived in Punta Gorda in the 1890s. He said that he was with a circus and was an animal trainer. He actually trained a whooping crane to march up and down Marion Avenue following his commands. This gimmick was to let his customers know that Little had a new batch of moonshine ready and waiting. (Blanchard House Museum of African-American History and Culture of Charlotte County.)

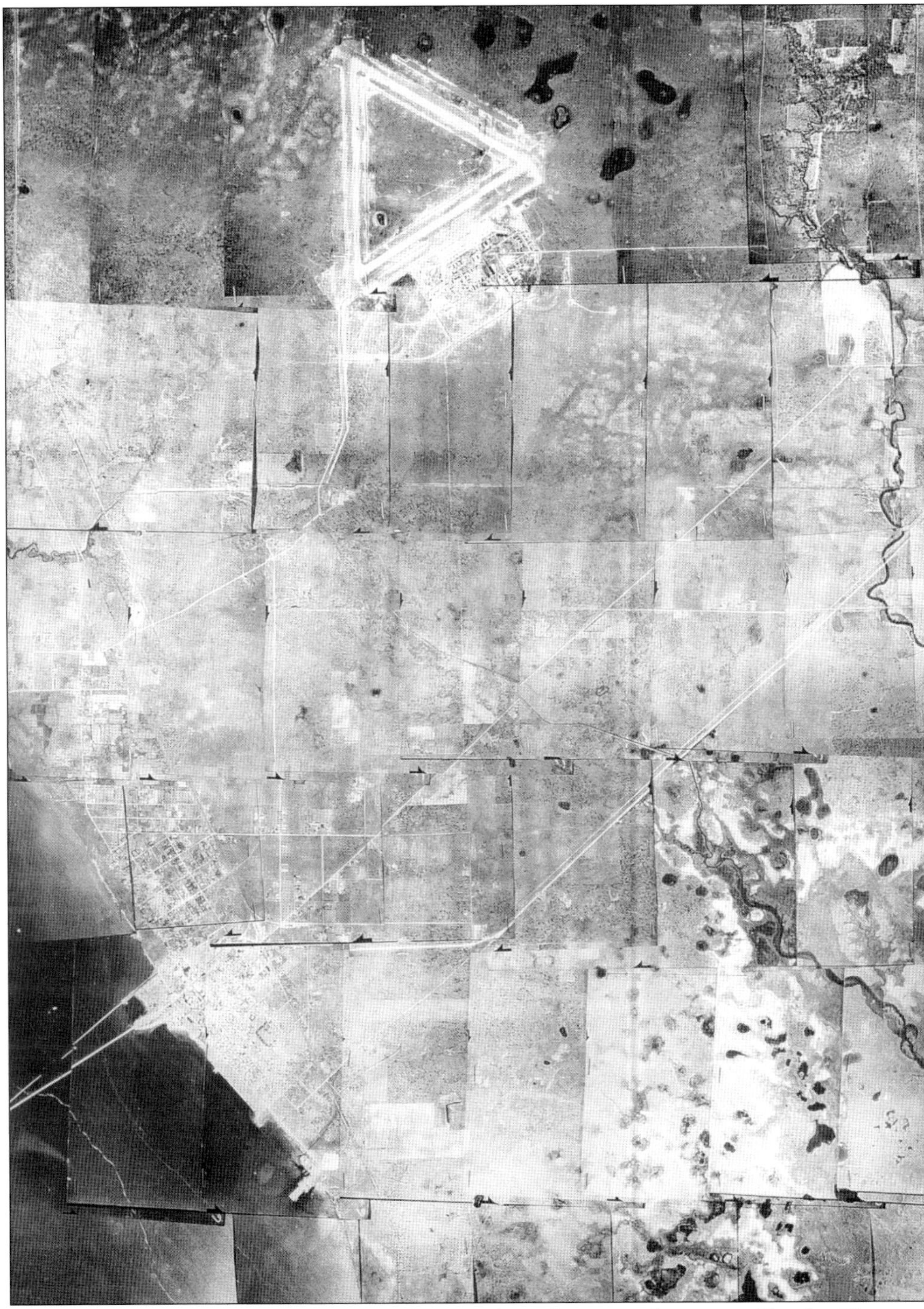

Punta Gorda Army Airfield I. World War II brought many changes to Florida. The army selected Punta Gorda to build an airbase for the purpose of training pilots. The training began on September 1943. The airbase was also an auxiliary airfield to the Third Air Force base at Sarasota. Pilots trained at Punta Gorda were taught to fly the P-40 Warhawk, the P-47 Thunderbolt, and the P-51 Mustang. (Military Heritage Museum.)

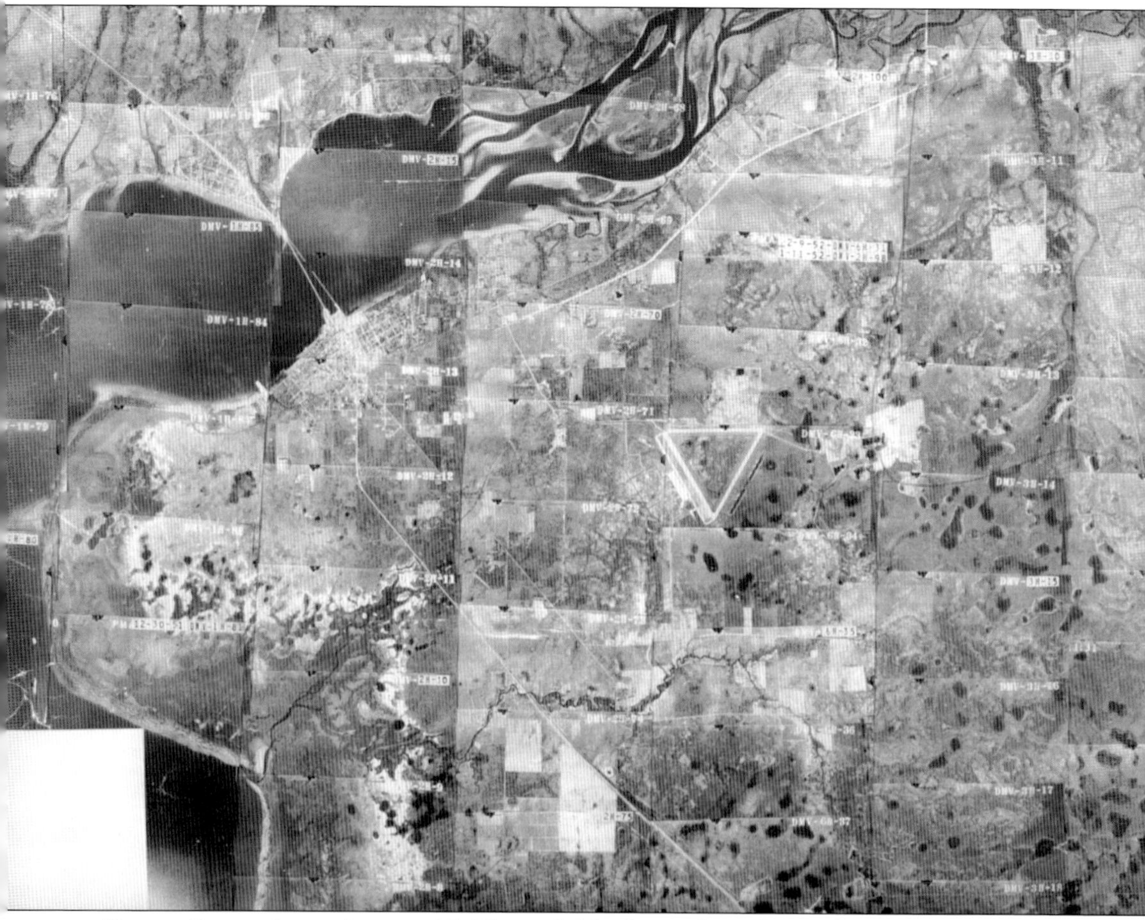

Punta Gorda Army Airfield II. The airfield is located 2 miles south of the Peace River and just east of Punta Gorda. The airfield is at 25 feet of elevation, which is the highest in Charlotte County. Following the war, the government transferred all of the fixtures and improvements on the airfield property over to the county. Charlotte County is one of the few airfields in the area that remains in service to this day. (Military Heritage Museum.)

Six

Activities

Visitors and residents who came to the area could enjoy the peace and quiet offered in natural settings at local parks and other nature areas. Sailors, boaters, and fishermen could enjoy the waters in the Peace River or Charlotte Harbor, as they offered some of the best fishing around. Hunters could also enjoy the game, as they would come for quail, deer, and wild turkeys. The wealthier visitors would stay for extended periods in the local hotels, while the less wealthy ones would stay at the "tin can" trailer park. Because the temperature in the area is often in the 80s or higher during the summer months and mild during winter months, often in the 60s, outdoor activities such as golf, tennis, and swimming were enjoyed throughout the year. Strolling, biking, and hiking were also partaken in, as was sunbathing on the white sandy beaches that line the Gulf of Mexico. The Gulf waters offer abundant marine life, including nearly 300 species of fish, such as snook, tarpon, and redfish; 100 species of birds, such as egrets, spoonbills, and seagulls; and many other animals, such as sea turtles, alligators, manatees, and dolphins. So it isn't surprising that animal and marine lovers have long come to the area to enjoy the natural beauty. However, it wasn't until 1935 that Charlotte County started its mosquito control program, so no doubt the outdoor activities during those early years were marred by bug bites.

Indoor activities included watching picture shows at the Hotel Charlotte Harbor or at the Dixie Theater in downtown Punta Gorda on Marion Avenue. The Marion Avenue theater was built by Vernon and Julian Jordan and could seat about 300 people. In 1936, it was sold and renamed New Theatre. In the 1950s, a drive-in theater was located in Charlotte Harbor. The drive-in was also used as a church on Sundays.

Visitors came to Punta Gorda to relax, rest, and vacation, so dancing and dining were often part of the evening's activities, as was enjoying a drink or a night of gambling at Ward's Bar. Residents and visitors alike may have also kicked back and relaxed with reading the daily news and gossip in the *Herald*, the local newspaper.

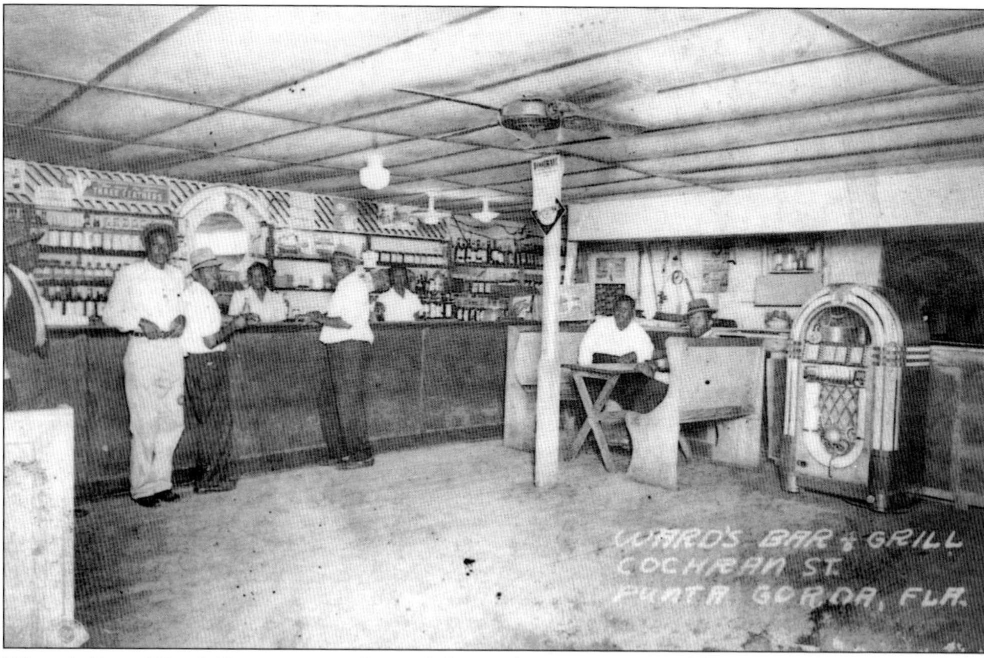

WARD'S BAR. Ward's Bar was one of two African American–owned bars in Punta Gorda. People from all over southwest Florida came to Punta Gorda to drink, dance, and play cards. Ward's Bar was located on Cochran Street (now Martin Luther King Jr. Boulevard). (Blanchard House Museum of African-American History and Culture of Charlotte County.)

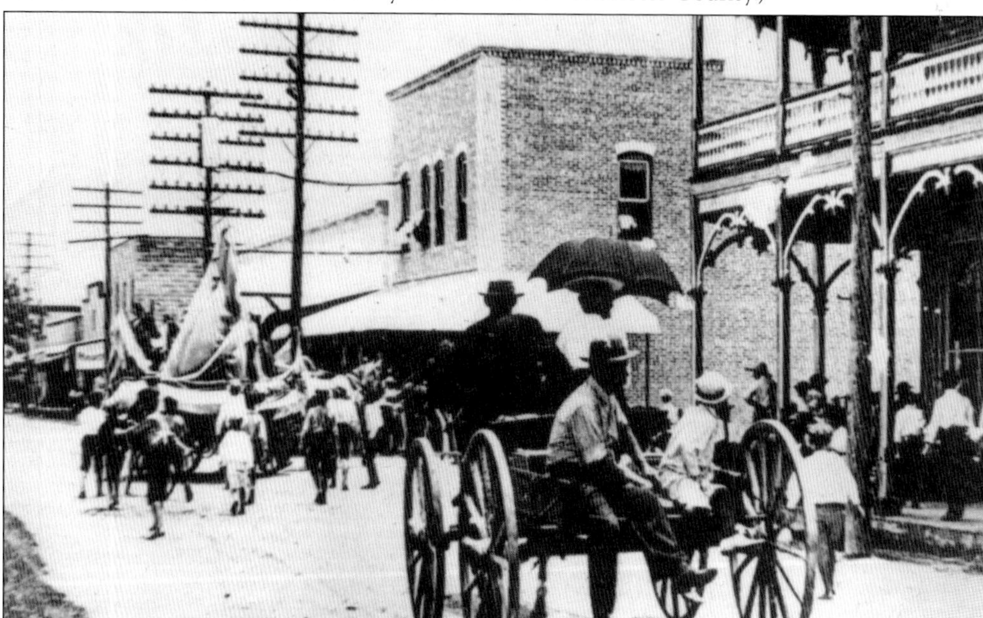

EMANCIPATION DAY PARADE DOWN MARION AVENUE, MAY 1908. Punta Gorda's African American community has always celebrated the anniversary of Emancipation on May 20. The parade is traveling through the center of Punta Gorda, down Marion Avenue, and has drawn a crowd of spectators. (U. S. Cleveland Collection.)

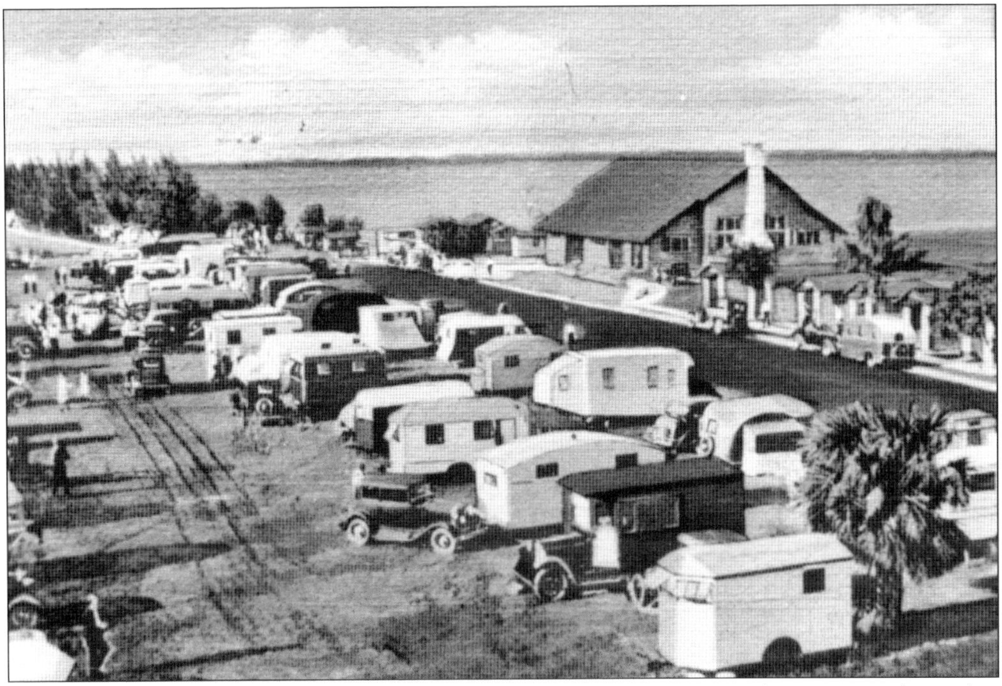

THE "TIN CAN" TRAILER PARK. The "tin can" trailer park, as it was referred to, was once located in what was Laishley Park. The Municipal Community Hall is shown in the background. Vacationers would come to stay for months on end at the park.

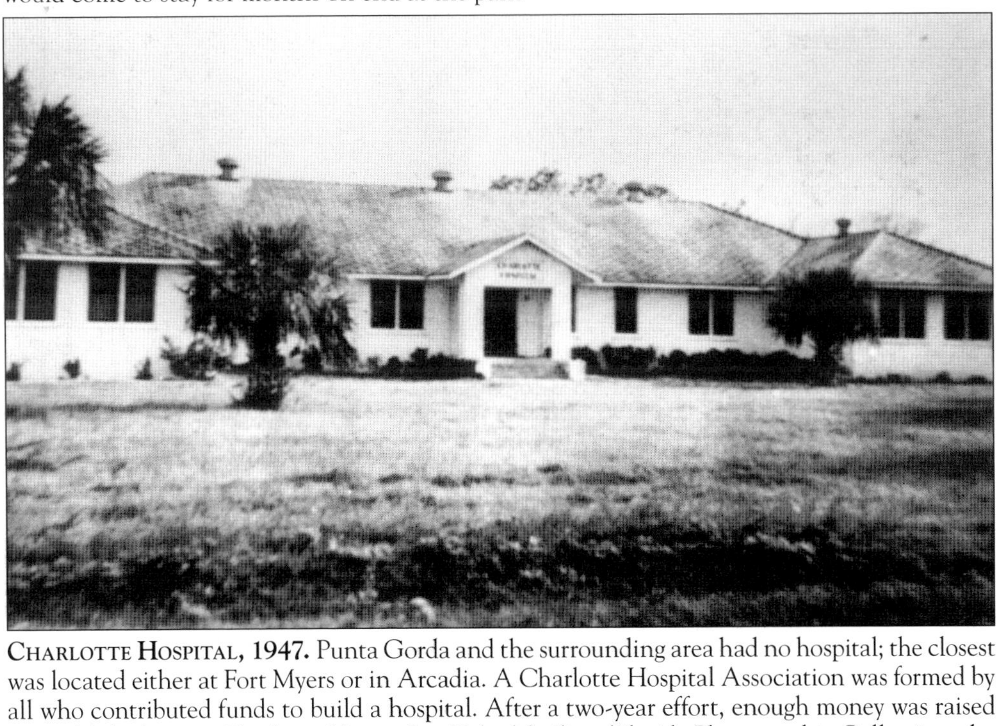

CHARLOTTE HOSPITAL, 1947. Punta Gorda and the surrounding area had no hospital; the closest was located either at Fort Myers or in Arcadia. A Charlotte Hospital Association was formed by all who contributed funds to build a hospital. After a two-year effort, enough money was raised to establish the new Charlotte Hospital, a 22-bed facility. (Florida Photographic Collection, the Florida Memory Project.)

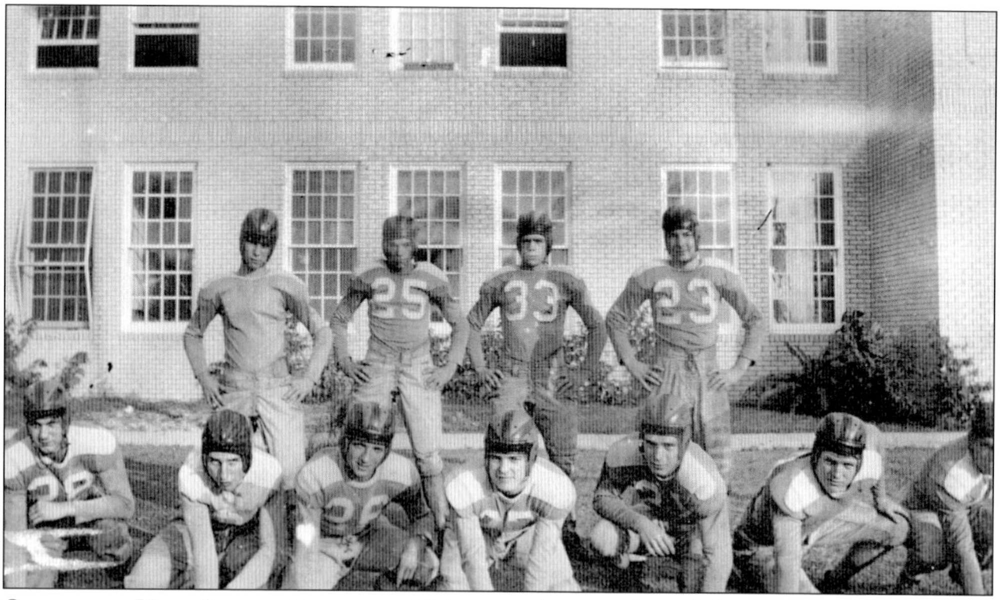

CHARLOTTE HIGH SCHOOL FOOTBALL. This team photograph is of the Charlotte High School varsity football squad of 1936. They were called "The Tarpons." Construction for the new high school building in Punta Gorda was started in April 1926. Charlotte High School opened on August 19, 1927, and housed the first students a few weeks later. In 1990, the building was added to the National Register of Historic Places. The school building was heavily damaged during Hurricane Charley on August 13, 2004. (U. S. Cleveland Collection.)

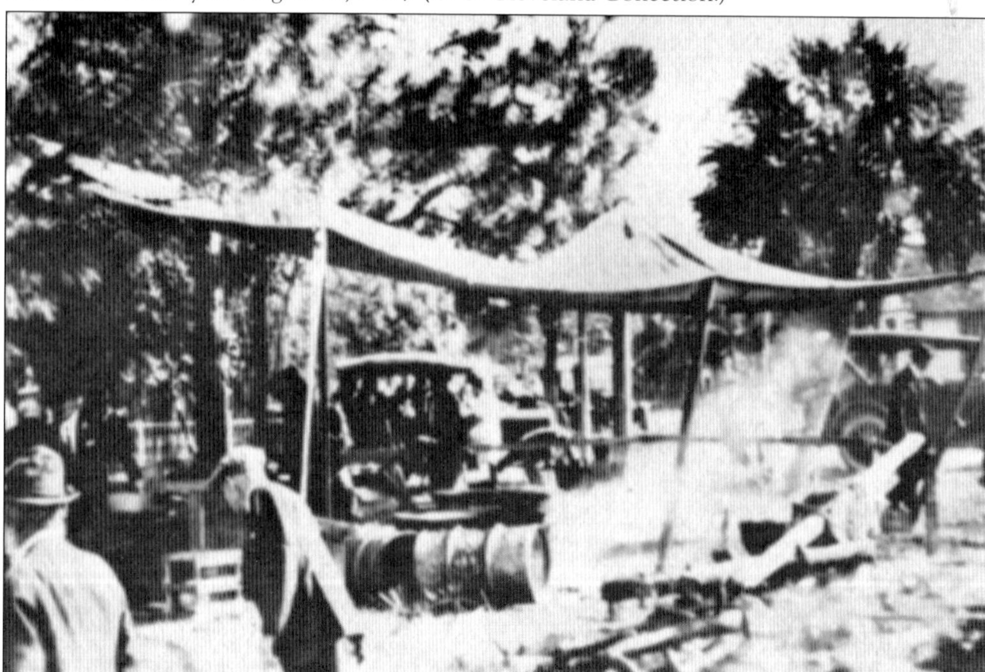

BRIDGE DEDICATION ON JULY 4, 1931. Over 14,000 people came to enjoy a free fish fry and entertainment in order to dedicate the Barron Collier Bridge. A special excursion train was brought in by the Atlantic Coast Line Railroad.

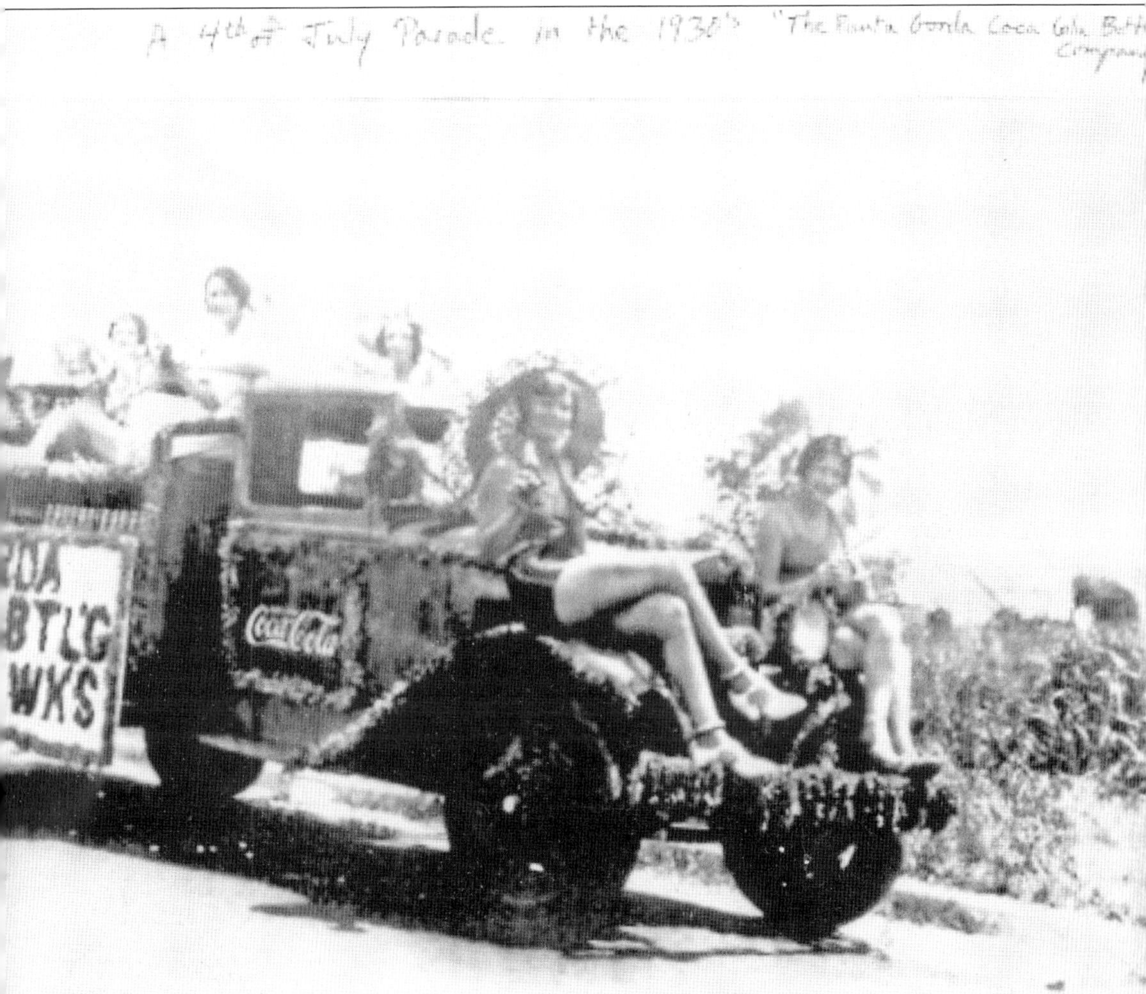

Coca-Cola Bottling Company Truck. In 1915, a Coca-Cola bottling plant opened in Punta Gorda. In the 1930s, this Coca-Cola Bottling Company truck carried young women aboard during the Fourth of July parade. No doubt it was a refreshing sight during a hot summer day. (Florida Photographic Collection, the Florida Memory Project.)

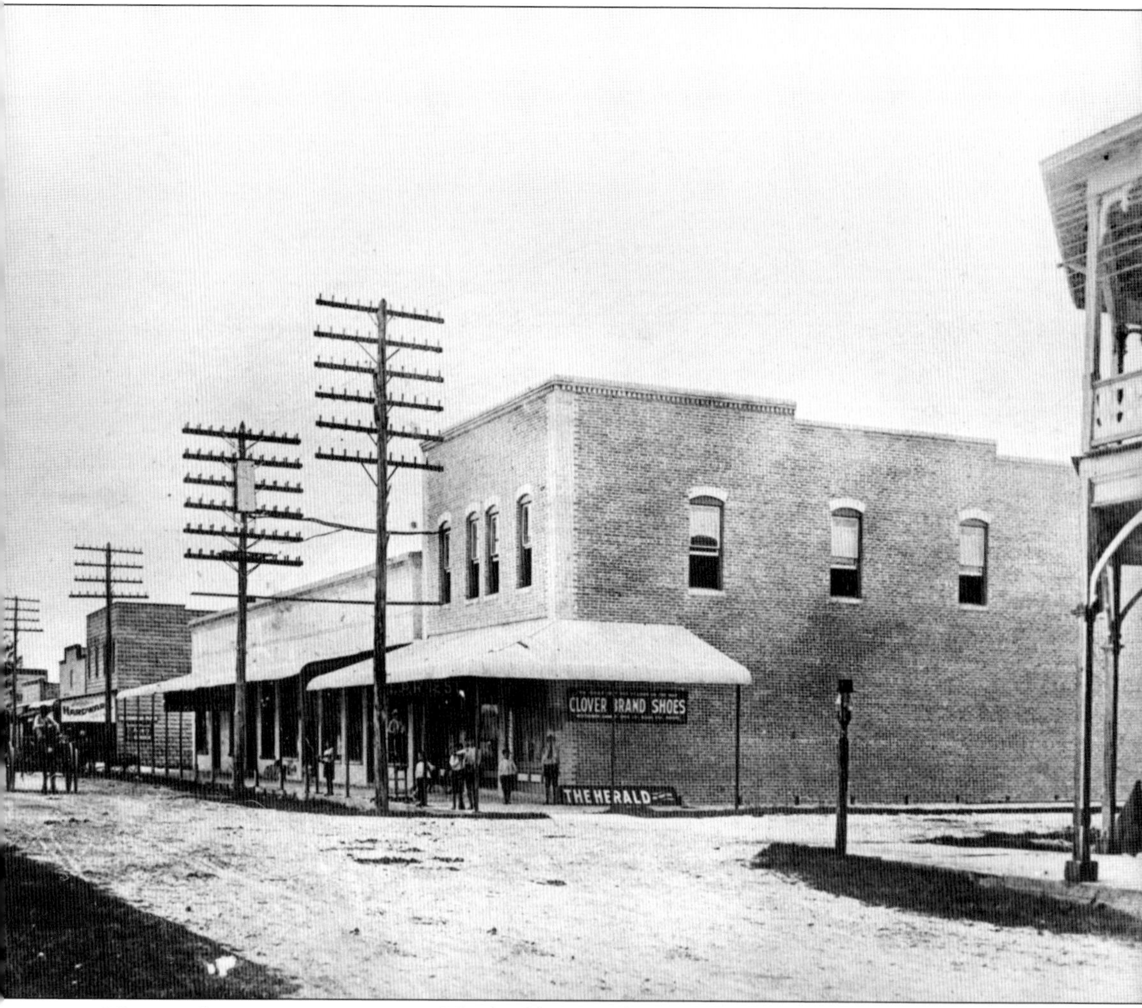

Marion Avenue around 1908. The building on the corner of Marion Avenue and Taylor Street in downtown Punta Gorda housed a general store downstairs and the telephone company and the *Punta Gorda Herald* upstairs. Gentlemen who were passing time on rocking chairs are sitting under the porch of the Dade Hotel (far right). (U. S. Cleveland Collection.)

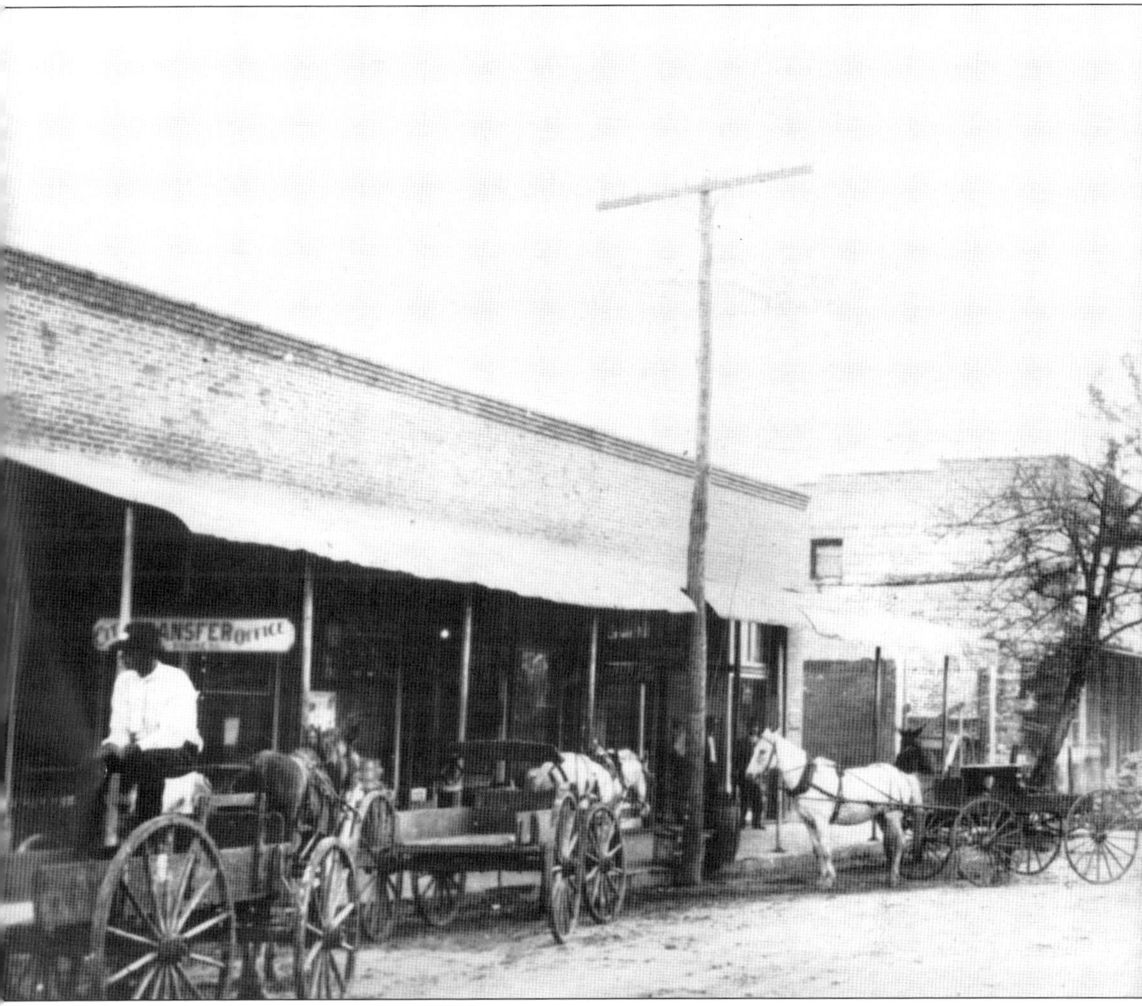

MARION AVENUE, 1890S. This early photograph shows horses and buggies lined up in front of the City Transfer Office along Marion Avenue. Marion Avenue was named for Marion Trabue, town founder Isaac Trabue's brother. Marion Avenue was Punta Gorda's main downtown street, where the majority of early businesses were located. The photograph was taken from East Punta Gorda. (U. S. Cleveland Collection.)

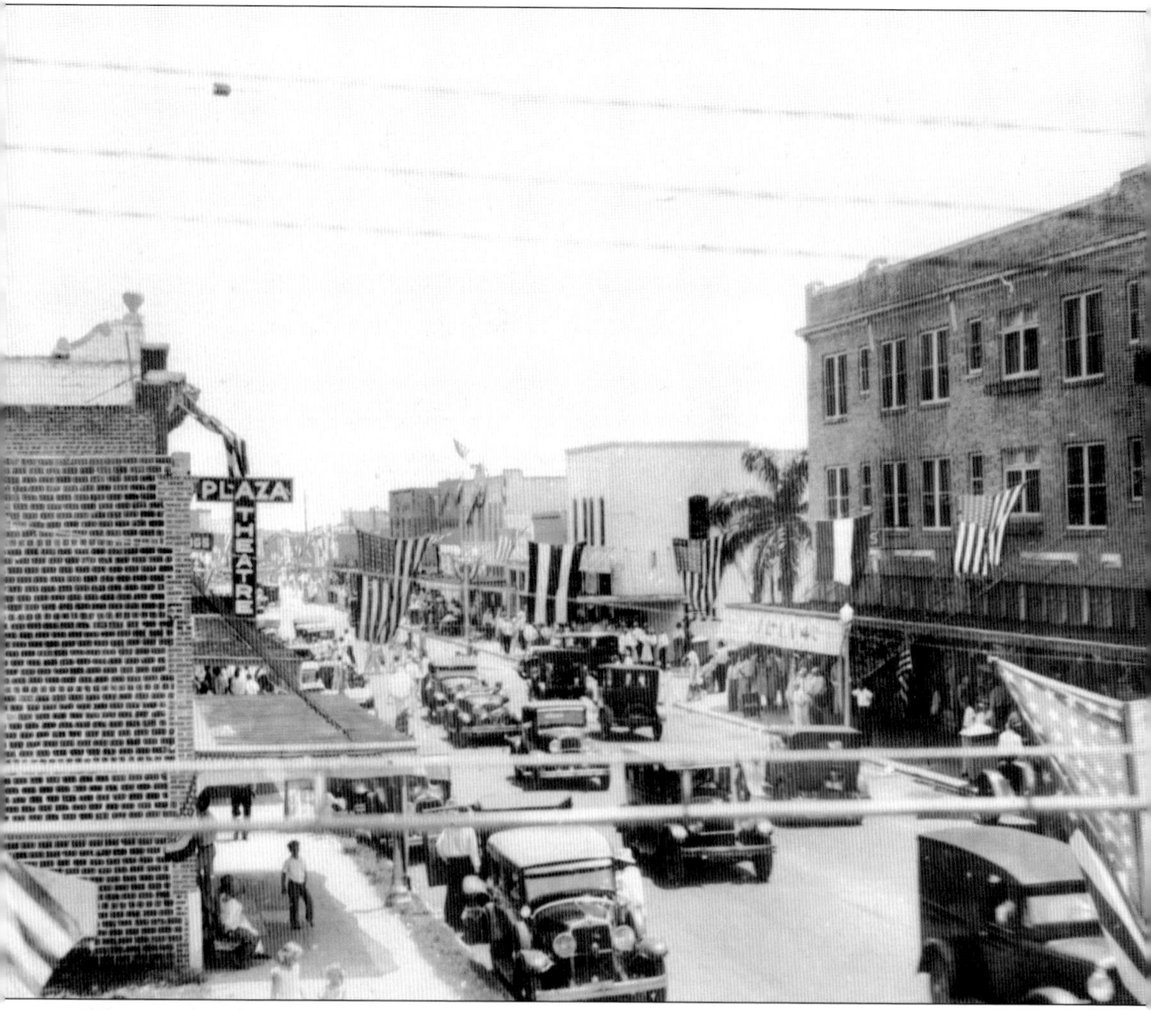

MARION AVENUE ON FOURTH OF JULY, 1930S. Punta Gorda's patriotically decorated street was adorned with 48-star American flags. The Charlotte Bay Hotel, shown here, has flags stretched over Marion Avenue to the Plaza Theater. Crowds of spectators are standing on the street corners preparing for the traditional Fourth of July parade. (Bernice A. Russell Collection.)

Merchants Bank of Punta Gorda. The Merchants Bank of Punta Gorda commenced business on April 9, 1912, with holdings of over $75,000. The Merchants Bank was a competitor to the already existing Punta Gorda Bank, which had operated since 1899. The new bank building was constructed of brick with white columns and presented a new image to the growing city of Punta Gorda. The cost of the land and the construction of the building was $3,500. The Merchants Bank converted its state charter in 1914 and became the First National Bank of Punta Gorda, under which it grew and prospered until the stock market crash of 1929. The crash caused the bank to close its doors, as it did many other banks in Florida and across the nation. Since then, the building has been occupied by various professional businesses.

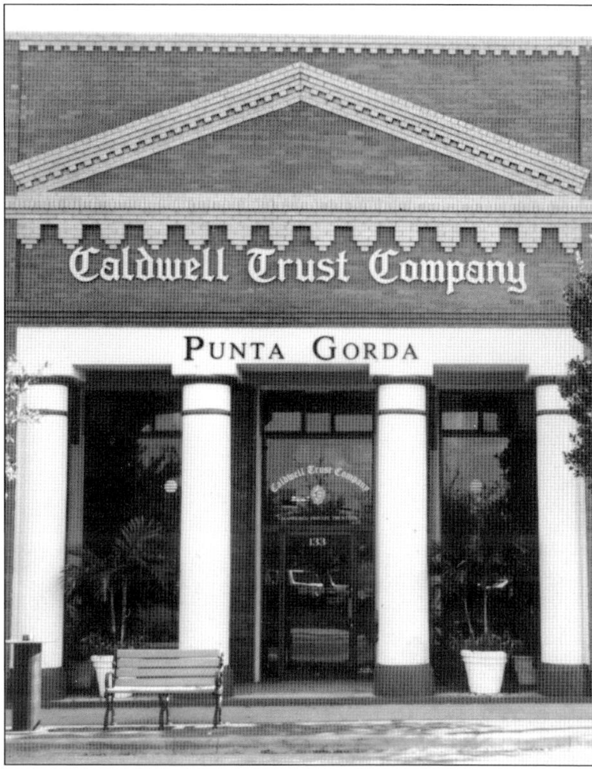

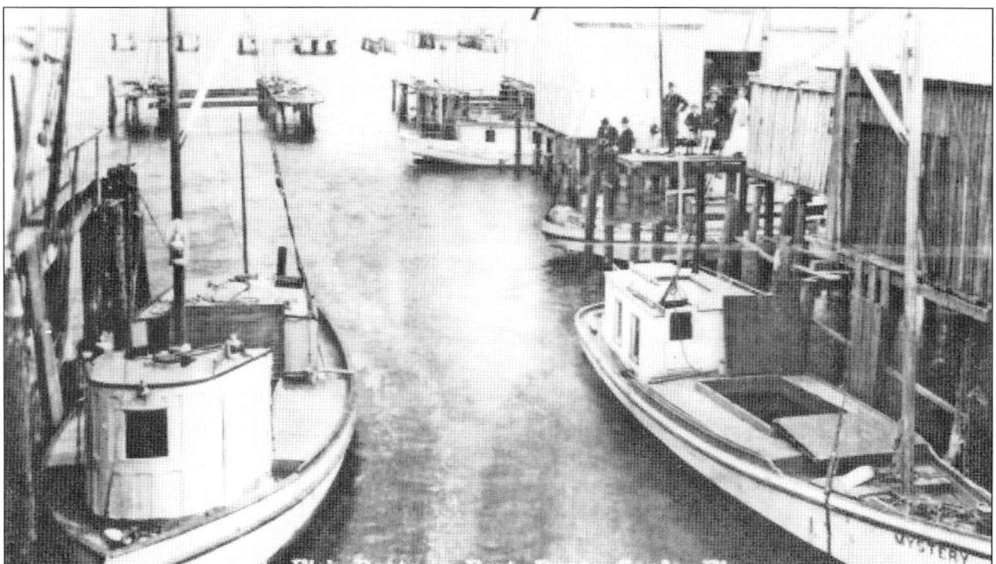

Fish Boats at the Dock in Punta Gorda. While fishing was a key industry to the area since its inception, fishing was, and still is, a favorite pastime of residents and guests. Charlotte Harbor is located between the islands of Gasparilla and Cayo Costa. This area in the Gulf of Mexico is known as Boca Grande Pass and is an ideal location for fishermen. (Florida Photographic Collection, the Florida Memory Project.)

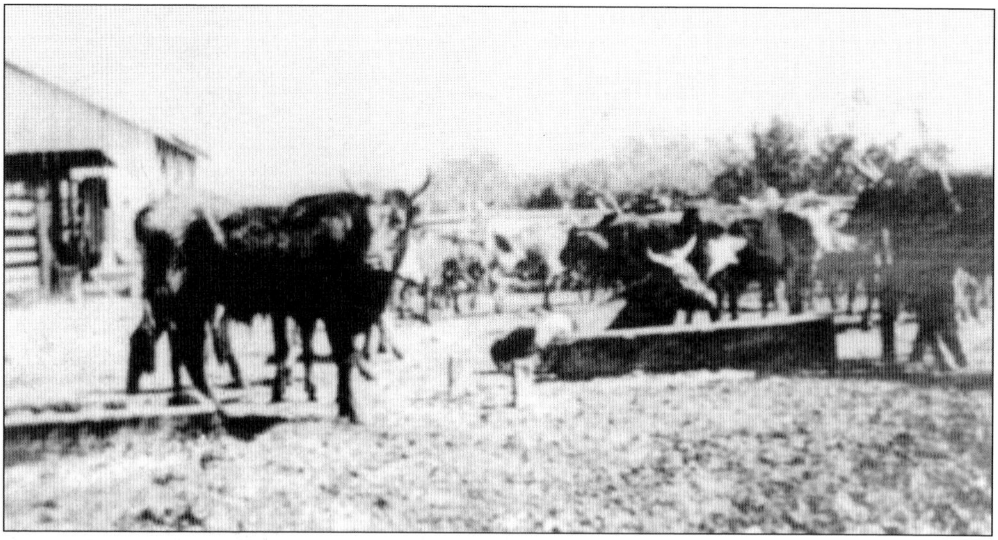

FLORIDA RANGE CATTLE. Cattle came to America with Juan Ponce de León in 1521, when he brought a small herd of Andalusian cattle and horses with him to Florida. By the late 1800s, Florida was a leading exporter of cattle, many of which were going to Havana, Cuba. In the late 1800s, breeds of northern European origin arrived and were bred with the cattle already in the area. The result was the Florida Cracker cattle. (Cracker cattle later bred with other breeds, such as Brahman, so few of the old stock remain.) The name "Florida Crackers" comes from the cracking sound of bullwhips used by Florida cattlemen, or "Cracker Cowboys," to drive cattle and oxen. (Florida Photographic Collection, the Florida Memory Project.)

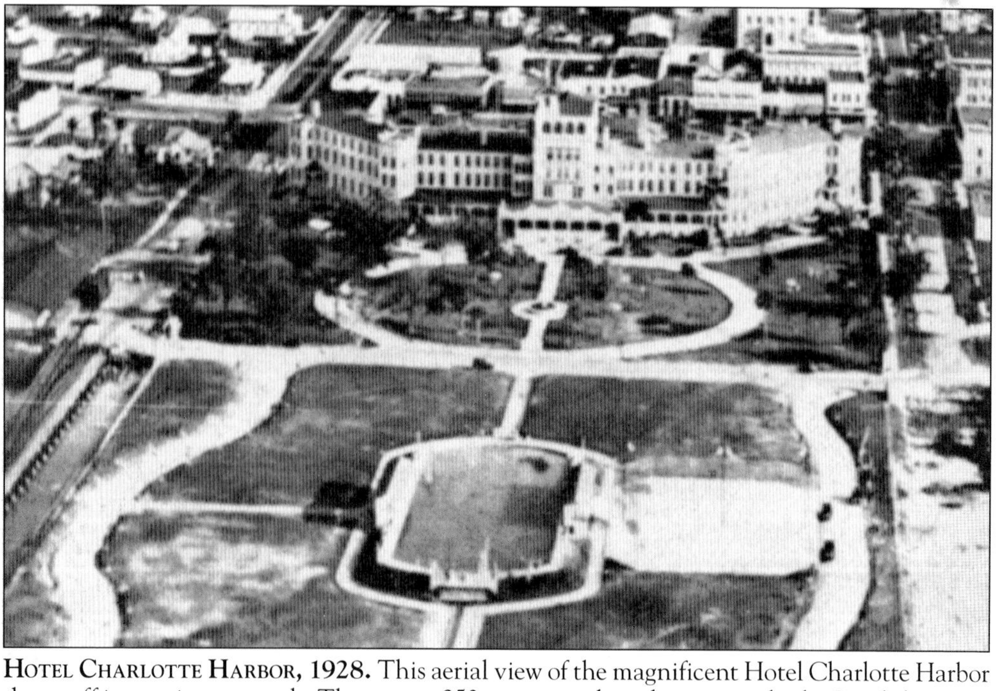

HOTEL CHARLOTTE HARBOR, 1928. This aerial view of the magnificent Hotel Charlotte Harbor shows off its spacious grounds. There were 250 rooms, each with a private bath. Quail shooting, fishing, tennis, and golf on the hotel's 18-hole golf course were all enjoyed in the daytimes, while evenings brought dances and the showing of movie pictures.

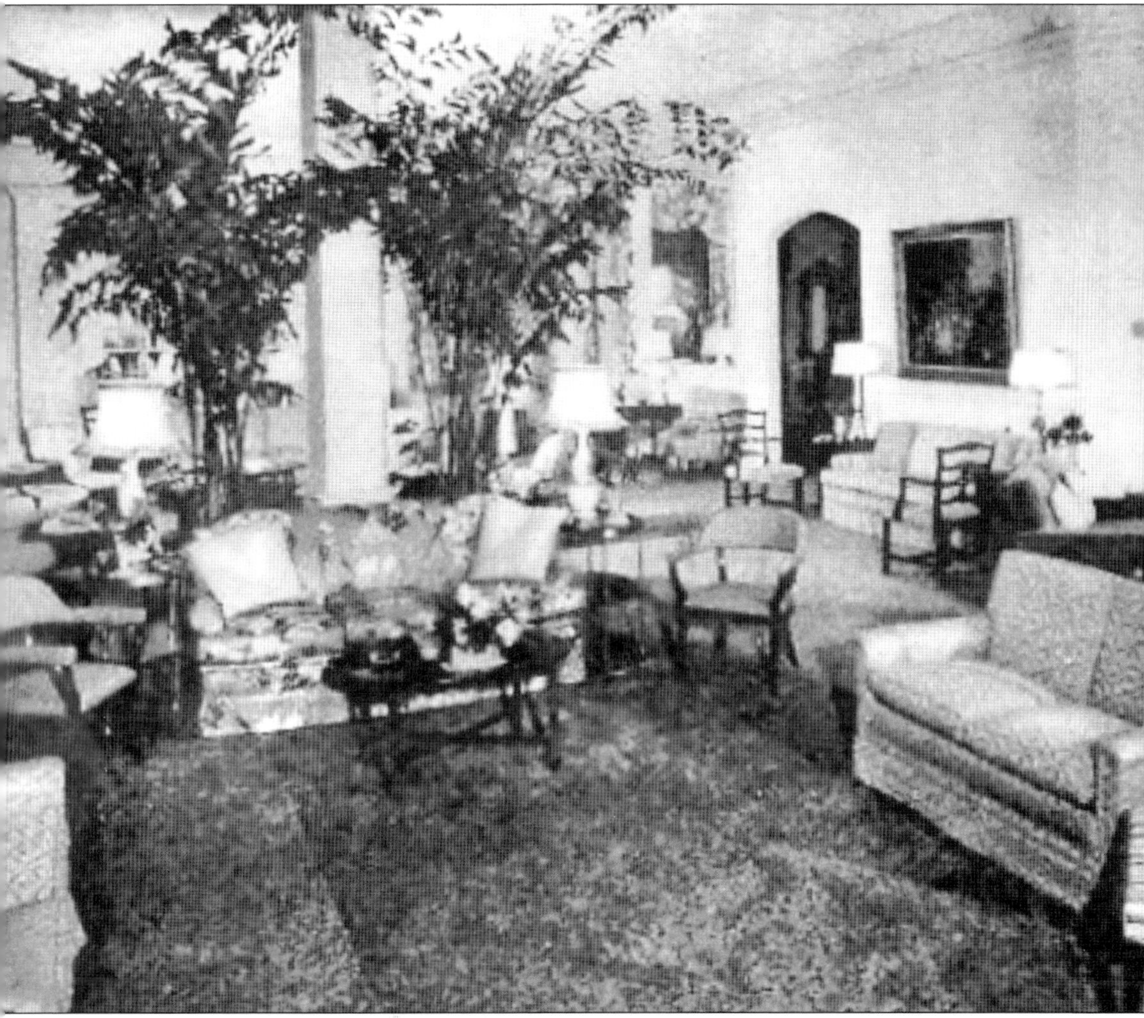

Hotel Charlotte Harbor. The summer days in Florida were oftentimes hot, so guests of Hotel Charlotte Harbor would sometimes enjoy a refreshing drink in the lounge at the hotel. A favorite indoor pastime of guests was also playing cards, and the hotel offered a separate card room where guests could kick back and enjoy bridge, solitaire, or rummy. (Punta Gorda Historical Society.)

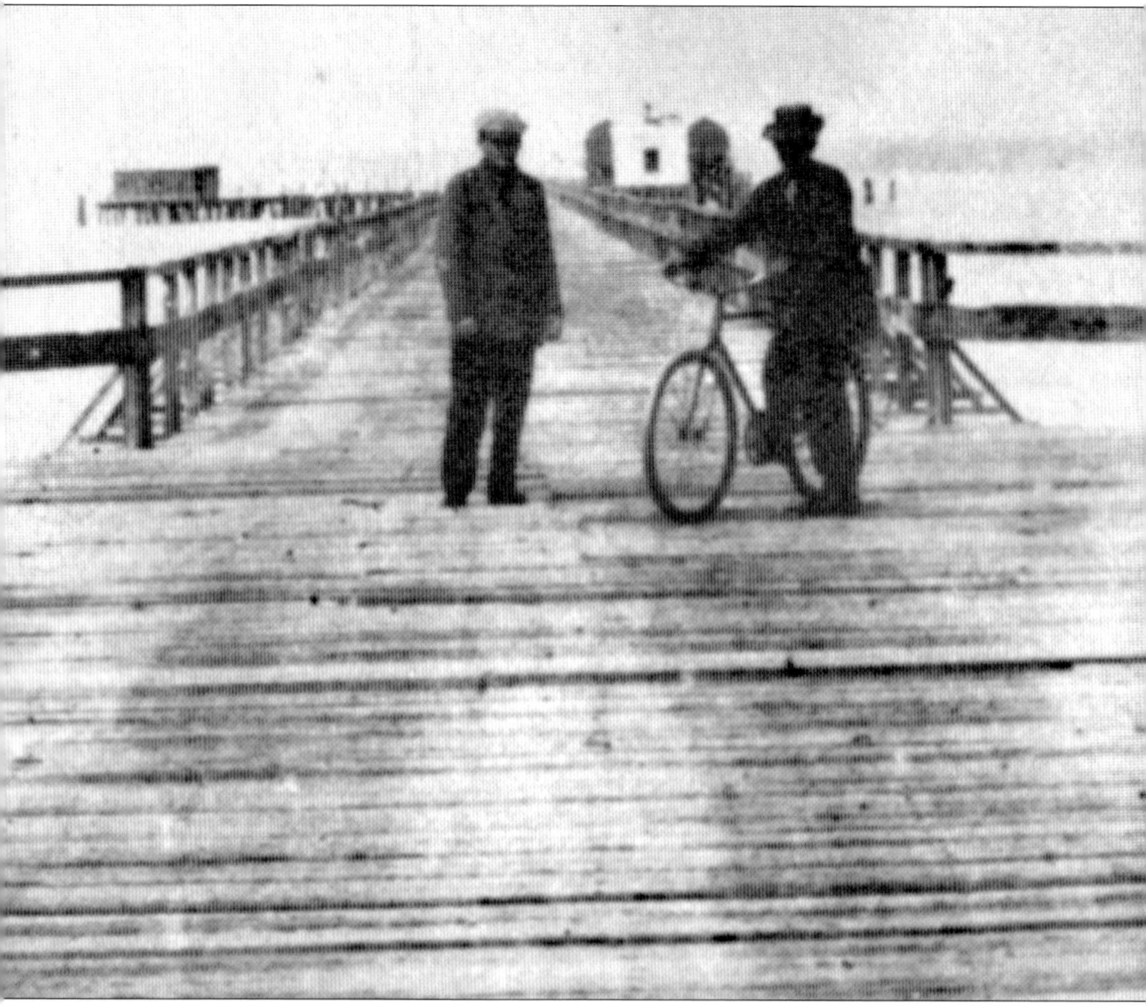

The City Dock on Sullivan Street, 1914. The city began the City Dock building project in October 1908 and completed the 1,800-foot dock in 1909. The entire project was completed by volunteer labor and with donated materials. Residents and tourists were able to enjoy the outdoor activities as much as they could—thanks to the warm weather in Florida. Here young men are biking on City Dock.

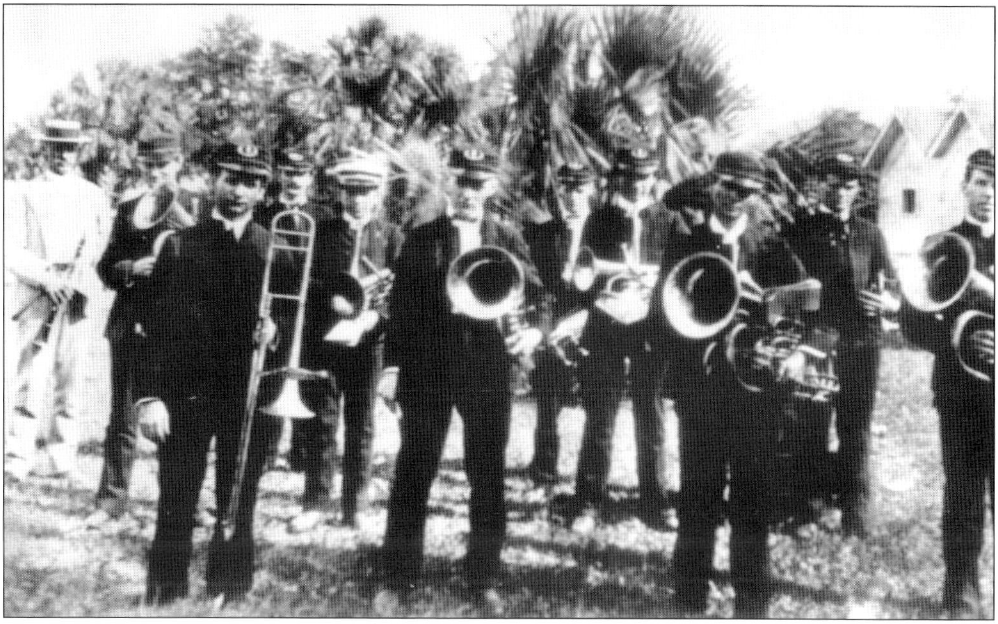

The Punta Gorda Brass Band. The Punta Gorda Brass Band was organized by local musicians and was operated on a volunteer basis. The band provided music for parades on patriotic holidays, played during scheduled concerts in the park, and entertained guests at the local hotels during the season. The bandstand built in the bay-front park was said to be one of their favorite places to play.

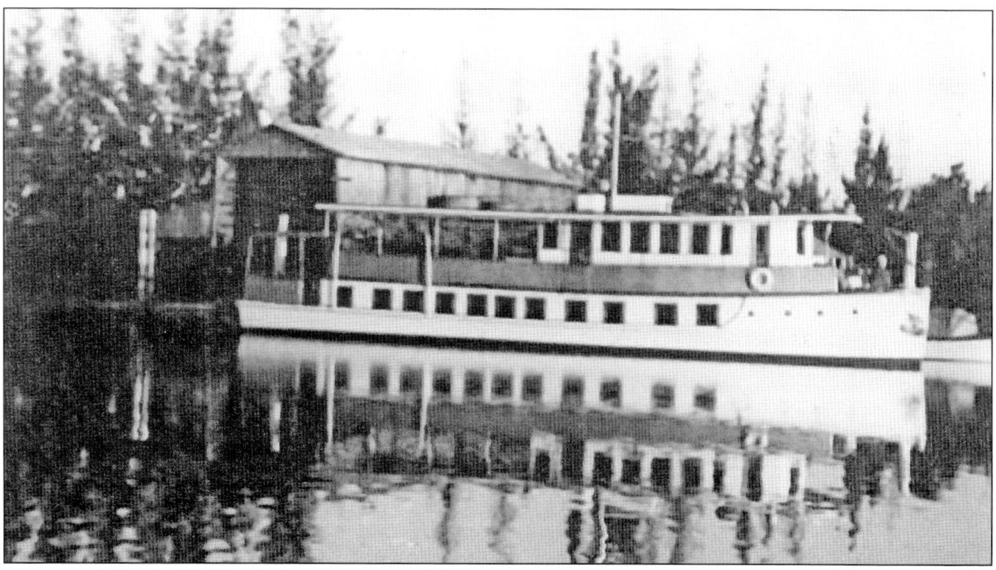

Houseboat in Punta Gorda. While some visitors enjoyed the waters of Charlotte Harbor for an afternoon of fishing, others stayed longer in houseboats that provided passengers with a dwelling. Passengers enjoyed a change of scenery, as well as the opportunity to be out on the water for longer periods of time. Recreational house boating gained popularity in the 1940s. This photograph was taken by Lt. Col. David S. Breece while on leave from primary flight training at Dorr Field in Arcadia, Florida, between 1942 and 1945. (Florida Photographic Collection, the Florida Memory Project.)

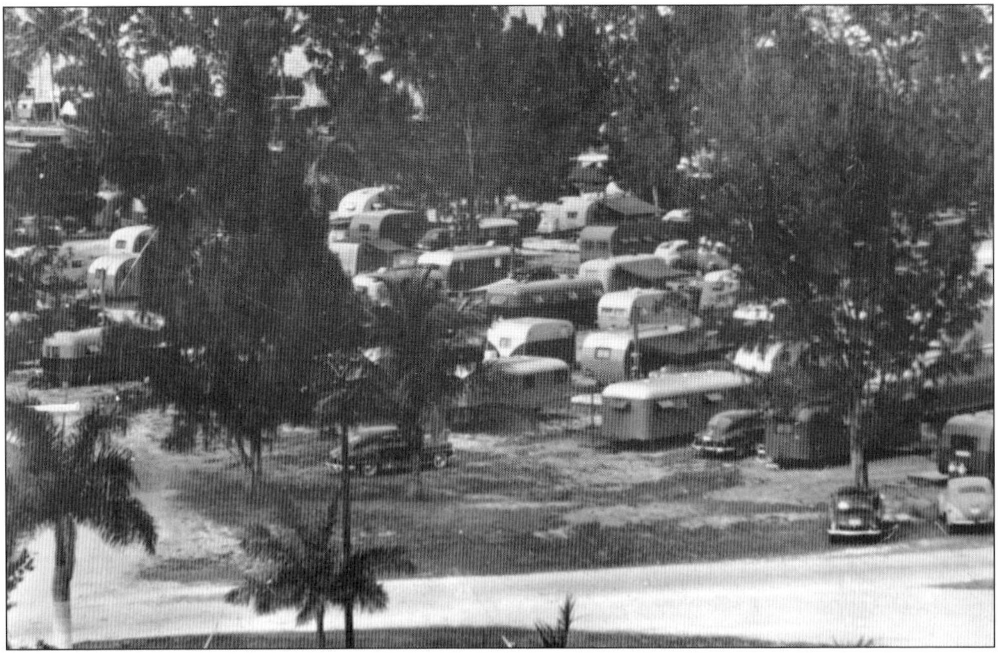

Tin Can Tourists. Tourists came down from the North to stay in the local hotels and to camp out in their own trailers, often for the entire winter season. The tin can trailer park was once located in what was Laishley Park. It was later moved by the City of Punta Gorda to Buttonwood Park, where it still stands today.

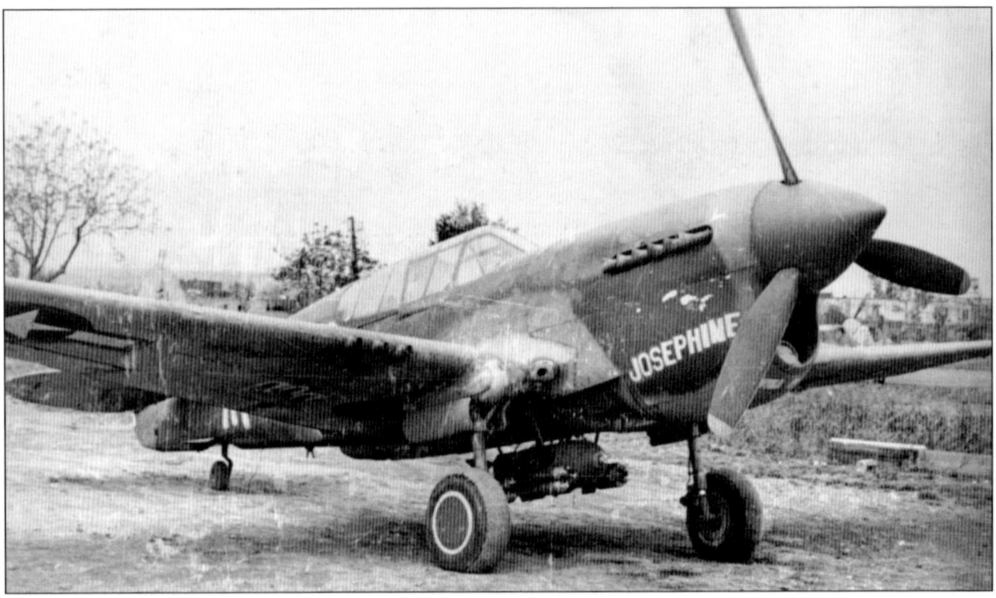

Lt. Charles P. Bailey, Tuskegee Airman. Punta Gorda's own Lt. Charles Bailey served with distinction as a famous Tuskegee Airman. He piloted a P-40 Warhawk and later a P-51 Mustang in the European theater. Charles was credited with shooting down two German fighters and logged 133 combat missions. He was one of six brothers to serve at the same time during World War II. He named his airplane "Josephine" for his mother. (Blanchard House Museum of African-American History and Culture of Charlotte County.)

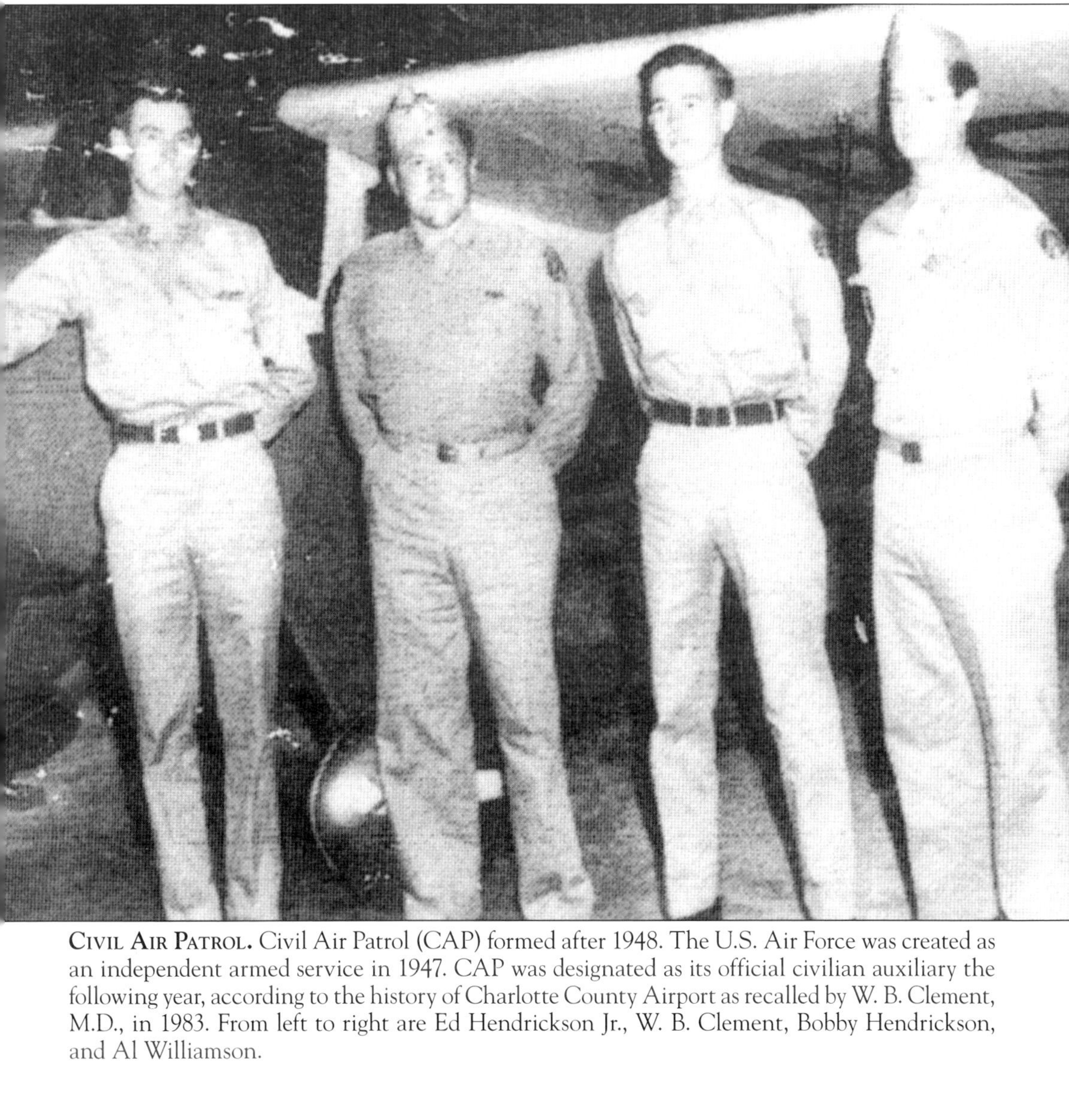

Civil Air Patrol. Civil Air Patrol (CAP) formed after 1948. The U.S. Air Force was created as an independent armed service in 1947. CAP was designated as its official civilian auxiliary the following year, according to the history of Charlotte County Airport as recalled by W. B. Clement, M.D., in 1983. From left to right are Ed Hendrickson Jr., W. B. Clement, Bobby Hendrickson, and Al Williamson.

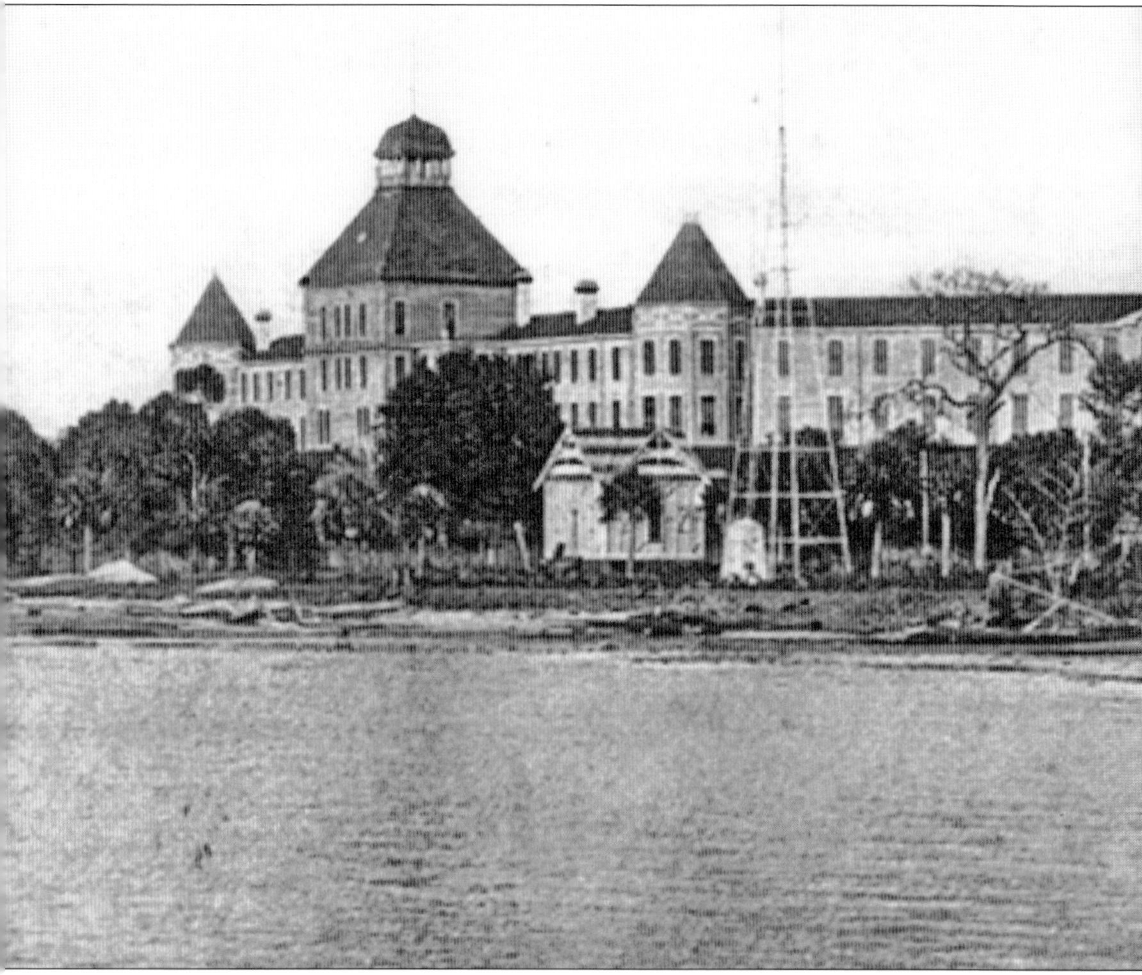

HOTEL PUNTA GORDA. Resting on the shores of Charlotte Harbor, the impressive Hotel Punta Gorda offered guests the opportunity to enjoy the beautiful bay just steps away. Hotel guests would walk by the shoreline, soak up the sun, stroll along the dock, swim, and of course fish in the waters that were filled with redfish, snook, tarpon, mackerel, and pompano. (Florida Photographic Collection, the Florida Memory Project.)

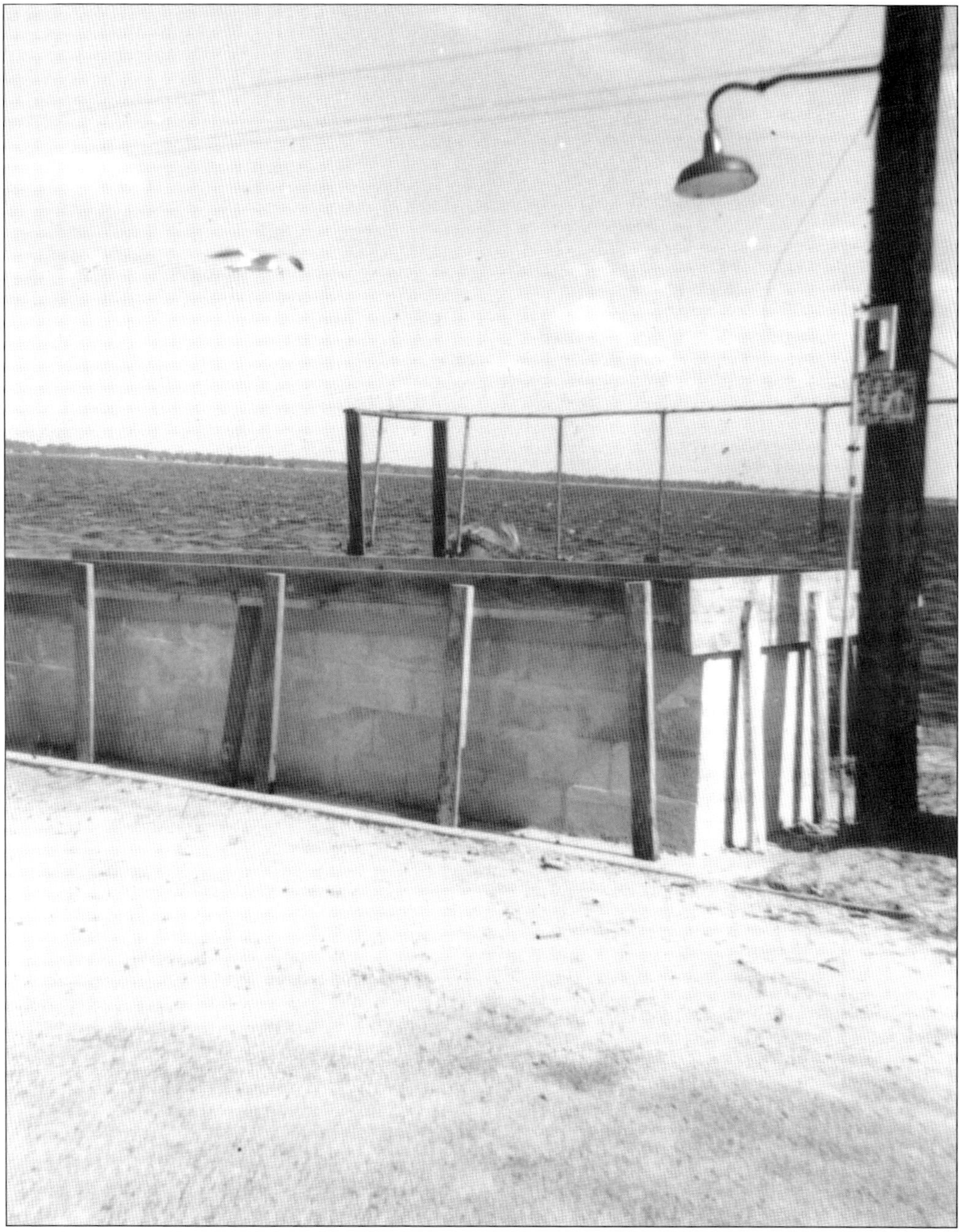

FISH CLEANING STATION. Commercial and sports fishing have always been key to the development and history of Punta Gorda. Small fishing villages, like Charlotte Harbor, began appearing up and down the Gulf Coast, as well as fish cleaning stations near the docks. Fishing for tarpon was a sport said to be invented in Boca Grande Pass.

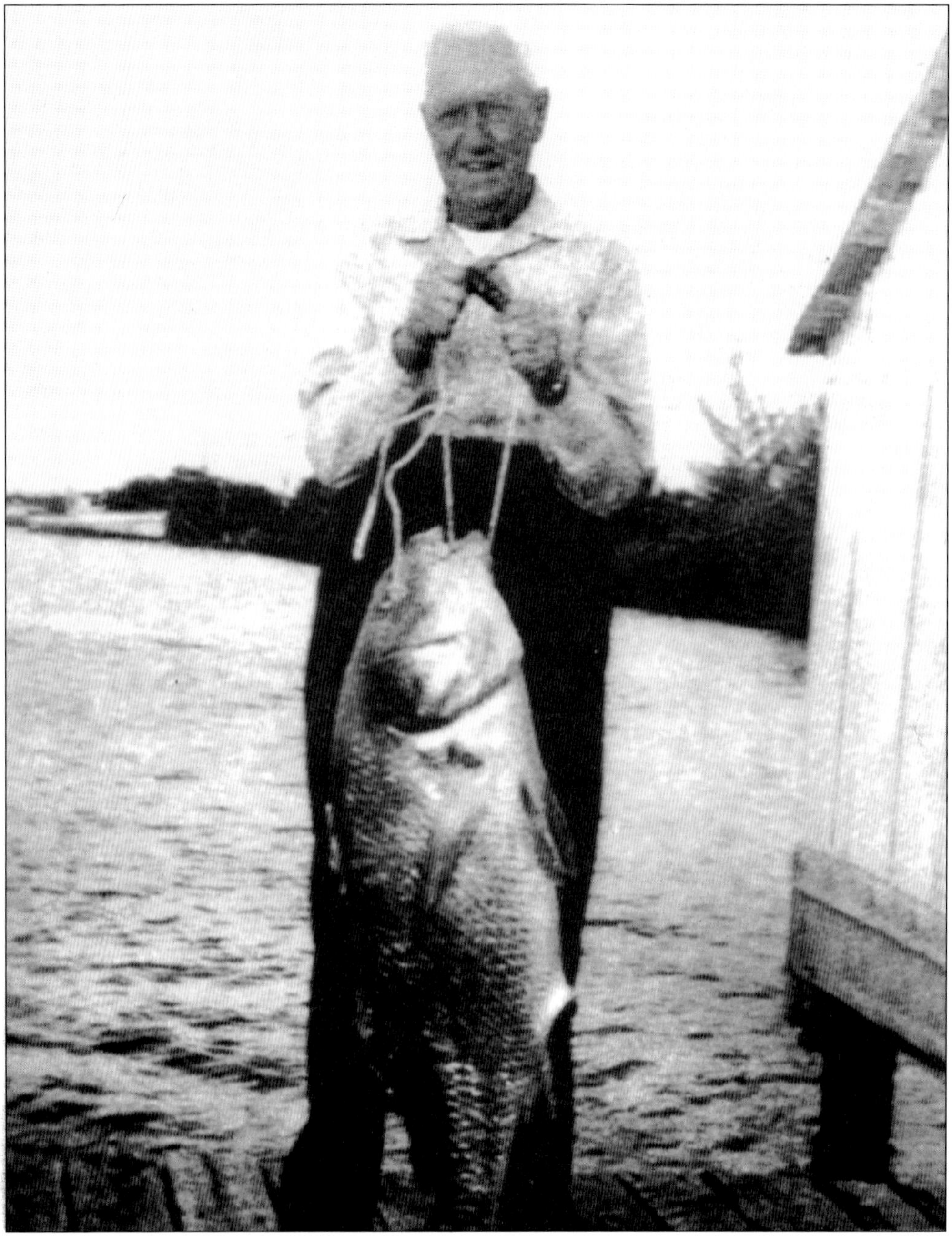

CARL WAGNER WITH HIS CATCH. This 1956 photograph shows Carl Wagner with a black drum caught off the Charlotte Harbor Bridge in Punta Gorda. The photograph was taken at Palms and Pines Trailer Park on U.S. 17. This first Charlotte Harbor Bridge was constructed in 1921.

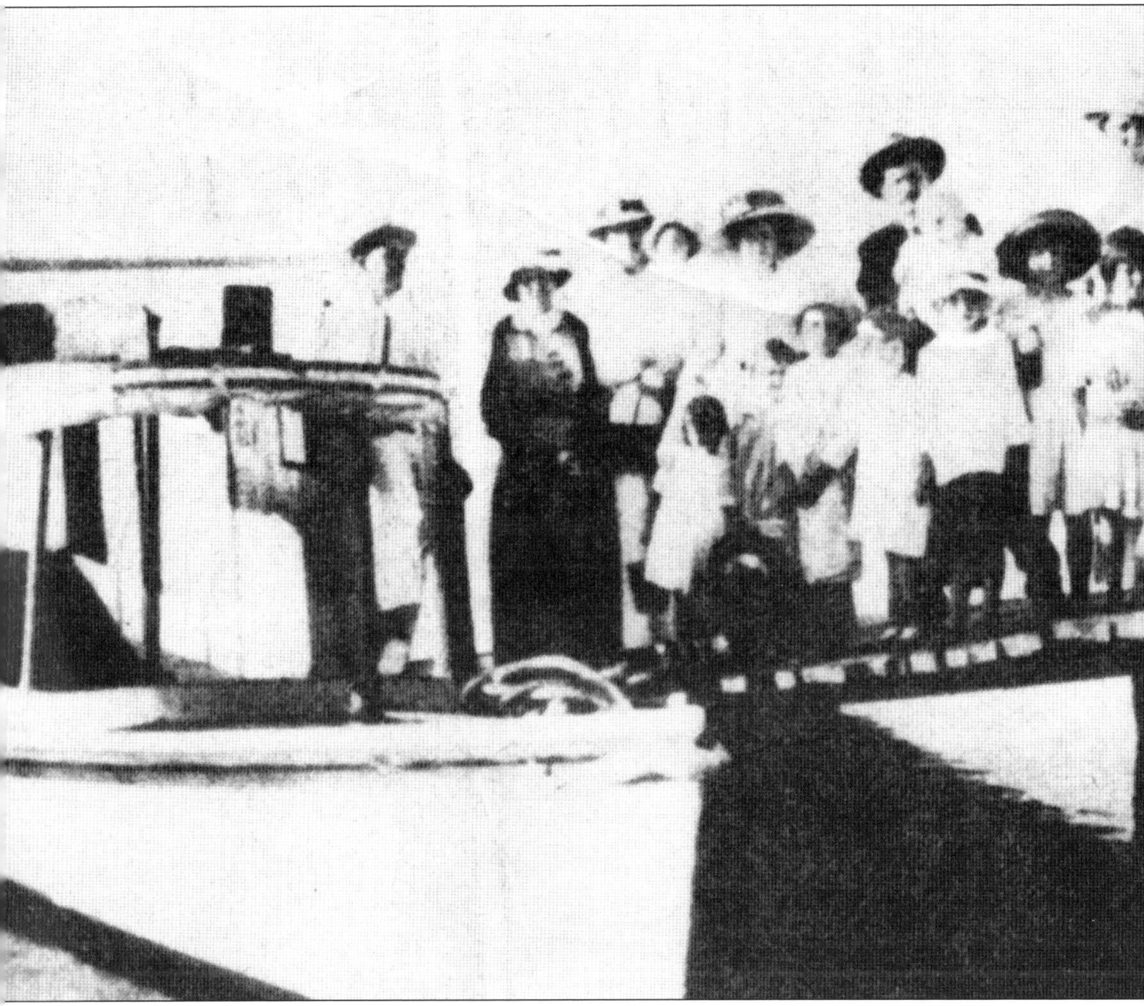

SCHOOL "BUS" BOAT. There are many islands in the Charlotte Harbor area, so in order to transport those children to school, boats were used to ferry them from the islands to Boca Grande, a community located on the barrier island Gasparilla. A dock was located near the school, and the ferry was docked all day in order to bring the children back home after school. (*Ceremonial Journal*, Punta Gorda Historical Society.)

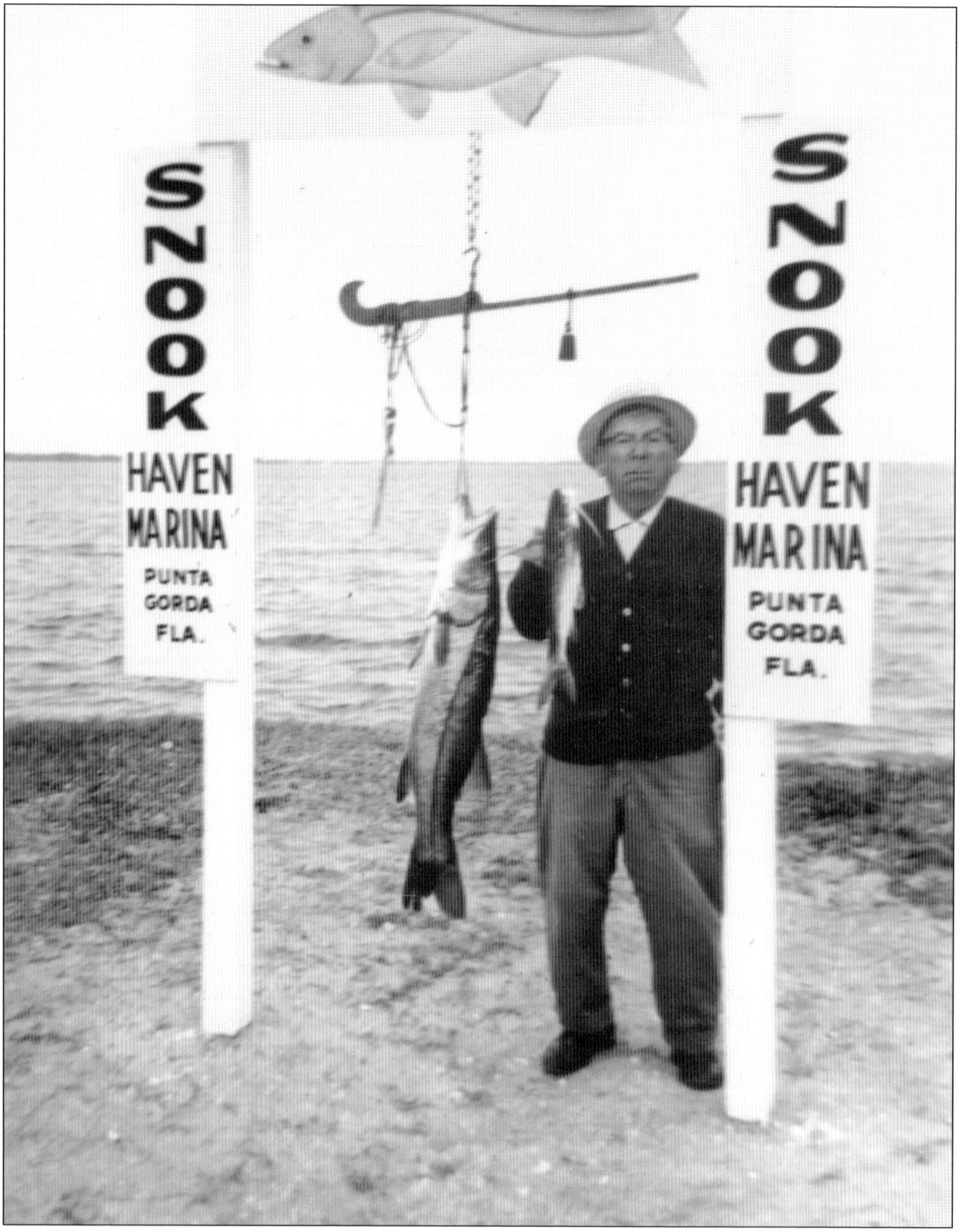

Fisherman with His Snook Catch. Charlotte Harbor's miles of mangrove shorelines, shallow grass flats, and sand and oyster bars make it the perfect home for snook, trout, redfish, and tarpon. The area's earliest commercial fishermen were the Spaniards. Pedro Menendez D'Aviles, a Spaniard, brought commercial fishing to the area in 1566. Charlotte Harbor is still renowned as offering some of the best fishing in the world.

Seven

The Later Years

In 1987, Punta Gorda celebrated its centennial with a parade, various ceremonies, exhibits, shows, and many other town events. The town has always been greatly loved by its residents and visitors alike as it is both picturesque and charming. There are several organizations in Punta Gorda that work tirelessly to preserve its history and charm. The Punta Gorda Historical Society works to preserve historic buildings, landmarks, streets, and other important aspects of Punta Gorda. In fact, one of the society's first works included preserving the quaint brick streets in the historic district. The society also regularly sponsors tours of the area's historical buildings and the Punta Gorda Historical District. Some of what the society has done is restore the Railroad Depot and the Trabue Land Sales Office, and they also established the Punta Gorda History Park. Punta Gorda's City Streetscape Program is working to restore the area's old Florida atmosphere to central district streets, such as Marion Street and Virginia Avenue, by adding brick lanes, street lamps, benches, brick planters, flowers, and shade trees. The Punta Gorda Historical Mural Society, formed in late 1994, paints historic and educational murals (23 to date), which help make Punta Gorda an even more beautiful community. The Blanchard House Museum of African-American History and Culture of Charlotte County serves as a museum. The Military Heritage Museum works to educate the public about our rich military heritage while honoring those who served to preserve our country's freedom. (The museum has over 50,000 artifacts on display.) There are also plenty of events at the Fisherman's Village, arts exhibits and programs at the Visual Arts Center, and Gallery Walks offered by downtown merchants. Furthermore, all of the new buildings in the downtown area are designed to maintain the beauty of Punta Gorda's downtown historical district. Although much time has passed since Ponce de León set foot in the area, Punta Gorda works to keep the changes pleasing to the eye.

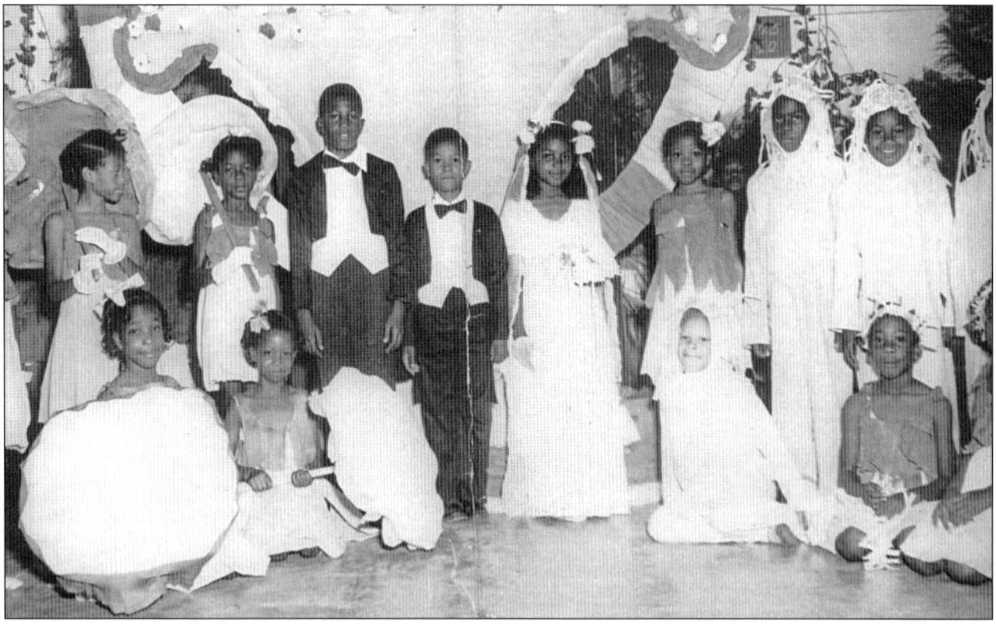

A Baker Academy School Play, 1950s. The African American students at the Baker Academy performed school plays as an important part of their curriculum. The plays date back to as early as 1904, when Benjamin Baker first arrived in Punta Gorda as the school's first teacher. The plays were announced in the newspaper, were always well attended, and were open to the public. (Blanchard House Museum of African-American History and Culture of Charlotte County.)

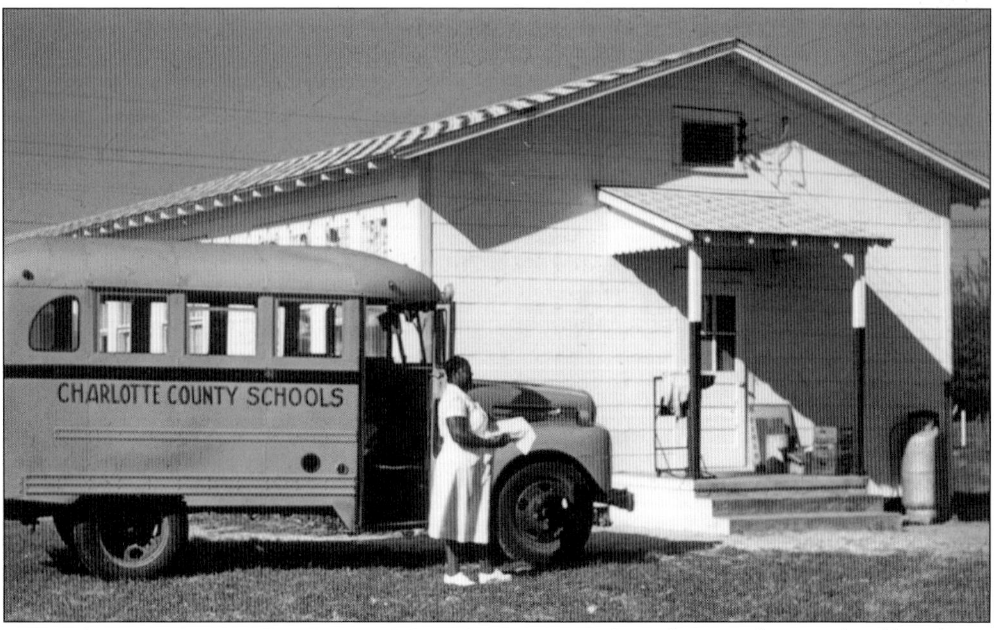

Baker Academy School Bus Driver Mary Goodnight. The Baker Academy's school bus driver was Mary Goodnight. She drove the only bus that served the African American community during the days of segregation. Mary was also the school's lunch lady, and once she arrived at the school, she began preparing lunch for the students. (Blanchard House Museum of African-American History and Culture of Charlotte County.)

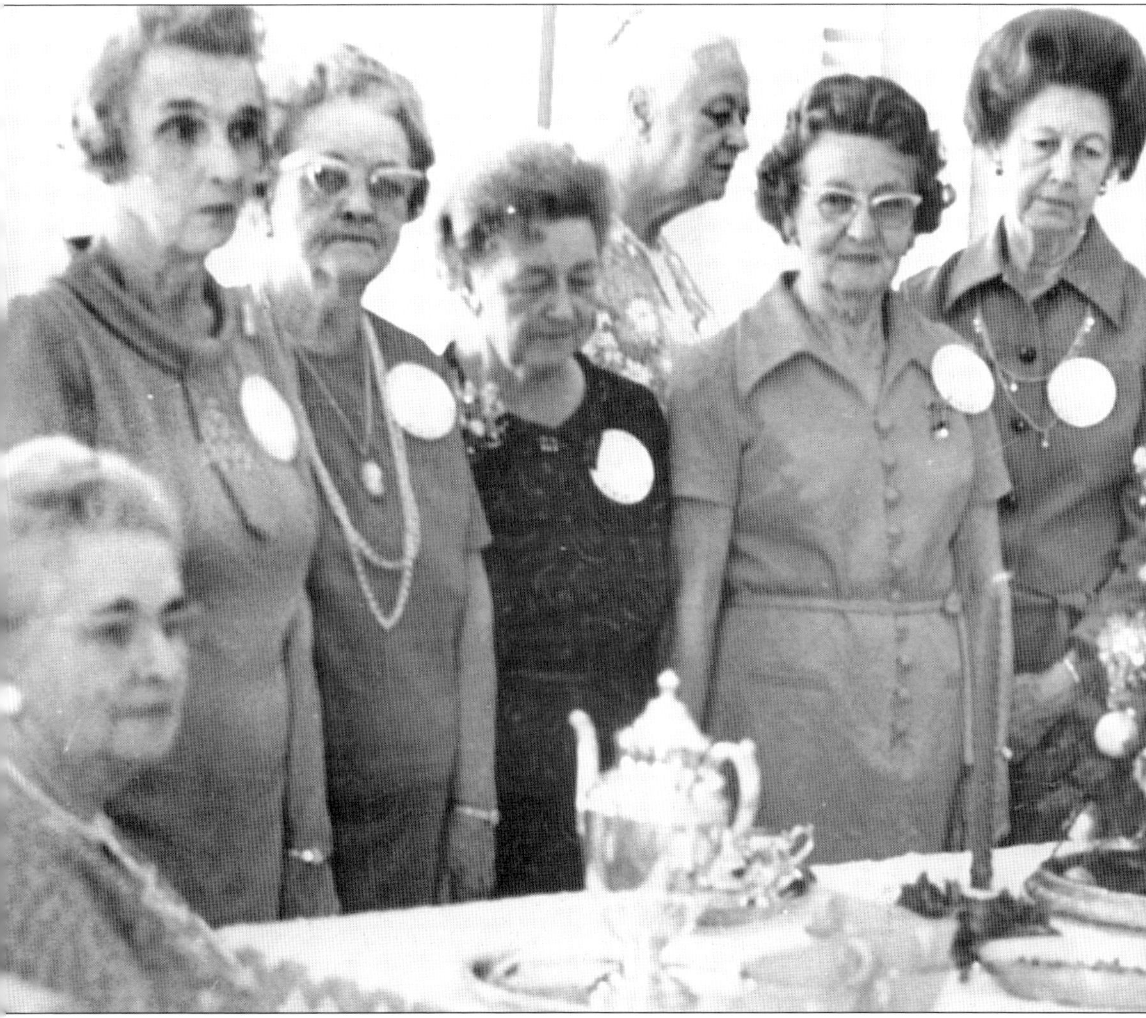

Punta Gorda Woman's Club around 1974. This 1974 photograph is of the Punta Gorda Woman's Club members. Shown from left to right are (seated) Esther McCollough; (standing) Grace Snyder, Areta Yeager, Velma Brayton, Mildred Sandlin, Helen Sexton, and Thelma King.

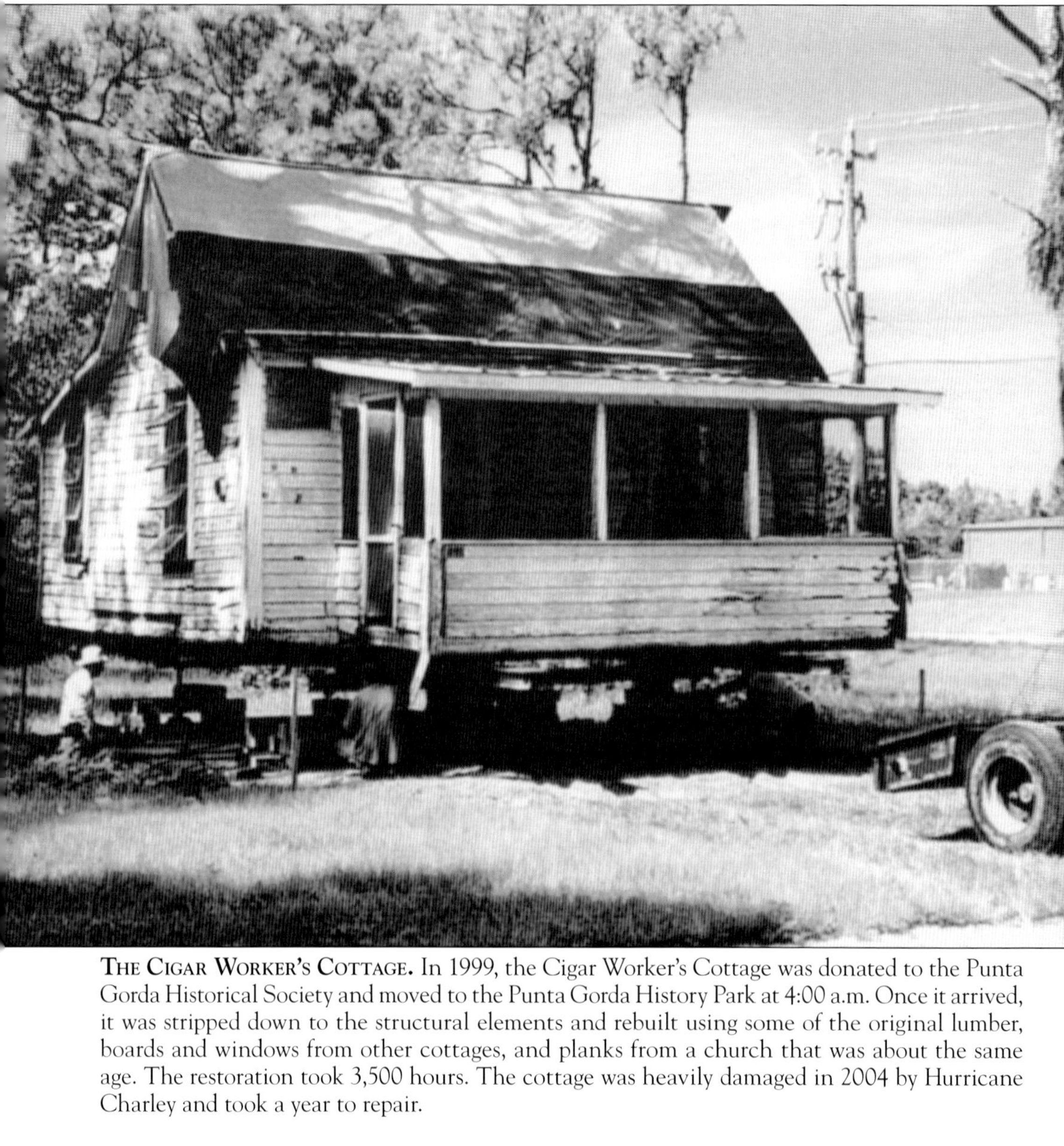

The Cigar Worker's Cottage. In 1999, the Cigar Worker's Cottage was donated to the Punta Gorda Historical Society and moved to the Punta Gorda History Park at 4:00 a.m. Once it arrived, it was stripped down to the structural elements and rebuilt using some of the original lumber, boards and windows from other cottages, and planks from a church that was about the same age. The restoration took 3,500 hours. The cottage was heavily damaged in 2004 by Hurricane Charley and took a year to repair.

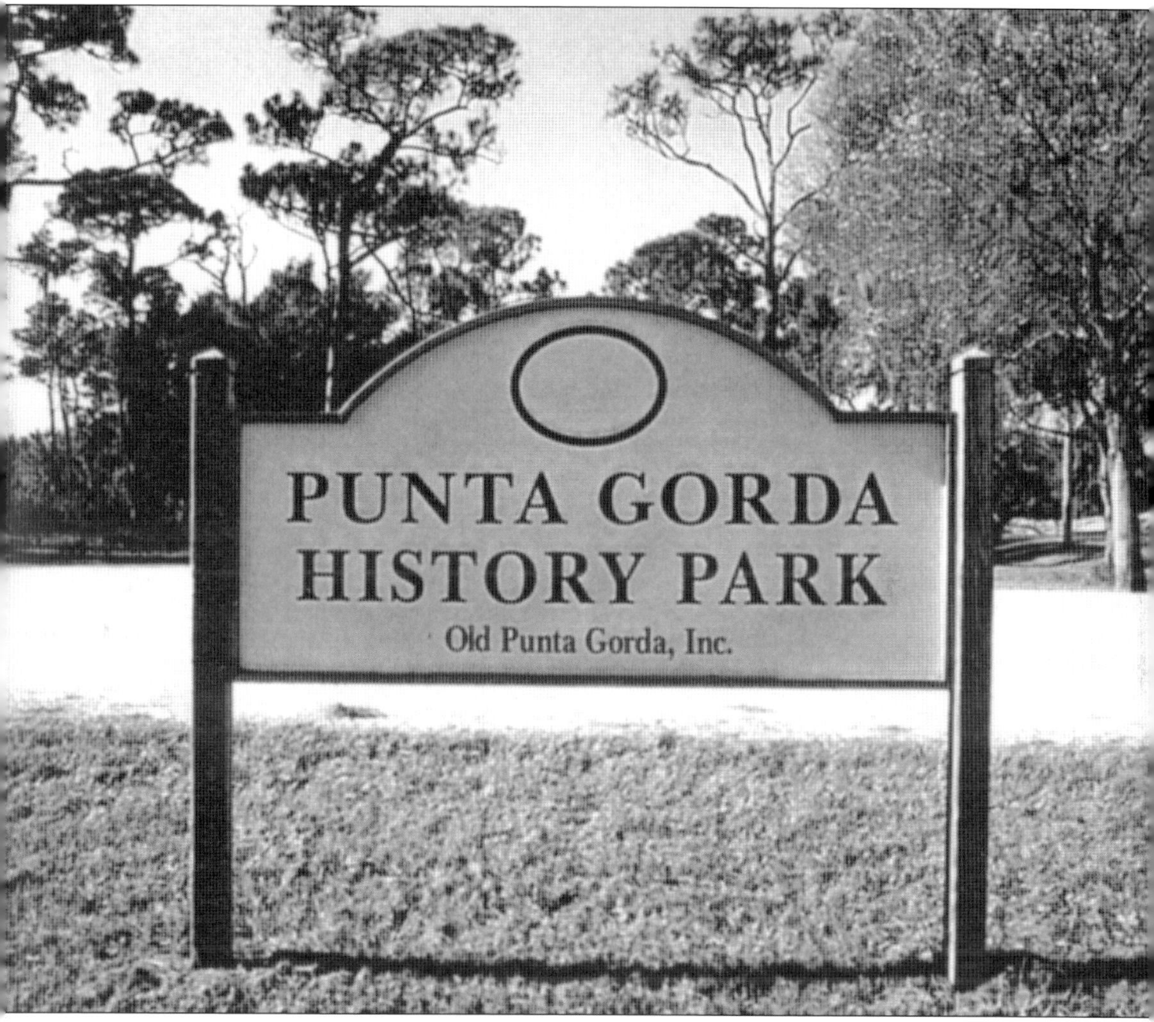

THE PUNTA GORDA HISTORY PARK. The Punta Gorda History Park is about a 2-acre park that was created for development as a historical relocation site. Now at the park are an 1890s cigar cottage and the Trabue law and land sales office building (which also houses the Peace River Center for Writers), along with the newly restored Price House. The park is located at 501 Shreve Street, Punta Gorda.

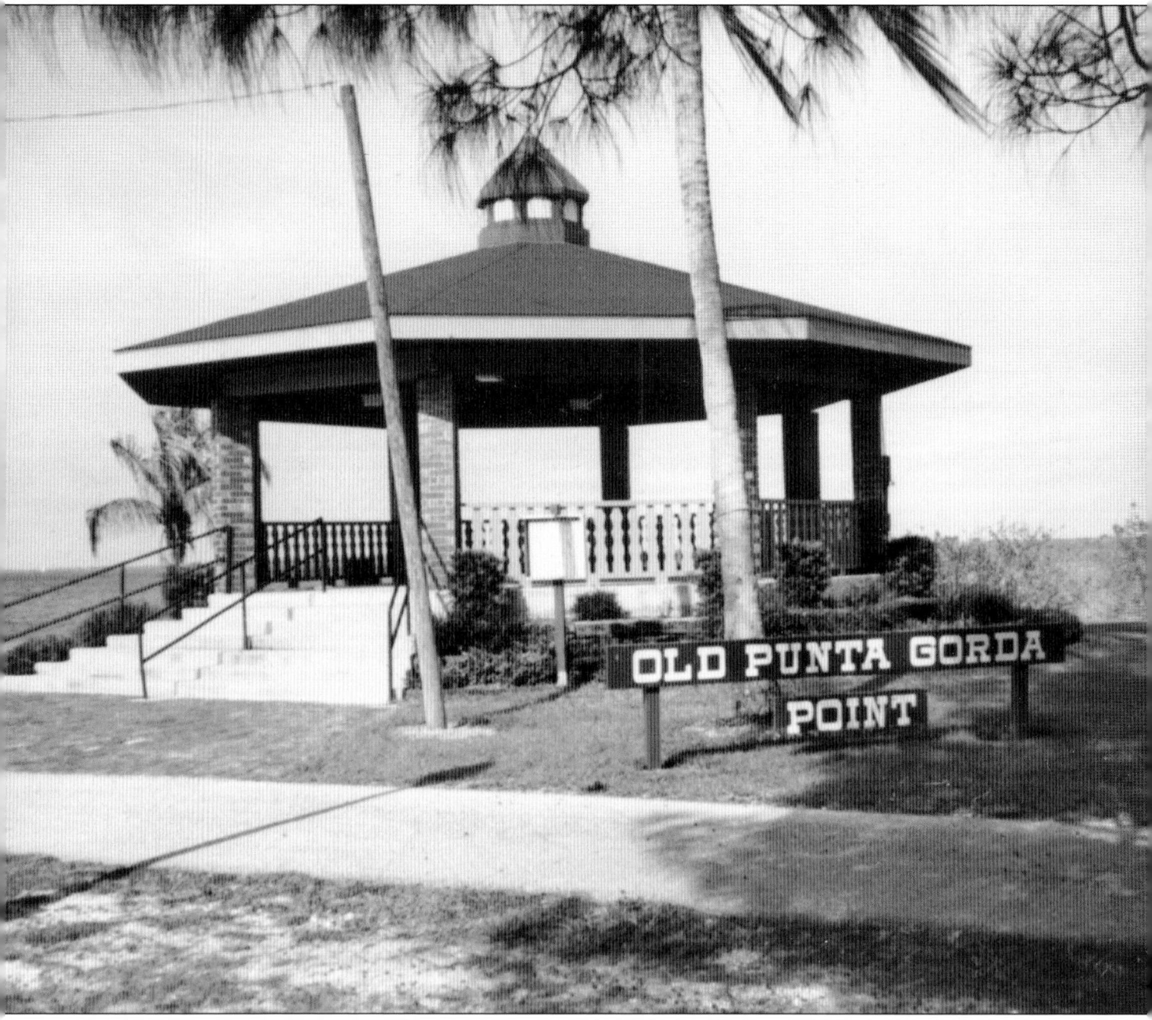

GILCHRIST PARK GAZEBO. The gazebo was built with funds from the Punta Gorda Historical Society. Gilchrist Park is 11 acres and runs along Charlotte Harbor. A statue of Ponce de León also is located at the park. Gilchrist Park is located 400 West Retta Esplanade.

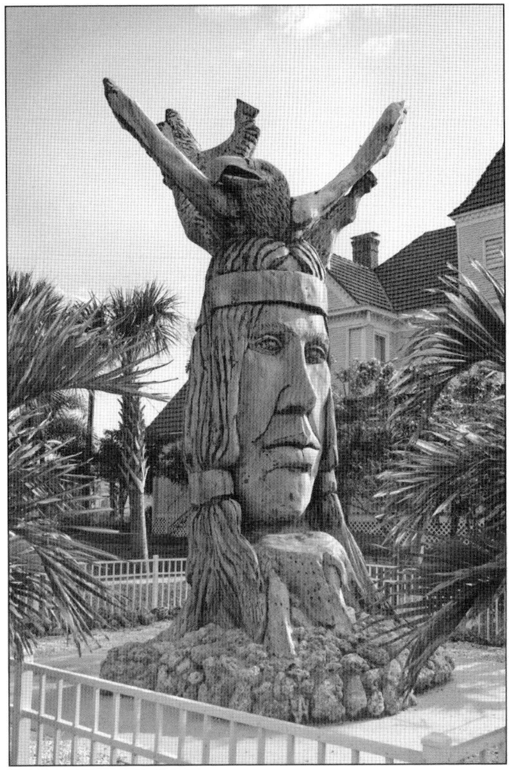

CALOSTIMUCU. This American Indian sculpture is carved from the trunk of a monkey pod tree that died in 1973. It was carved by Peter Toth, an artist who has vowed to create an American Indian statue in all 50 states. The artist spent three months creating this unusual carving. It depicts a brave on one side and a maiden on the other. Over their heads is an emerging dream of a dying bison and an eagle trying to honor the American Indian and to raise awareness of the damage prejudice and injustice have caused. (Photograph by Scot Shively; Blanchard House Museum of African-American History and Culture of Charlotte County.)

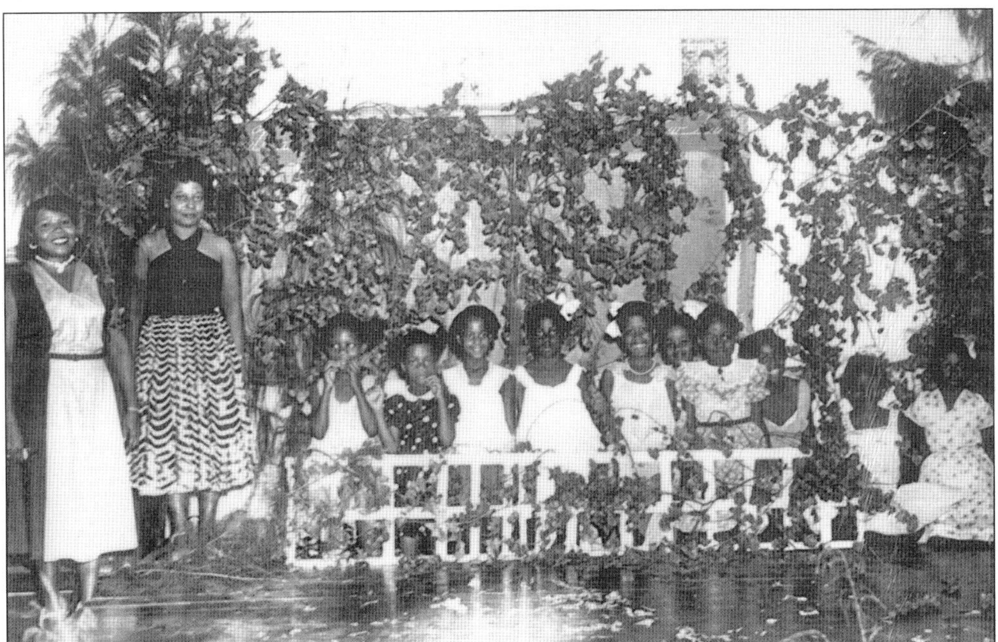

BAKER ACADEMY SCHOOL PLAY. Baker Academy teacher Lorene Bailey stands next to her students during a school pageant. School plays were an important part of the curriculum and were well attended by family members and members of the community. (Blanchard House Museum of African-American History and Culture of Charlotte County.)

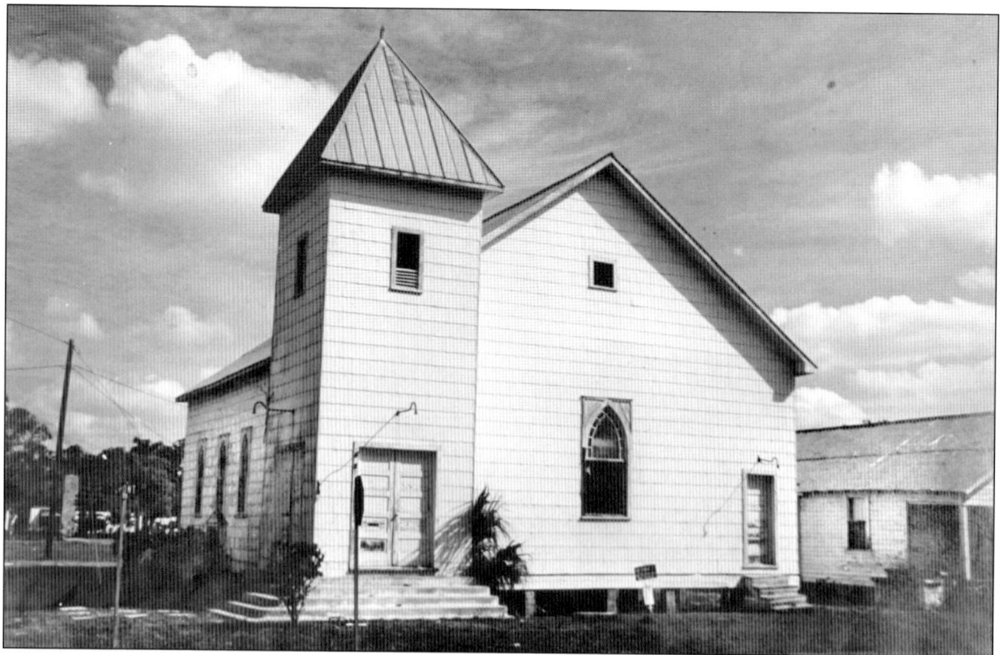

St. Mark Progressive Baptist Church. The church was founded by Punta Gorda African American pioneer Dan Smith and was attended by both blacks and whites. The first St. Mark Church was built in 1893. (Blanchard House Museum of African-American History and Culture of Charlotte County.)

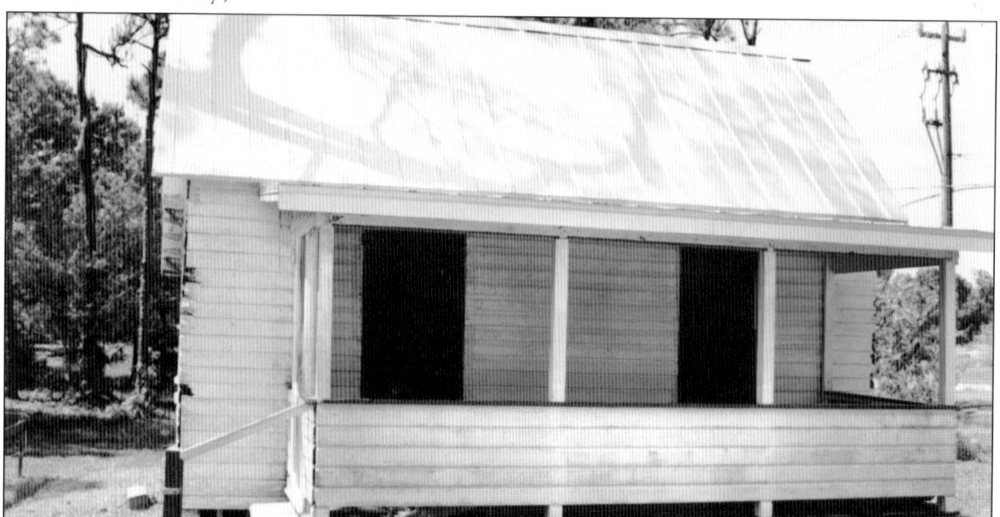

The Cigar Worker's Cottage Being Renovated. In the 1890s, the Cigar Worker's Cottage was built by El Palmetto Cigar Factory. The company built several cottages near its factory, located on the corner of Virginia and Cochran Avenues. Cigar rollers were skilled laborers and highly desired workers, so the housing was likely built for the workers to have an incentive to stay and work. The cottage is actually a set of rooms, or a duplex. One worker lived in each side of the cottage. Bathroom and cooking facilities were located outside of the building. In the 1920s, this cottage and another like it were both moved to Brown Street. Front porches were later added, and they were turned into single-family homes.

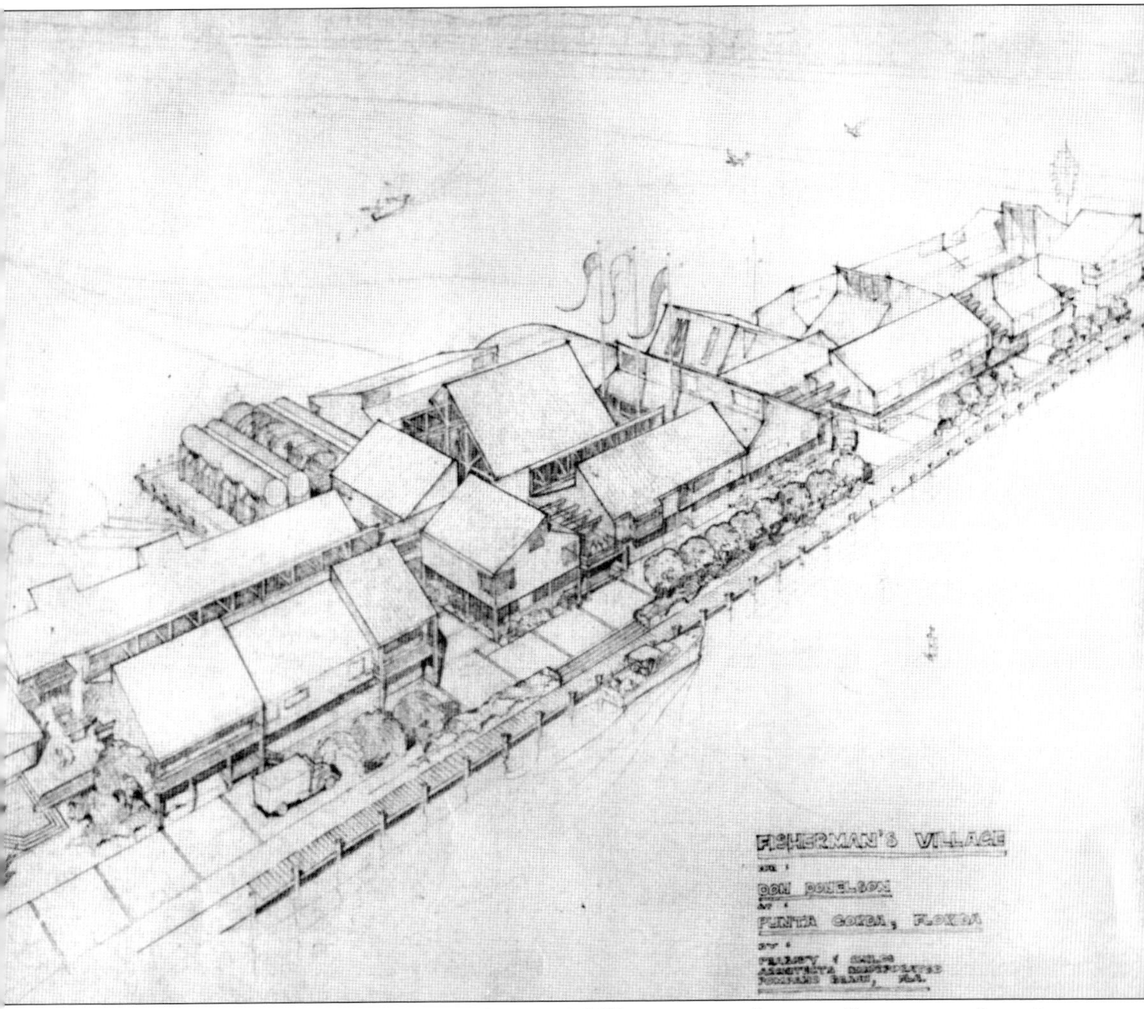

Plans for Fisherman's Village. Fisherman's Village, a waterfront mall, resort, and marina, was built on the site of the old City Dock in Punta Gorda in the late 1970s. The village received the Pinnacle Achievement Award from the Punta Gorda Chamber of Commerce in 2008. The village features boutiques, shops, dining, day spa, villa vacation rentals, harbor cruises, fishing charters, boat and Jet Ski rentals, live entertainment, and special events. The name and location are a tribute to the town where fishing was a key business. (Fisherman's Village.)

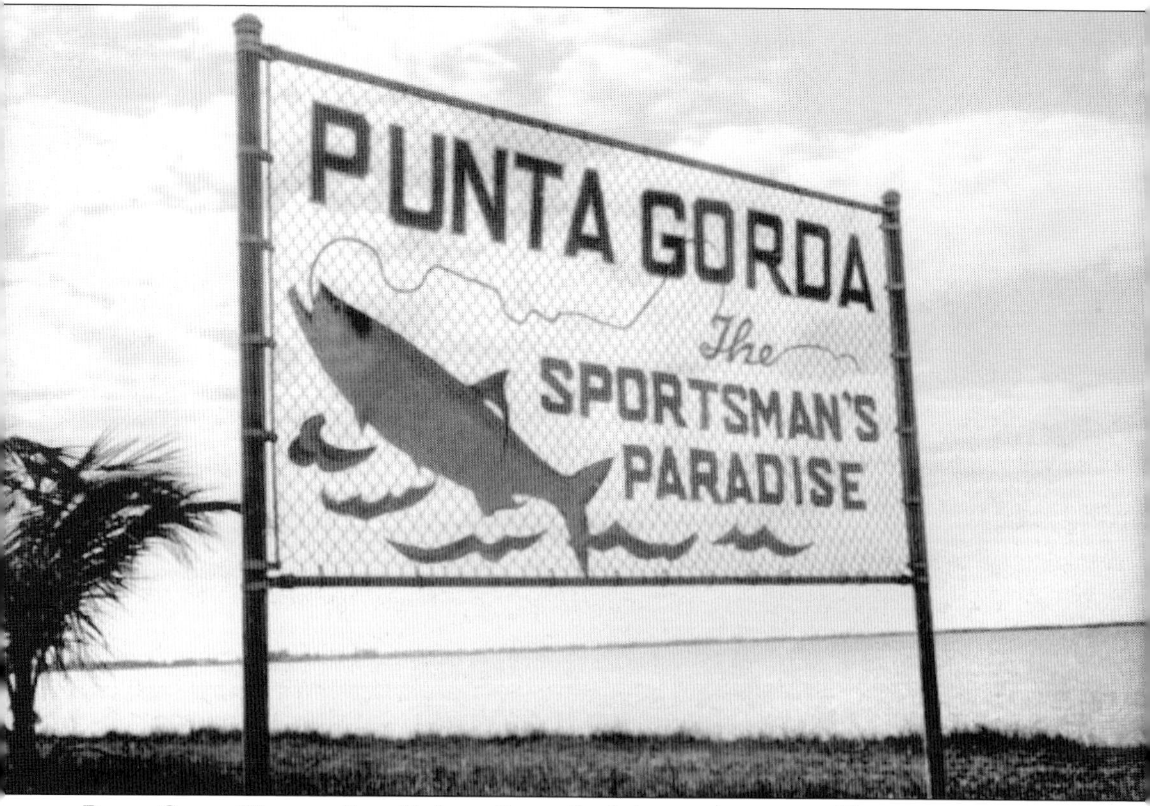

Punta Gorda Welcome Sign. Early on, Punta Gorda became known as a "Sportsman's Paradise." Many of the early Hotel Punta Gorda guests came down specifically to enjoy the abundant fishing. Tarpon quickly became one of the most sought-after game fish. Many tarpons, known as "Silver King" tarpons, caught in the local waters were in the impressive 80-90-pound range. (Florida Photographic Collection, the Florida Memory Project.)

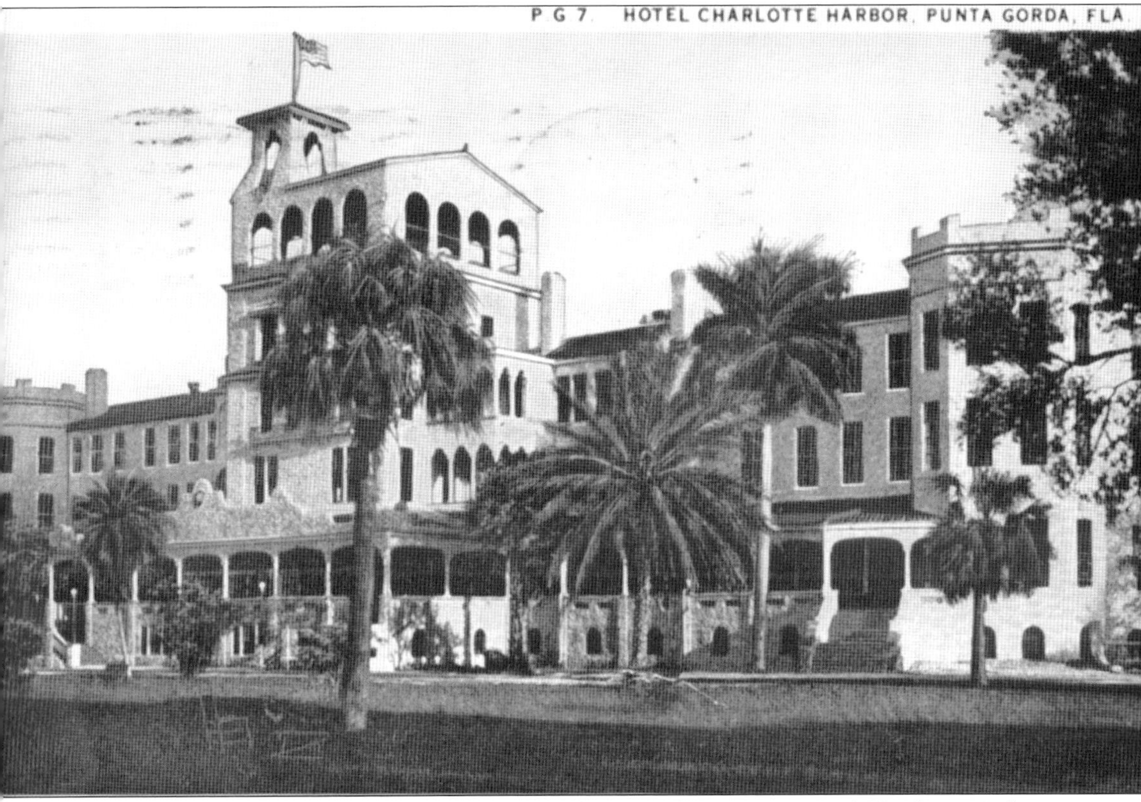

HOTEL CHARLOTTE HARBOR. This early postcard shows off the majestic Hotel Charlotte Harbor, which is situated waterside. Hotel Punta Gorda was known as Hotel Charlotte Harbor after it was sold in 1924 and refurbished by Barron Collier and Cornelius Vanderbilt. They spent three years enlarging and modernizing the hotel. Dignitaries and the wealthy would come to stay at the grand hotel. Pres. Theodore Roosevelt visited Punta Gorda and was a guest at the hotel.

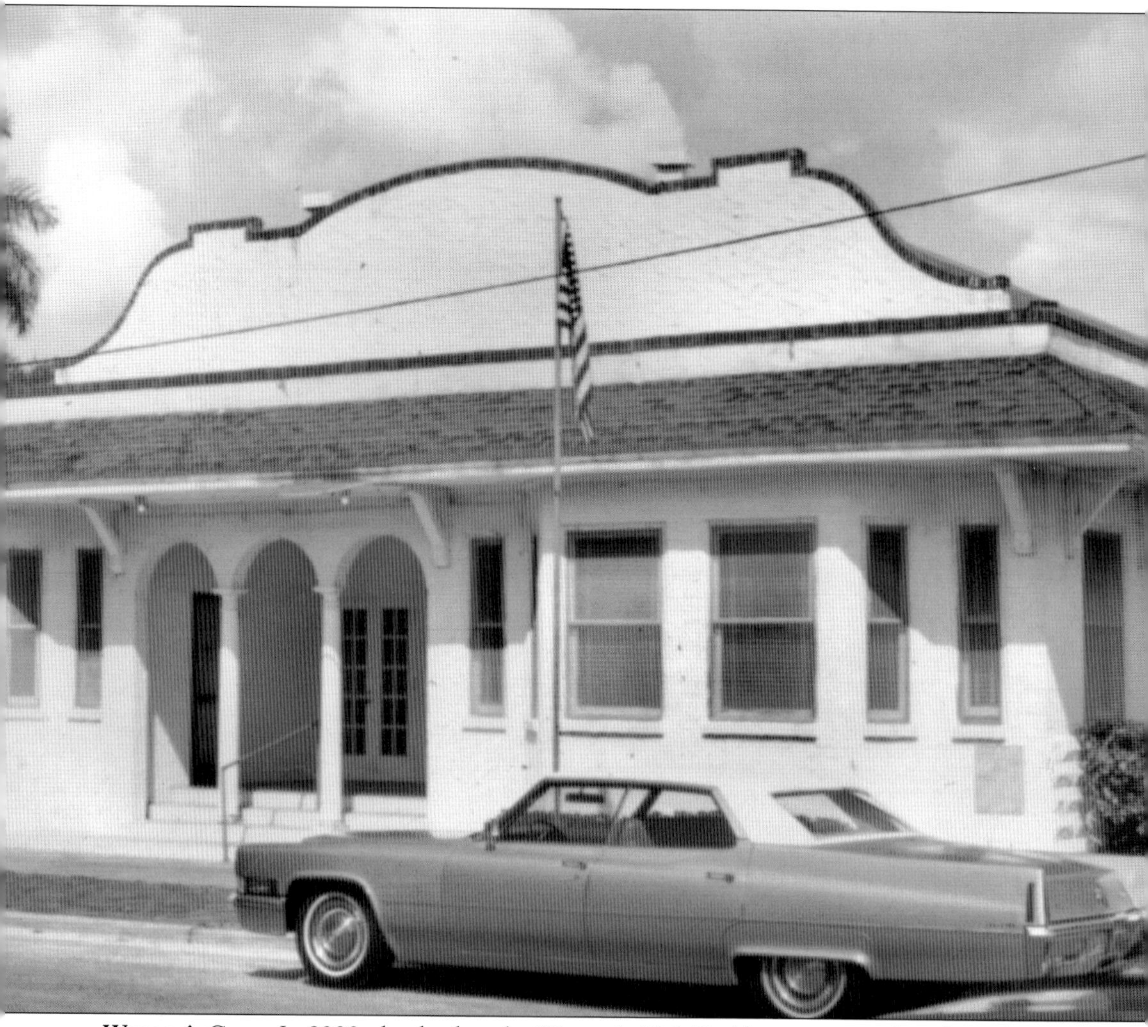

WOMAN'S CLUB. In 2000, the deed to the Woman's Club Building was transferred to Old Punta Gorda, Inc., now the Punta Gorda Historical Society, whose office is located in one of the front rooms of the building. The Punta Gorda Historical Society has been preserving historic buildings in Punta Gorda for over 20 years. Some of the building restorations include the Railroad Depot, the Trabue Land Sales Office, and the Cigar Worker's Cottage. The society also raises funds for other projects, such as building the Gilchrist Park Gazebo and for the establishment of the Punta Gorda History Park. They also regularly sponsor tours of the area's historical buildings and the Punta Gorda Historical District.

Joseph A. Blanchard Home. The Blanchard House was built in 1925 and was originally home to Joseph and Minnie Blanchard. Joseph was a fisherman and a boat pilot, and Minnie was a mail-order bride. The house was purchased by Bernice Russell in 1997 after all of the Blanchard heirs were deceased. At Bernice's death in 1999, the house was donated to the Bernice A. Russell Center, Inc., by her daughter, Dr. Martha R. Bireda, and her children. The house was moved from its original location at 613 Fitzhugh Avenue to its present location on Emancipation Day, May 20, 2002.

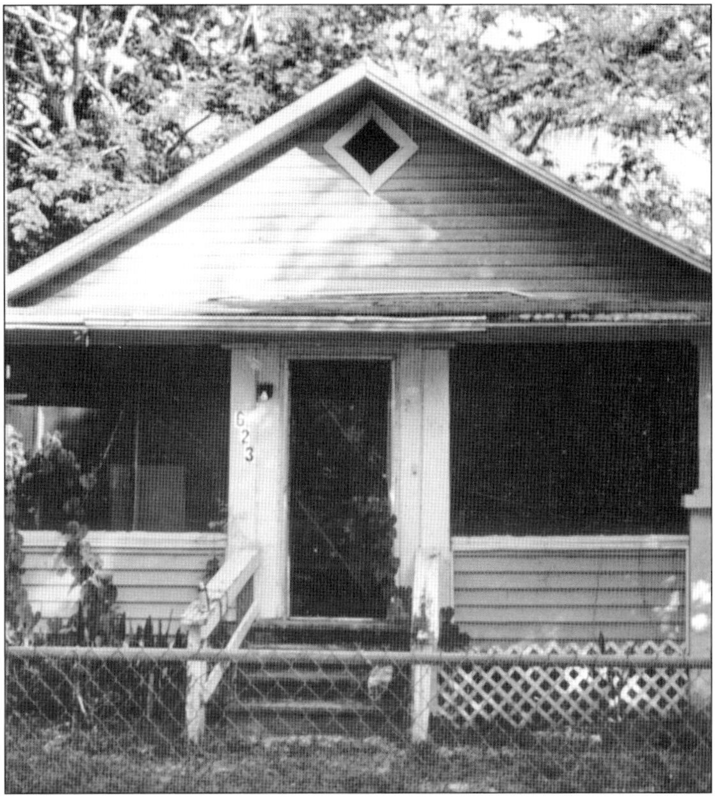

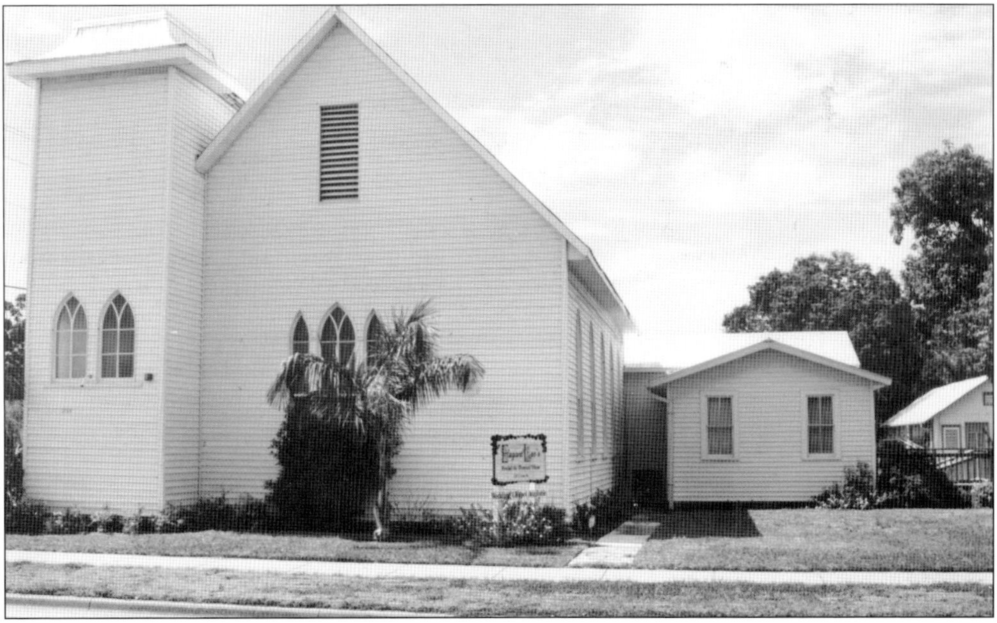

The First Baptist Church. The First Baptist Church was organized in 1899. The nine-member congregation initially met in the ice-skating rink above a downtown livery stable. A building site at Olympia Avenue and Cross Street was purchased in 1891, and the church was completed in 1895. (*Fact and Fable: Charlotte County*.)

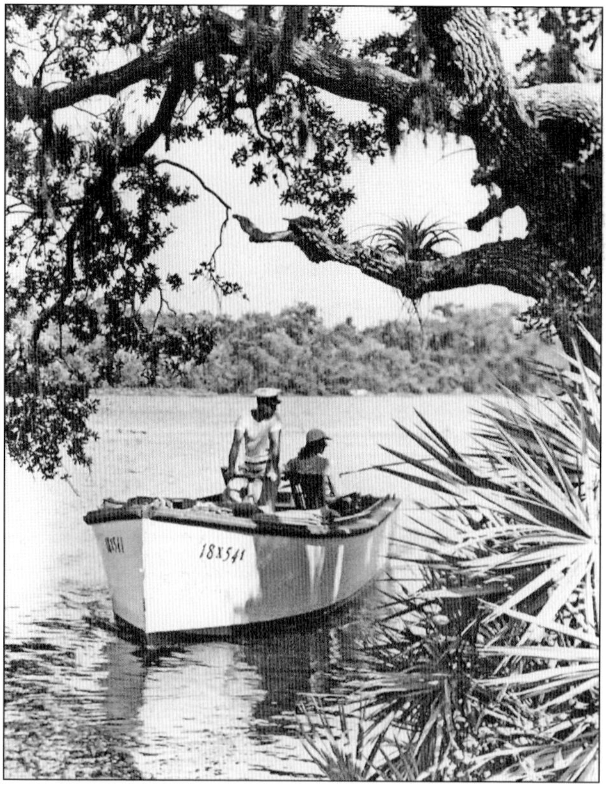

Fishing Guide Roy Nicely and Mildred Allen Trolling for Tarpon in the Peace River. The scenic Peace River is over 100 miles long and outpours into Charlotte Harbor. The Spaniards referred to the Peace River as Rio de la Paz—"river of peace." The Peace River has long been known for its abundance of largemouth bass, bream, and catfish, along with tarpon, that can be found in the lower part of the river. (Florida Photographic Collection, the Florida Memory Project.)

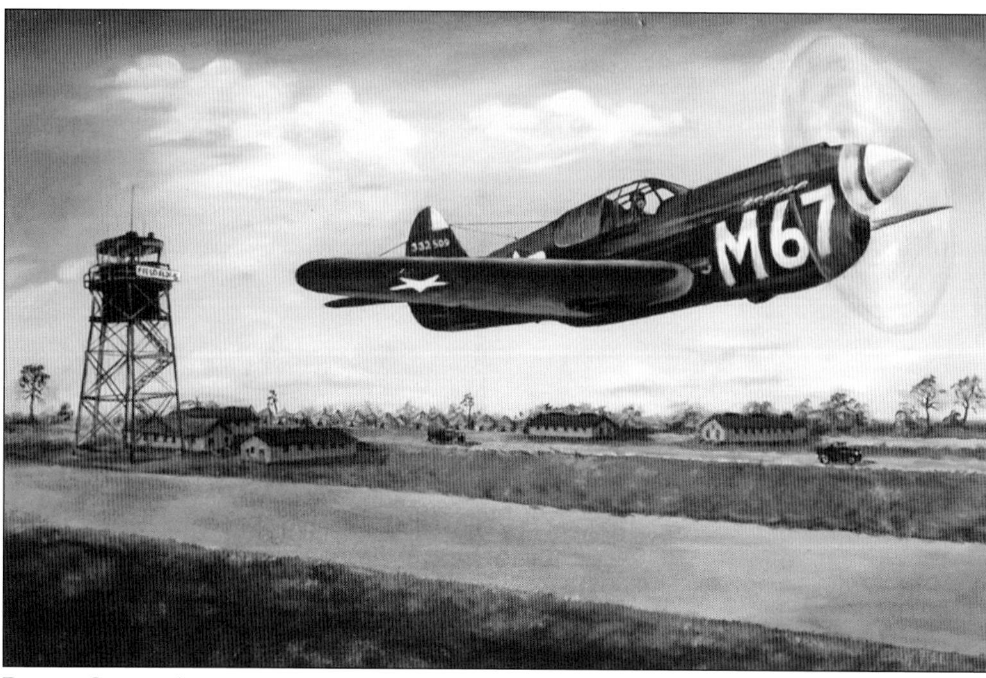

Punta Gorda Airfield during World War II. The pilots at the airfield trained on P-40 Warhawks, P-47 Thunderbolts, and P-51 Mustangs during World War II, according to the history of Charlotte County Airport as recalled by W. B. Clement, M.D., in 1983.

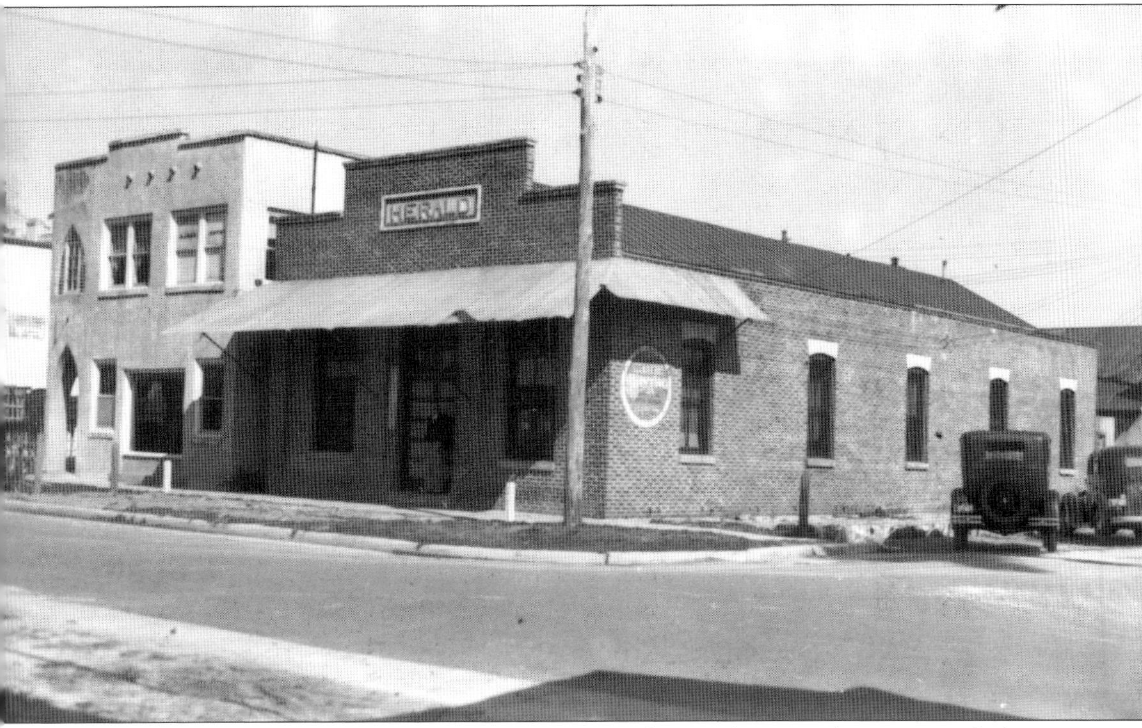

THE *HERALD* BUILDING. The *Herald* was founded by Robert Kirby Seward in 1893. Back then, newspapers incorporated local gossip along with regular local news stories. Under the paper's masthead was "In God We Trust, All Others Cash." The newspaper was only two pages long.

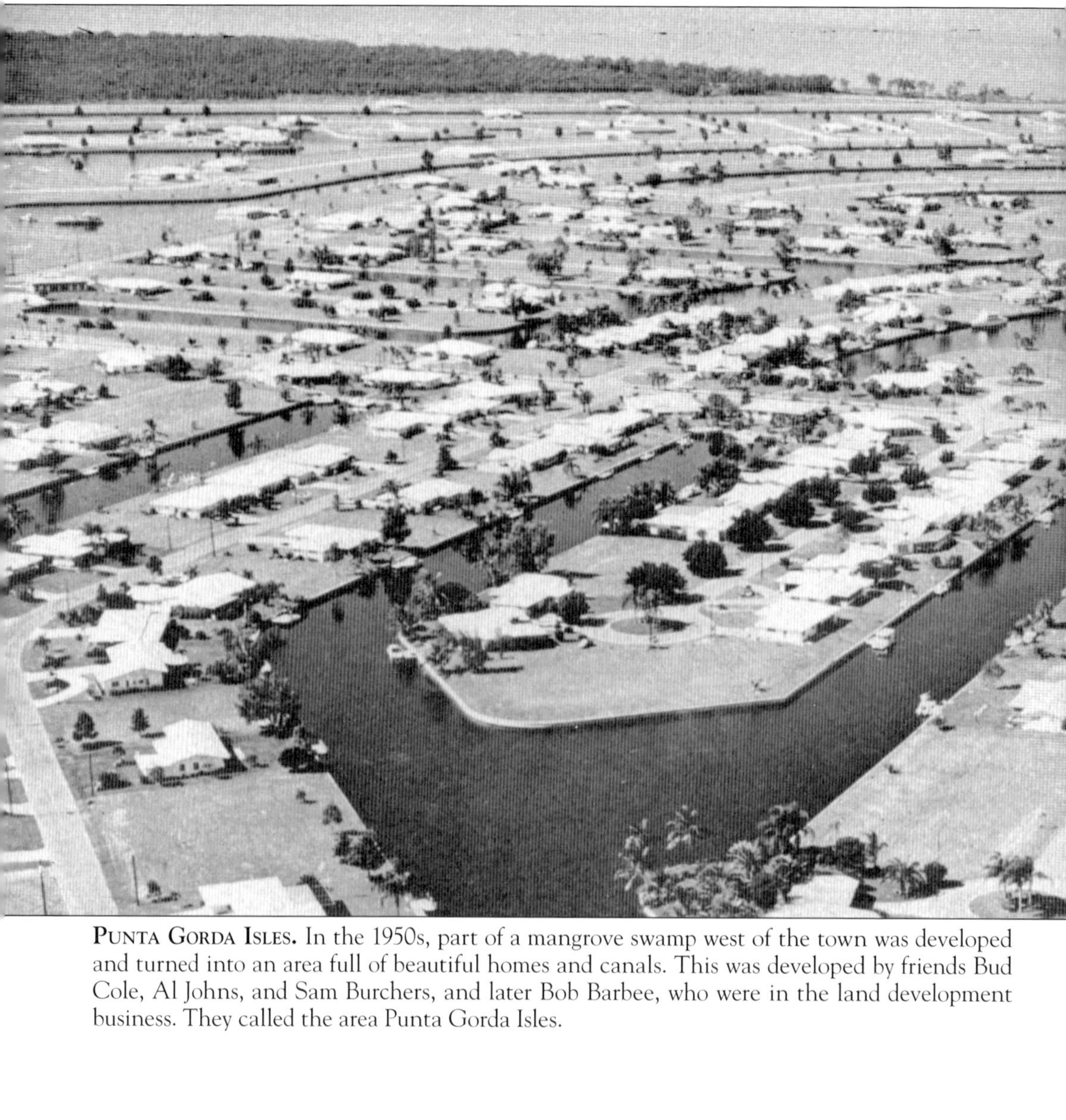

Punta Gorda Isles. In the 1950s, part of a mangrove swamp west of the town was developed and turned into an area full of beautiful homes and canals. This was developed by friends Bud Cole, Al Johns, and Sam Burchers, and later Bob Barbee, who were in the land development business. They called the area Punta Gorda Isles.

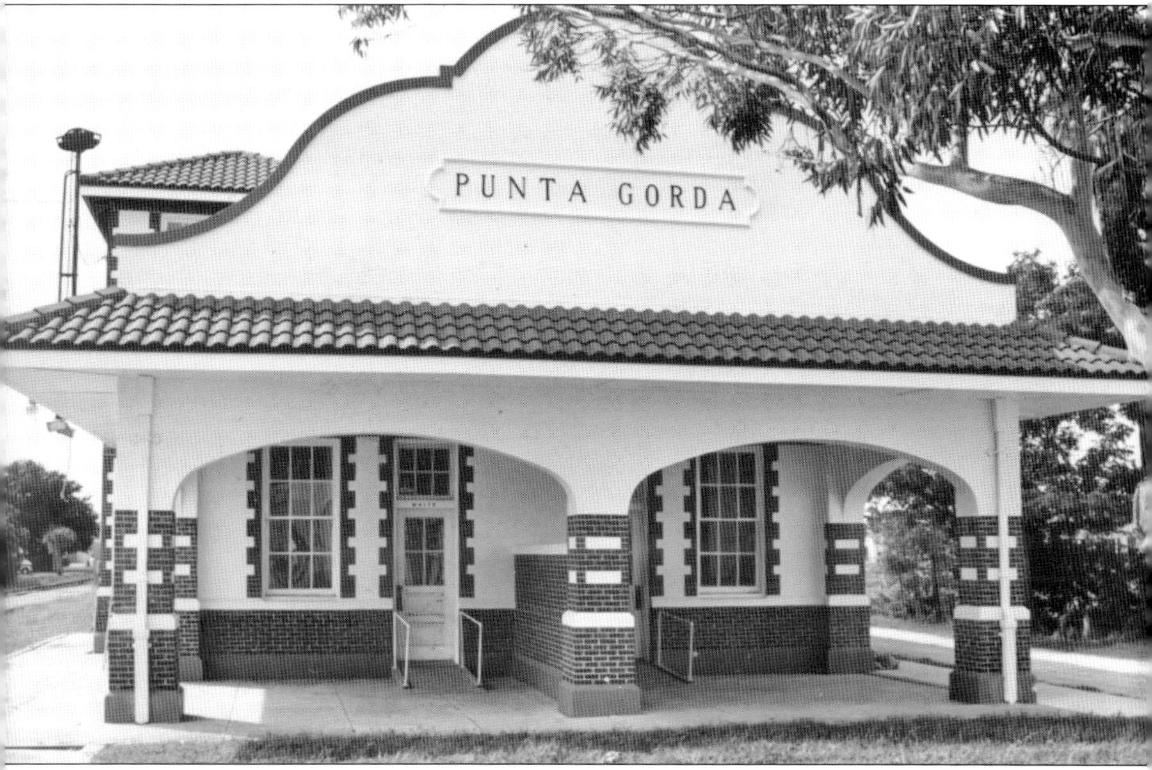

PUNTA GORDA'S HISTORIC RAILROAD DEPOT. The late Fred Babcock, industrialist and rancher, gave the Punta Gorda Historical Society money to purchase the depot from him in 1996. Since then, the building has been restored, and the freight room now serves as the Punta Gorda Historic Railroad Depot and Antique Mall. A railroad museum is planned for the ticketing area. The building was listed on the National Register of Historic Places in 1990, and in 2008, a historical marker was placed on the grounds. The Punta Gorda Historic Railroad Depot and Antique Mall is located at 1009 Taylor Road.

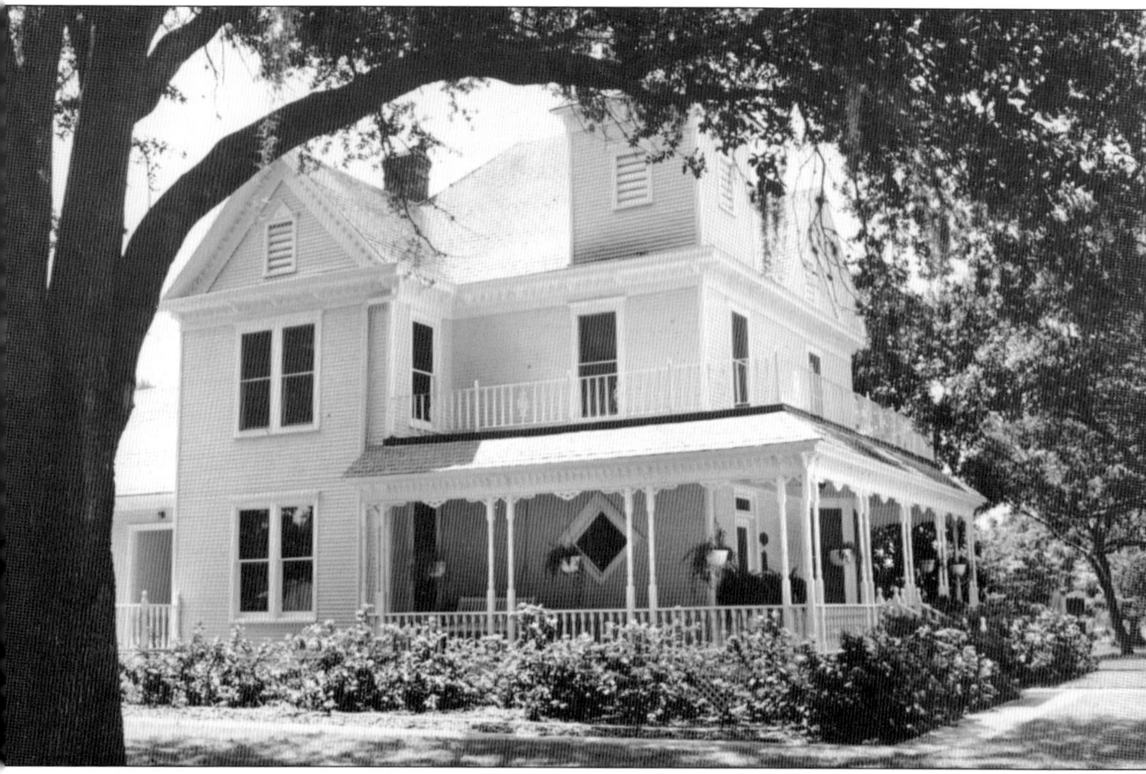

A. C. Freeman House. The 1903 A. C. Freeman House is now open for tours conducted by volunteers. Inside one will find period furnishings by the Mr. and Mrs. John Morrison collection. In 1985, the house was slated for demolition, but a major committee, coordinated by the Medical Center Foundation, relocated the house to its present location at 311 West Retta Esplanade in Punta Gorda.

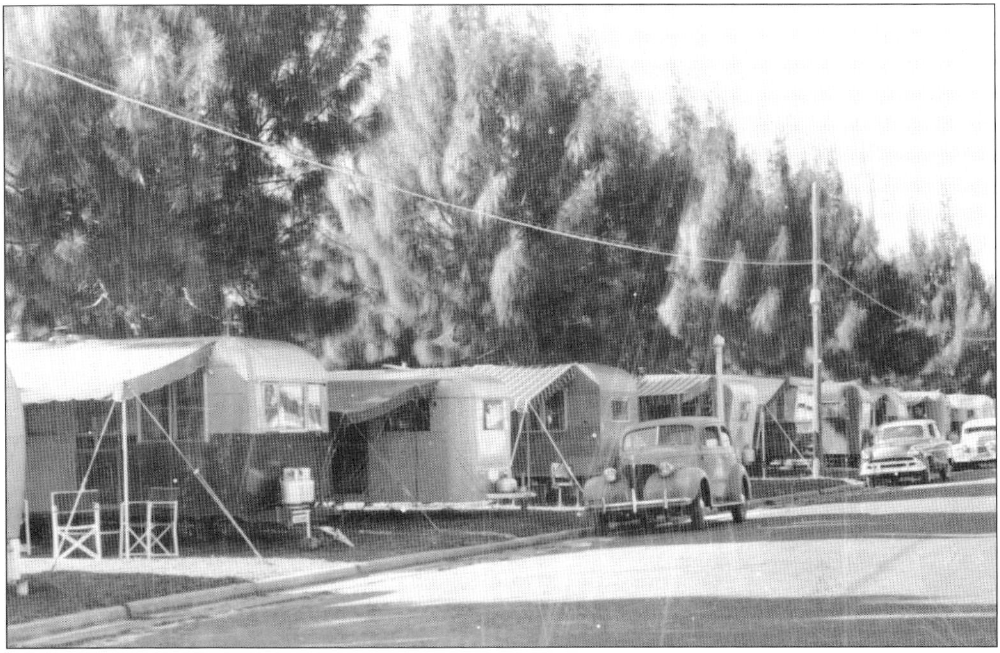

EARLY SNOWBIRDS. Traveling via trailer was a popular choice, as it was more comfortable than a tent, and Northerners could bring many of their belongings down for an extended stay. Back in the early 1920s, visitors who enjoyed traveling this way were often referred to as "tin can tourists," as the trailer was towed on the back of the vehicle.

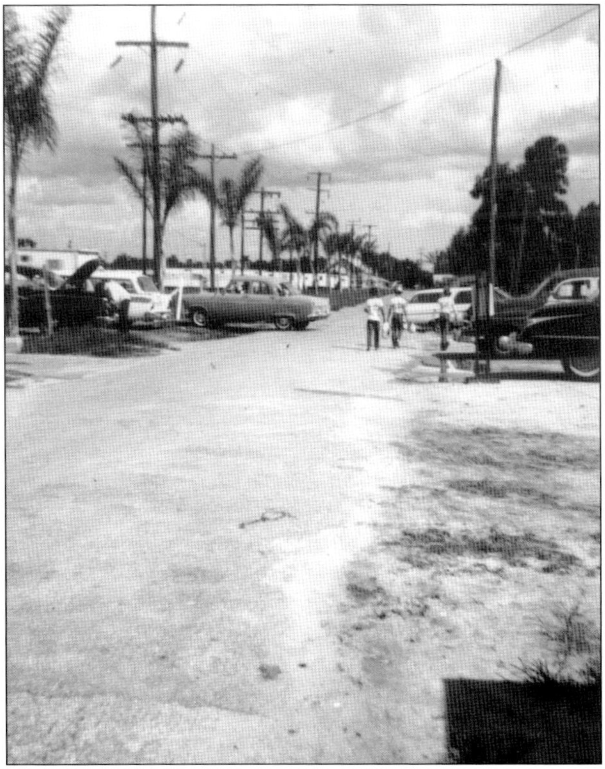

SEASONAL RESIDENTS ENJOY PUNTA GORDA. As the trailers become more modern in the 1930s and 1940s, they were called "house trailers." In the 1950s and 1960s, the recreational vehicle (RV) and mobile home industries came about, both of which are still found in the Punta Gorda area. This photograph dates back to the 1950s.

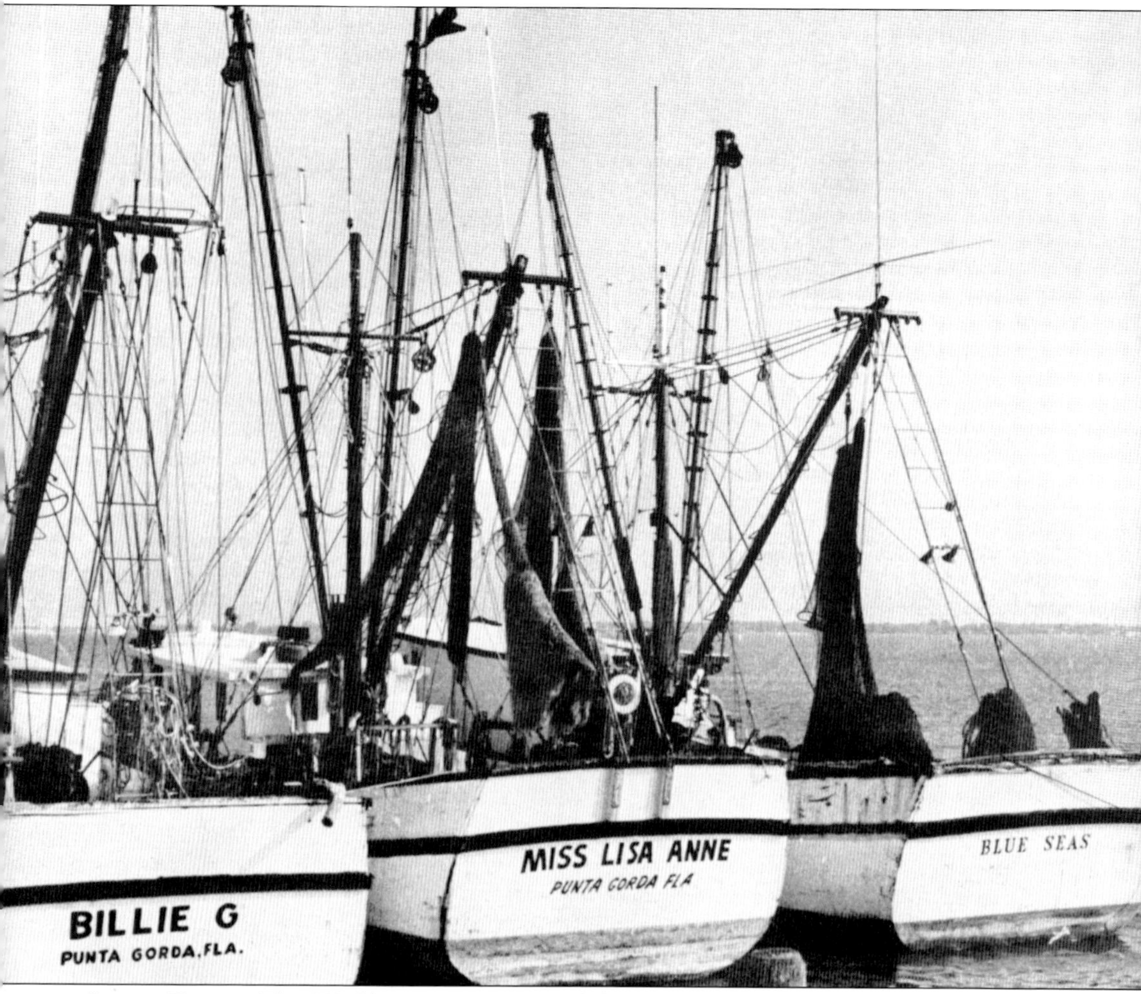

Shrimp Boats. After World War II, commercial shrimping became popular in the local waters. Although it wasn't the main part of the fishing industry, it contributed to the local economy. Shrimp boats tied up at Punta Gorda were a common sight in the 1950s and 1960s.

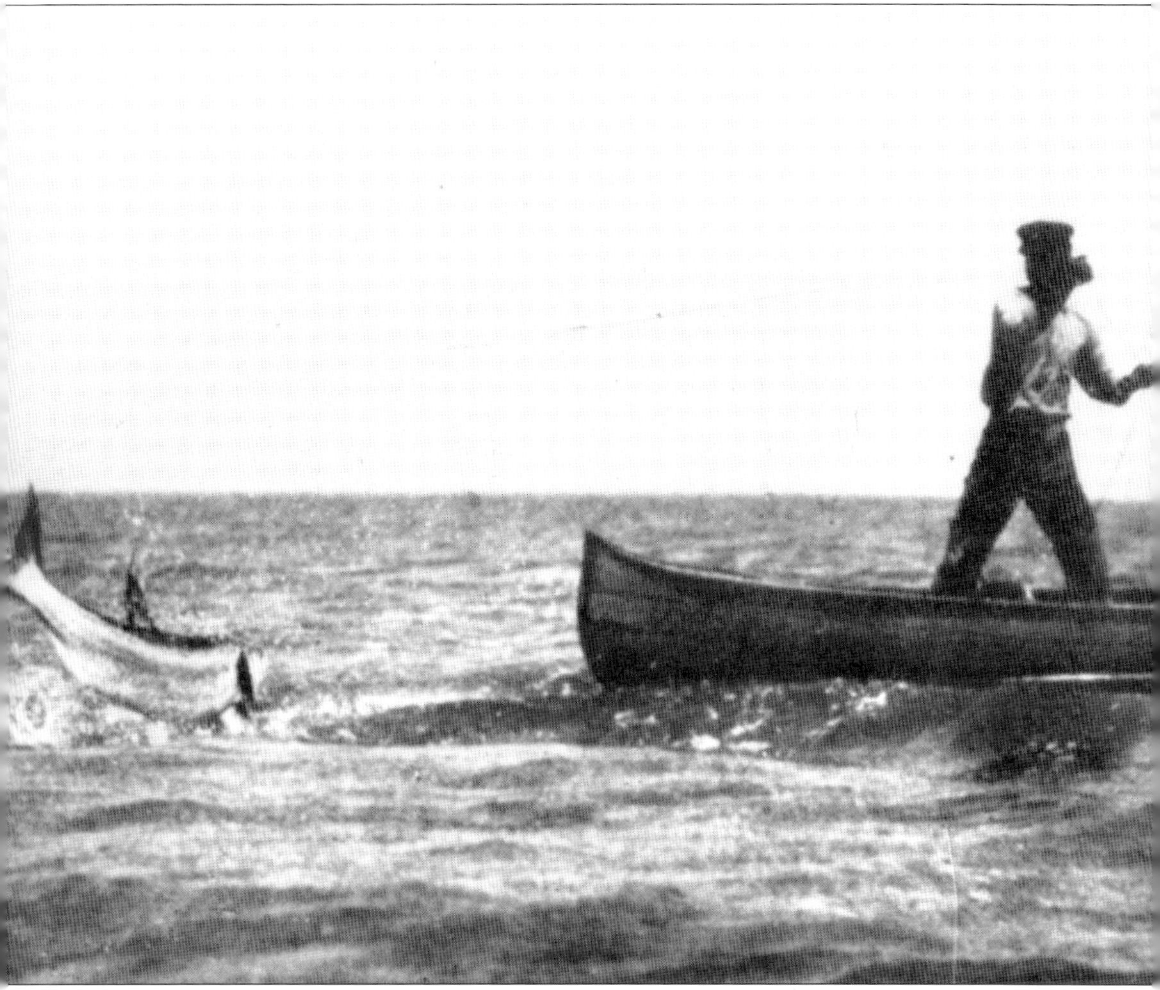

Tarpon Fishing in Charlotte Harbor. Charlotte Harbor offers 120 square miles of cruising waters in the harbor and access to the Gulf of Mexico, as well as inland passages north and south, so it is perfect for tarpon fishing. Charlotte Harbor is fed by the Myakka River and the Peace River, both of which are navigable. (Blanchard House Museum of African-American History and Culture of Charlotte County.)

Discover Thousands of Local History Books Featuring Millions of Vintage Images

Arcadia Publishing, the leading local history publisher in the United States, is committed to making history accessible and meaningful through publishing books that celebrate and preserve the heritage of America's people and places.

Find more books like this at
www.arcadiapublishing.com

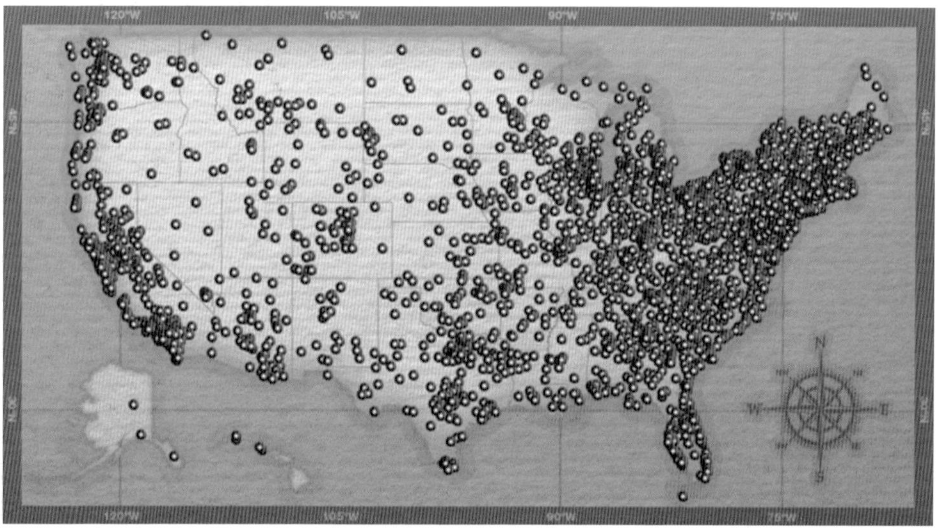

Search for your hometown history, your old stomping grounds, and even your favorite sports team.

Consistent with our mission to preserve history on a local level, this book was printed in South Carolina on American-made paper and manufactured entirely in the United States. Products carrying the accredited Forest Stewardship Council (FSC) label are printed on 100 percent FSC-certified paper.

MADE IN THE USA